Global Dialogues on Law and Technology

This book explores how technology today shapes every aspect of human life, from communication and commerce to governance and justice. Its rapid growth presents not only technical challenges but also profound legal and ethical dilemmas, such as:

- How do we safeguard privacy in a world of constant data collection?
- What kind of legal protection should exist for digital rights in the age of artificial intelligence?
- And how can legal frameworks keep pace with innovations that move faster than regulations?

The volume draws connections between law, technology, and education, offering perspectives that are both globally relevant and contextually grounded. It invites readers to reimagine how legal and policy frameworks can be reshaped to safeguard rights, foster innovation, and ensure justice in a rapidly evolving digital world.

Covering broad subject areas such as digital privacy, data protection, artificial intelligence, legal innovation, and technology-driven education, this book is designed for scholars, policymakers, legal practitioners, educators, and anyone interested in the intersection of law, technology, and society.

The chapters in this book were originally published as a special issue of *International Review of Law, Computers & Technology.*

Sweta Lakhani is Assistant Professor and Assistant Dean (LLM Blended Programme) at Jindal Global Law School, O.P. Jindal Global University, Sonipat, Haryana, India. Her interdisciplinary research lies at the intersection of law, technology, and behavioural science, with a particular focus on how emerging technologies shape legal norms, regulatory frameworks, and human decision-making.

Subhajit Basu is Professor of Law and Technology at the University of Leeds, Leeds, UK, and Editor-in-Chief of the *International Review of Law, Computers & Technology*. His research focuses on AI, big data, autonomous systems, online harms, privacy, and access to justice, with particular attention to the Global South.

Global Dialogues on Law and Technology

Bridging Policy, Innovation, and Rights

Edited by
Sweta Lakhani and Subhajit Basu

Routledge
Taylor & Francis Group
LONDON AND NEW YORK

First published 2026
by Routledge
4 Park Square, Milton Park, Abingdon, Oxon OX14 4RN

and by Routledge
605 Third Avenue, New York, NY 10158

Routledge is an imprint of the Taylor & Francis Group, an informa business

British Library Cataloguing in Publication Data
A catalogue record for this book is available from the British Library

ISBN13: 978-1-041-22550-8 (hbk)
ISBN13: 978-1-041-22554-6 (pbk)
ISBN13: 978-1-003-73287-7 (ebk)

DOI: 10.4324/9781003732877

Typeset in Myriad Pro
by Newgen Publishing UK

Publisher's Note
The publisher accepts responsibility for any inconsistencies that may have arisen during the conversion of this book from journal articles to book chapters, namely the inclusion of journal terminology.

Contents

Citation Information vii
Notes on Contributors ix

Introduction: global dialogues on law and technology 1
Subhajit Basu and Sweta Lakhani

1 Transparency as the defining feature for developing risk assessment AI technology for border control 12
Jonida Milaj and Jeanne Pia Mifsud Bonnici

2 ChatGPT for good? Taking 'beneficence' seriously in the regulation of generative artificial intelligence 24
Krishna Deo Singh Chauhan

3 Patents in metaverse: an analysis of scope and challenges 47
Prajakta Kale

4 Contours of data protection in India: the consent dilemma 66
Aafreen Mitchelle Collaco

5 Standardised cookie banner: a solution to the cookie consent problem 85
Paarth Naithani

6 When it's cute but also dark: critical analysis of *FarmVille 3*'s game design in the digital economy 103
Caroline Stockman, Anthony O'Connell and Emma Nottingham

7 Getting global cooperation right on internet governance: strategic roadmaps for the future 126
Miriam F. Weismann

8 Minimising unnecessary restrictions on cross-border data flows? Indonesia's position and challenges post personal data protection act enactment 153
Faiz Rahman and Cora Kristin Mulyani

Index 173

Citation Information

The chapters in this book were originally published in the *International Review of Law, Computers & Technology*, Volume 39, Issue 2 (2025). When citing this material, please use the original page numbering for each article, as follows:

Chapter 1

Transparency as the defining feature for developing risk assessment AI technology for border control
Jonida Milaj and Jeanne Pia Mifsud Bonnici
International Review of Law, Computers & Technology, Volume 39, Issue 2 (2025), pp. 140–151

Chapter 2

ChatGPT for good? Taking 'beneficence' seriously in the regulation of generative artificial intelligence
Krishna Deo Singh Chauhan
International Review of Law, Computers & Technology, Volume 39, Issue 2 (2025), pp. 152–174

Chapter 3

Patents in metaverse: an analysis of scope and challenges
Prajakta Kale
International Review of Law, Computers & Technology, Volume 39, Issue 2 (2025), pp. 175–193

Chapter 4

Contours of data protection in India: the consent dilemma
Aafreen Mitchelle Collaco
International Review of Law, Computers & Technology, Volume 39, Issue 2 (2025), pp. 194–212

Chapter 5

Standardised cookie banner: a solution to the cookie consent problem
Paarth Naithani
International Review of Law, Computers & Technology, Volume 39, Issue 2 (2025), pp. 213–230

Chapter 6

When it's cute but also dark: critical analysis of FarmVille 3*'s game design in the digital economy*
Caroline Stockman, Anthony O'Connell and Emma Nottingham
International Review of Law, Computers & Technology, Volume 39, Issue 2 (2025), pp. 231–253

Chapter 7

Getting global cooperation right on internet governance: strategic roadmaps for the future
Miriam F. Weismann
International Review of Law, Computers & Technology, Volume 39, Issue 2 (2025), pp. 254–280

Chapter 8

Minimising unnecessary restrictions on cross-border data flows? Indonesia's position and challenges post personal data protection act enactment
Faiz Rahman and Cora Kristin Mulyani
International Review of Law, Computers & Technology, Volume 39, Issue 2 (2025), pp. 281–300

Notes on Contributors

Subhajit Basu, School of Law, University of Leeds, UK.

Jeanne Pia Mifsud Bonnici, Security, Technology and e-Privacy Research Group (STeP), University of Groningen, Groningen, The Netherlands.

Krishna Deo Singh Chauhan, Jindal Global Law School, O.P. Jindal Global University, Sonipat, Haryana, India.

Aafreen Mitchelle Collaco, Jindal Global Law School, O.P. Jindal Global University, Sonipat, Haryana, India.

Prajakta Kale, Jindal Global Law School, O.P. Jindal Global University, Sonipat, Haryana, India.

Sweta Lakhani, Jindal Global Law School, O.P. Jindal Global University, Sonipat, Haryana, India.

Jonida Milaj, Security, Technology and e-Privacy Research Group (STeP), University of Groningen, Groningen, The Netherlands.

Cora Kristin Mulyani, Faculty of Law, Universitas Gadjah Mada, Yogyakarta, Indonesia.

Paarth Naithani, Jindal Global Law School, O.P. Jindal Global University, Sonipat, Haryana, India.

Emma Nottingham, Law, University of Winchester, Winchester, UK.

Anthony O'Connell, English Literature Research, University of Winchester, Winchester, UK.

Faiz Rahman, Faculty of Law, Universitas Gadjah Mada, Yogyakarta, Indonesia; The Van Vollenhoven Institute for Law, Governance and Society, eLaw Center for Law and Digital Technologies, Leiden; Law School, Universiteit Leiden, Leiden, The Netherlands.

Caroline Stockman, Education Studies, University of Winchester, Winchester, UK.

Miriam F. Weismann, Clinical Professor of Business Law and Tax, Florida International University, Miami, FL, USA.

Introduction: global dialogues on law and technology

Subhajit Basu and Sweta Lakhani

Introduction

Digital technologies now function as infrastructures of governance. They filter and rank what we see and what we never encounter. They screen and sort people at borders. They determine which transactions are frictionless and which are treated as suspicious. They normalise continuous extraction of behavioural data in ordinary environments—work, school, leisure, care. They intervene to "assist," to "optimise," to "protect," but in doing so, they categorise, escalate, and sometimes exclude. All of this is presented as service design. In practice, it is an exercise of power.

However, if we treat this as a mere "technological disruption," it would radically understate what is happening. Technology is no longer a sequence of external shocks to legal systems. We are past the point where a new technology emerges, creates a regulatory puzzle, and waits for the law to catch up. We now inhabit an environment in which computational systems are woven directly into how decisions are made, justified, and enforced. The boundary between "legal order" and "technical system" has thinned to the point of near collapse.

A border screening model that assigns a "risk score" to an individual using scraped social media data is not just a tool that helps an immigration officer decide. It has already pre-structured who is presumed truthful, who is treated as potentially dangerous, and whose claims will be met with suspicion. A child-facing game that deploys highly stylised, soft "cute" aesthetics to cultivate attachment and normalise recurrent micro-spend is not simply entertainment. It is a behavioural environment that trains habits of attention, buying, and disclosure. A so-called personal assistant built on a generative artificial intelligence (AI) model is not merely filling out drafts and scheduling meetings. It is taking on communicative, cognitive, and relational labour that used to require explicit judgement and responsibility, while operating according to values that are not democratically negotiated. In each case, the technology is not simply enabling an existing legal or economic structure. It is reconfiguring it.

This edited volume begins from that position. It treats modern digital infrastructures—border AI systems, generative AI platforms, mixed-reality/immersive environments, behavioural design in game economies, consent interfaces, data transfer regimes—as sites in which legality, legitimacy, and accountability are already being renegotiated. The volume claims that if we continue to frame these domains as regulatory afterthoughts or specialist "tech law" problems, we will fail to grasp a more basic development: digital infrastructures have become constitutional in effect. They allocate burdens, benefits, privileges, exposure, and voice. They draw the practical boundaries of autonomy. They shape who must explain themselves, and to whom. That is the very terrain on which law has historically claimed authority.

The aim here is both analytic and normative. Analytically, the volume maps how computational infrastructures embed modes of decision-making that look like law—classifying, authorising, forbidding, nudging, allocating—while bypassing some of law's disciplines: publicity, the possibility of refusal, and the right to contest. Normatively, it asks what must follow. If these infrastructures are already governing, then they must meet standards traditionally reserved for public power. If they refuse those standards, or if we decline to insist on them, then legality will shift from something collectively articulated and challengeable to something privately embedded and practically unaccountable.

The argument proceeds in seven parts. First, it explains why familiar accounts of "law catching up with technology" are no longer adequate. Second, it offers a way of understanding how law and technology now co-produce institutional reality. Third, it specifies how the commitments associated with the rule of law are strained by computational governance. Fourth, it outlines the substantive contributions of each chapter in this collection. Fifth, it identifies the structural tensions that recur across these domains. Sixth, it explains the volume's originality and significance for scholars, regulators, practitioners, and educators. Finally, it states what is at stake.

Moving past the "catching up" story

For several decades, the mainstream approach to law and technology has followed a familiar pattern. A new or intensified technology is identified: large-scale data analytics, reproductive intervention, online platforms, biometric surveillance, and AI. We are told this development poses unprecedented risk. Scholars locate doctrinal gaps that "existing law" has not addressed. Policymakers are urged to intervene, and the regulatory machine is expected, eventually, to "catch up." We know that this model is comfortable because it preserves a reassuring hierarchy: technology moves quickly; law follows with deliberation and fixes the problem. It paints technology as the active force and law as the corrective. It imagines a world in which social order remains, in the end, legally underwritten. It is now inadequate on its own terms.

First, the "gap then patch" narrative treats each technology as a discrete shock. This fragments analysis into isolated sub-questions: AI and hiring, AI and policing, AI and education; the metaverse and IP; online games and child protection; data localisation and trade. The wider recomposition of authority, legitimacy, and accountability is backgrounded. What is missed is that each of these controversies reflects the same structural development: computational infrastructures are assuming functions that look and feel like governance.

Second, the narrative assumes that law suits outside technological systems, ready to intervene. This is often no longer true. Law is already engineered into these systems. An AI supplier to a border agency will design a system that meets (or appears to meet) procurement standards, human rights risk assessments, and internal audit requirements from day one. A platform will build a consent interface expressly to qualify as "freely given, informed choice" as that concept has been interpreted by data protection regulators, even if that "choice" has been carefully steered. A company filing broad, anticipatory patents for immersive digital environments is not waiting for legislatures to decide how the metaverse should be governed: it is using existing IP law to determine, in advance, who will have the right to exclude, license, and monetise within that environment.

Third, and most important, the narrative quietly preserves a comforting separation: "technology" over here, "law" over there. The assumption is that technology's job is to innovate and law's job is to respond. This description is no longer empirically accurate. Technical systems now implement legal concepts (such as risk, accountability, and proportionality) in code. Legal norms now incorporate technical assumptions (data-driven objectivity, optimisation, efficiency) in doctrine. Neither can be understood in isolation. They are co-produced.

This co-production matters. When a government authority uses an algorithmic "risk assessment" model to flag individuals for detention or further scrutiny at the border, that authority is not simply augmenting human judgement with a neutral tool. It is allowing the classification logic of that model to set the evidentiary baseline and frame the narrative of suspicion. Downstream actors—tribunals, oversight bodies, courts—are then asked to review the "reasonableness" of decisions that were, in reality, pre-structured by an opaque pipeline. The legal contest has already been channelled.

When a child spends hours inside a "free-to-play" game whose entire economic model depends on affective bonding, intermittent reward, and normalised micro-payment, any subsequent consumer protection analysis that focuses solely on whether the billing terms were sufficiently prominent is selecting the wrong moment in time. By the point of payment, the behavioural environment has already done its work. "Choice" is an end-stage performance, not a free-standing act of will. When a state in the Global South decides whether to permit foreign companies unrestricted cross-border access to locally generated data, that is not a minor technical decision about privacy compliance. It is a geopolitical decision about economic self-determination, bargaining leverage, and institutional independence in a data-driven world economy. The law on data flows is, in that moment, a tool of industrial policy and national strategy.

In short, the story in which "law lags" and then "catches up" is not only incomplete. It obscures how much of modern legal ordering has already moved inside computational infrastructures, and how much of modern computational design is already an exercise in legal positioning.

Rule-of-law disciplines under computational governance

The modern rule-of-law tradition rests, in simplified terms, on three demands. First, power must be publicly articulable. Those subject to it should be able to know, in comprehensible terms, what standards are being applied to them. Second, refusal must at least be conceptually available. Law is not a physical constraint but a normative demand. People can breach it, defend their reasons, and force the system to justify itself; that possibility is what keeps legal power accountable and revisable. Third, decisions that affect rights and interests must be open to challenge before a forum that is not wholly captured by the decision-maker. There must be somewhere to contest not only the outcome, but the basis on which the outcome was produced. They are the mechanisms through which law distinguishes itself from arbitrary administration, coercive custom, or private fiat. They express a view that power, to be legitimate, must be publicly justifiable, reviewable, and contestable.

Computational governance strains each of these disciplines. Opacity is engineered in. Large-scale models used in border control, fraud detection, welfare eligibility screening, or predictive policing are regularly described as commercially confidential, operationally sensitive, or technically incomprehensible to non-specialists. The ability to interrogate how they work is narrowed by design. The person classified by the system cannot access the logic by which they were placed in a high-risk category. They cannot test whether the training data was accurate, biased, or even lawfully collected. Even oversight bodies often get only managed visibility into a system's internals. The standard becomes "trust us, it's sophisticated," not "here is how we exercised power over you."

Refusal is structurally disabled. Access to essential infrastructures—communications platforms, financial services, educational portals, health triage tools—is increasingly conditional on accepting continuous tracking and profiling. The individual is said to "choose" to share location data, biometric identifiers, and behavioural telemetry. However, in practice, declining often means exclusion from meaningful participation in work, social connections, or basic services. A right that can be exercised only at the cost of self-exile is not, in any serious sense, a right.

Contestability is displaced. When an output is presented as "what the system determined," it is framed as a neutral fact—a signal—rather than as a discretionary act. Disputes are redirected into opaque escalation channels, internal "appeals," or vendor-managed review, rather than into a publicly accountable legal challenge. The core move is subtle but potent: what would once have been recognised as a contestable decision is redescribed as an objective result, and therefore treated as outside the ordinary vocabulary of justification.

This is not to say that the law no longer matters. It is to say that legal commitments are being pushed into a position where they must either adapt or recede. A border agency that relies on opaque AI-driven classification is, in effect, asserting that physical entry, detention, and removal can be shaped by systems whose operation the affected individual cannot meaningfully contest. A data-driven behavioural advertising platform that "secures" consent through a deliberately coercive interface is, in effect, asserting that autonomy is satisfied by performance rather than reality. A child-facing game that yields revenue by systematically training compulsion and normalising micro-payment is, in effect, asserting that exploitation is acceptable if it is wrapped in an aesthetic of comfort.

This volume treats these developments as constitutional questions. Not "constitutional" in the narrow domestic sense of written charters and judicial review, but "constitutional" in the broader sense: how authority is distributed, what forms of power are normalised, which interests are structurally advantaged, and which safeguards we insist upon as non-negotiable in public life.

The contributions in this volume

The chapters that follow were originally published together in a special issue, and they have been curated here because they collectively map the sites where computational infrastructures and legal ordering now collide. They are grouped into six clusters.

AI in high-stakes public decision-making

The first cluster examines AI in migration, asylum, and border control—domains that sit at the edges of public law and at the heart of state sovereignty. These are precisely the areas where governments have historically claimed exceptional discretion and resisted intrusive scrutiny. Under proposed European regulatory frameworks, AI systems deployed in migration and border management are expressly categorised as "high-risk." This label is not rhetorical. It is intended to trigger demanding obligations around data quality, transparency, documentation, and rights safeguards.

In Chapter 1, Jonida Milaj and Jeanne Pia Mifsud Bonnici test whether those obligations can, in practice, be satisfied when such systems are trained on what is blandly called "open-source data": social-media content, scraped posts, behavioural traces, context-stripped fragments of identity performance. Social-media data is situational and strategic. It reflects performance, aspiration, fear, misdirection, humour, code-switching, and survival tactics. Treating it as unmediated evidence of "risk" imports all of that situatedness into border decision-making, while stripping it of protective social context.

Their analysis advances two claims. First, if the training data is structurally noisy, biased, and performative, then automated "risk-assessment" models at the border may fail to meet the minimum legal standard of data integrity required for deployment. Second—and more fundamentally—they treat transparency as a constitutional threshold. If an AI system is informing or driving decisions that determine who is stopped, detained, admitted, or expelled—and if neither the affected individual nor any independent body can meaningfully interrogate how that classification was reached—then the deployment of that system is not simply "high-risk." It becomes incompatible with the minimum conditions of lawful governance in a rights-intensive domain. The conclusion is uncompromising: where transparency and data integrity cannot be guaranteed, such systems should not be deployed at all. This claim matters beyond migration. It asserts a baseline for all AI used in high-stakes public functions: opacity is not a feature to be managed; it is a reason to prohibit.

Generative AI and the duty to serve the public good

The second cluster turns to generative AI—large-scale, general-purpose systems that produce text, images, and other content on demand. These systems are already being integrated into education, creative production, knowledge retrieval, administrative triage, and advice provision. Debate around them has, so far, been dominated by risk mitigation: preventing discrimination, blocking overt fraud, suppressing obvious misinformation, and guarding against malicious use.

In Chapter 2, Krishna Deo Singh Chauhan argues that this harm-reduction-only posture is normatively weak once such systems become infrastructural. When a technology is purely optional and marginal, it may be sufficient to ensure it does not cause serious harm. When a technology is embedded at scale in core communicative, cognitive, and relational infrastructures, the bar must be higher. At that point, the public is entitled not only to the absence of harm, but also to the presence of benefit.

The chapter, therefore, advances a positive regulatory demand: beneficence. In domains where systems claim authority over human welfare—medicine is the classic example—it is not enough to avoid harm; there is an affirmative obligation to promote well-being. The same, it is argued, should apply to generative AI systems that aspire to act as social infrastructure. "Does this system avoid the worst harms?" is no longer an adequate test. Regulators should also ask, "What identifiable public good does this system create, for whom, and how will that be verified?" The move is conceptually important: it reframes AI governance from triage ("stop the worst outcomes") to stewardship ("justify your inclusion in socially critical infrastructures") and forces specificity about who defines, measures, and can demand "benefit."

Patent strategy and enclosure of immersive environments

The third cluster turns to immersive, persistent environments often described—not always helpfully—as "the metaverse." The concern here is not hype but control.

In Chapter 3, Prajakta Kale observes that immersive environments are being marketed simultaneously as the next social commons, workplace, classroom, shopping mall, and therapeutic interface. If these environments do become persistent and economically significant, whoever controls core interaction modes, standards, and interfaces will hold extraordinary leverage over communication, labour, education, and care.

Patent law is already being used to stake those claims. Far from being a belated, reactive discipline, patent doctrine is functioning here as an anticipatory constitution. Companies are filing for exclusive rights over how bodies move, transact, signal intent, and experience presence in immersive space—locking in control over the building blocks of shared virtual environments before those environments have socially stabilised and long before their governance norms have been democratically negotiated.

Two problems follow. First, doctrine built around territoriality, discrete inventions, and conventional "use" is being stretched to cover transnational, continuous, experiential spaces that behave like hybrid public/private commons, workplaces, and marketplaces at once. Second, and more profoundly, pre-emptive enclosure means governance is being decided privately and in advance: the legal infrastructure of public life in augmented space is authored through early IP positioning, not public deliberation. Kale makes that anticipatory move visible and insists we treat it as constitutional in effect.

Data protection, consent, and engineered choice

The fourth cluster addresses data protection through two distinct but reinforcing lenses: high-level data protection law in a large jurisdiction in the Global South, and the humble cookie banner in the EU. Together, they amount to a frontal attack on one of the most entrenched fictions in digital governance: that people "freely choose" surveillance and extraction.

In Chapter 4, Aafreen Mitchelle Collaco situates statutory reform against a constitutional backdrop that recognises privacy as a fundamental right. The statute nevertheless relies heavily on consent as the legal basis for processing. In abstraction, this looks autonomy-respecting. In practice, consent is binary and non-negotiable, and saying "no" often means exclusion from platforms and services that are essential for economic participation, social interaction, education, or access to public goods. Consent is therefore formally voluntary but structurally coerced. A regime cannot proclaim privacy a fundamental right and then make its protection contingent on theatrical consent. Collaco calls for a shift away from consent-centricity and towards structural protections that do not presume symmetric bargaining with infrastructures individuals cannot avoid.

In Chapter 5, Paarth Naithani zooms in on the interface layer. In principle, cookie banners are supposed to secure "freely given, informed, specific" consent before non-essential tracking. In practice, they are built to extract acquiescence: "accept all" buttons are large and emotionally reassuring; "reject all" is hidden, linguistically ambiguous, or effortful. Repeated prompts wear down resistance. The claim is that interface design is part of the regulatory terrain. If a legal regime rests on the notion of consent, regulators must ask not only "was consent obtained?" but "under what designed conditions?" Naithani proposes regulatory standardisation—timing, placement, option symmetry, language clarity, refusal mechanics—as a structural assertion that autonomy requires real support, not formal words.

Behavioural design, affect, and consumer protection

The fifth cluster turns to manipulative design in ostensibly low-stakes spaces—casual gaming, particularly games aimed at or attractive to children. It develops the idea of "cute but dark" design.

In Chapter 6, Caroline Stockman, Anthony O'Connell, and Emma Nottingham show how soft aesthetics—warm palettes, rounded characters, comforting tone, reward loops dressed as kindness—cultivate attachment, encourage constant re-engagement, normalise spending, and smooth the surrender of data. What appears "cute" is a behavioural instrument. The game does not simply entertain; it conditions. It teaches that progression is purchased, frames micro-transactions as care, and blurs the boundary between social interaction and commercial extraction.

The legal claim is that traditional consumer and child-protection frameworks, which tend to focus on overt deception or coercion, are not equipped for this mode of influence. The manipulation is not a single misleading statement; it is an immersive environment calibrated to generate dependency and monetise it. The chapter calls for regulators to recognise certain aesthetic and affective strategies as dark patterns—deliberate manipulations of vulnerability that warrant treatment as regulatory violations in their own right.

Cybersecurity governance, data flows, and sovereignty

The final cluster scales up to the geopolitical and asks: who governs a digital infrastructure that is globally entangled, strategically invaluable, and deeply mistrusted?

In Chapter 7, Miriam F. Weismann explains the persistent failure to achieve a comprehensive, binding multilateral order for state conduct in cyberspace. The obstacle is not merely technical coordination but sovereign authority. States resist structures that would subject their conduct to meaningful external constraint, yet unilateral control is structurally impossible because infrastructures are transnational, layered, and mutually dependent. The result is an unstable patchwork of bilateral deals, voluntary guidelines, informal norms, and strategic ambiguity. Naming the problem as constitutional at the global scale—authority, accountability, and permission to act in shared infrastructures—is a precondition for credible institutional design.

In Chapter 8, Faiz Rahman and Cora Kristin Mulyani examine cross-border data governance from the perspective of a major jurisdiction in the Global South, following the adoption of a comprehensive data-protection law. The state faces three pressures: an economy dependent on data mobility; a public increasingly angry about breaches and misuse; and a political leadership unwilling to allow unrestricted offshore extraction of domestic data on terms set by external actors. The response is neither rigid localisation (which can throttle growth) nor laissez-faire outflows (which entrench dependency). It is conditional openness: data can leave on terms that preserve strategic autonomy, developmental interest, and negotiated reciprocity. Cross-border data governance, in this framing, is both privacy law and economic statecraft.

The significance is twofold. First, this rejects the assumption that high-standard data-protection norms inevitably diffuse from a single regulatory core and are merely "implemented" elsewhere. Second, it recognises jurisdictions outside traditional centres of norm production as active authors of digital constitutional order, not recipients of it.

Structural tensions

The chapters, read together, surface four recurring tensions. These tensions are not incidental. They trace the pressure lines along which the legal and institutional settlement for a computational society is currently being formed.

Transparency versus opacity: In high-stakes decision-making—border control, welfare eligibility, public security—legitimacy cannot rest on assurances of competence. It must rest on intelligibility. People affected by a decision must be able to ask: who decided, on what basis, using what data, and how can I challenge it? However, many computational systems are designed, contractually shielded, and politically defended to prevent precisely those questions. Vendors claim trade secrecy. Agencies claim operational necessity. Technical complexity is invoked as if it were a justification in itself. The first tension is therefore between the constitutional demand that power be publicly justifiable and the structural incentives to keep computational power opaque.

Autonomy versus engineered environments: Modern regimes of data protection and consumer protection are still written in the language of voluntariness. Users "consent." Children "engage." People "accept." However, digital environments are now actively engineered to produce those outcomes. Interface design punishes refusal with friction, delay, or exclusion. Affective design cultivates dependency and frames surrender as care. By the moment of "choice," the field of possible choices has already been shaped. The second tension is between a legal rhetoric of self-determination and an infrastructural reality of behavioural orchestration. If that gap is not closed—either by redesigning environments or by abandoning the fiction that consent legitimises extraction—then autonomy risks devolving into theatre.

Public authority versus private architecture: Many of the most consequential computational infrastructures sit in an unstable seam between public and private power. Border control uses proprietary AI supplied by private vendors. "Consent" interfaces, built by commercial actors, are treated as if they were legally meaningful declarations of will. Immersive environments pitched as the next public commons are being pre-structured by private patent portfolios. Traditional accountability doctrine splits cleanly: public law constrains states; private law constrains firms. That split no longer tracks where power is actually exercised. The third tension is between who holds the practical capacity to govern and where law, as currently configured, is prepared to impose accountability.

Sovereignty versus interdependence: Digital infrastructures are global. Infrastructure failures cascade across borders in real time. Data flows underpin economic activity across entire regions. However, states remain deeply and understandably attached to sovereignty—not only for reasons of national pride or constitutional form, but also because sovereignty remains the principal legal language through which governments assert developmental priorities, democratic legitimacy, and security obligations to their own populations. The fourth tension is therefore between the functional need for collective governance of shared infrastructures and the political imperative to retain bargaining power, narrative control, and institutional independence. This tension is most visible in cybersecurity governance and cross-border data regulation. It will define the next decade of digital public international law, whether we name it as such or not.

Original contribution, significance, and audience

The work collected in this volume makes three claims to originality and significance. First, it is doctrinally concrete in areas where doctrine is still forming. The analysis of AI in border control sets out conditions under which such systems must be treated not merely as "high risk" but as legally impermissible. The discussion of generative AI does not stop at "avoid harm"; it articulates why these systems, if they are to be embedded in social infrastructure, should be held to affirmative obligations to deliver public benefit. The chapter on immersive environments shows that patent strategy is already determining who will control interaction and presence in spaces being marketed as the next social commons. The two consent chapters expose how autonomy is being hollowed out and propose specific regulatory levers—including standardised interface design—to restore substance. The gaming chapter reframes soft, affective design as a site of manipulative commercial practice rather than harmless style. The chapters on cybersecurity and data sovereignty situate digital infrastructure governance within questions of constitutional authority and strategic independence, refusing to reduce them to technical coordination problems.

Second, it provides a general account of the relationship between law and technology that moves beyond crisis-driven gap-spotting. Across different domains, the same dynamics recur: computational infrastructures are assuming decision-making roles that look like law; law is already inscribed into these infrastructures, not simply applied to them from the outside; and actors with power are actively working to shape, limit, and in some cases pre-empt the forms of accountability that might otherwise attach. The volume offers language and structure for thinking about that condition. It treats border AI, consent banners, "cute but dark" game design, metaverse patenting, and cross-border data sovereignty as manifestations of the same transformation rather than as a string of unrelated novelties.

Third, it is unapologetically normative without collapsing into a slogan. It does not pretend that "ethics" alone will save us, or that we just need "better design," or that "more innovation" will resolve structural asymmetry. Instead, it states plainly where lines should be drawn. Opacity in high-stakes AI should be treated as disqualifying, not as an inconvenience. Generative AI that aspires to infrastructural status should be required to justify itself in terms of affirmative social good, not just in terms of reduced harm. Consent that is manufactured through interface pressure should not count as consent. Affective design targeting children to normalise extraction should be treated as a regulatory violation, not as an aesthetic preference. Cross-border data governance by states in the Global South should be recognised as strategic and legitimate, not dismissed as parochial protectionism. Cybersecurity governance should be recognised as a constitutional problem—who gets to act, at what scale, under what constraints—not merely as an engineering challenge.

The intended readership is deliberately broad and, at this point, unavoidable—constitutional and administrative lawyers who wish to understand how discretion and accountability now work in data-driven bureaucracies. Human rights lawyers are already encountering algorithmically shaped decisions on liberty, security, and migration status. Consumer and child protection lawyers confronting behavioural design as a mode of exploitation. Intellectual property lawyers advising clients seeking to territorialise immersive space. Data protection authorities under pressure to enforce "freely given" consent in environments optimised to eliminate refusal. Competition and trade lawyers who are being pulled into arguments about digital sovereignty. Public international lawyers who are watching states struggle to govern infrastructures that ignore borders but trigger national security reflexes at every turn. Legal educators who are responsible for training the next generation to operate credibly in systems in which legal and computational infrastructures are inseparable.

Conclusion

The chapters in this volume collectively insist on one claim: modern digital infrastructures are already constitutional in effect. They decide who is visible, who is profiled, who is delayed for questioning, who is taken seriously, and who is quietly deprioritised. They control the pathways through which people access credit, employment, welfare, education, healthcare, and even social visibility. They teach individuals—including children—what is normal, what is purchasable, and what is expected. They determine what counts as "consent." They structure how national sovereignty is asserted and how international coordination fails or succeeds. Above all, they determine how easily an exercise of power can be questioned. If that is true, then the governance of these infrastructures is not an optional specialism. It is the contemporary form of constitutional practice.

This has two immediate implications. First, legal analysis can no longer afford to treat "technology" as an optional appendix. The control logic of border AI, the extraction logic of platform consent, the enclosure logic of metaverse patenting, the conditioning logic of "cute but dark" design, the sovereignty logic of cross-border data regimes, and the authority logic of cybersecurity governance are already shaping, in practice, the scope of rights and the reach of accountability. They are reshaping administrative law, constitutional law, human rights law, consumer and child protection, intellectual property, competition, and international law in real time, whether we articulate that shift or not. Second, the law's own self-image must change. Law cannot proceed as if it were an external check that occasionally disciplines "technology." Nor can it give up, accepting an airless narrative of inevitability in which computational systems set the terms and public oversight merely tidies the edges. Law is already in these systems. Law is already invoked to justify them, to shield them, to market them, to resist them. The task is not to ask whether the law will govern technology. The task is to decide which legal commitments we are prepared to entrench—transparency, contestability, autonomy in fact rather than in fiction, protection against manipulation, distributive fairness, strategic self-determination—and to insist that those commitments run through the infrastructures that are, in practice, governing us.

The work collected here does not claim to have resolved that task. It does something both more modest and more ambitious. It names where the struggle is actually happening: at the border checkpoint where an opaque score tips a life one way or another; in the interface where a child is taught to accept extraction as care; in the patent claim that quietly asserts jurisdiction over future shared space; in the pop-up that converts surveillance into "choice"; in the treaty room where states fight to preserve leverage over infrastructures they no longer fully control. By naming those sites, and by offering tools to analyse them with doctrinal precision and normative clarity, this volume aims to shift the conversation from "What should we do about technology?" to the question we can no longer postpone: "On what terms, and for whose benefit, will we allow computational infrastructures to govern?"

OPEN ACCESS

Transparency as the defining feature for developing risk assessment AI technology for border control

Jonida Milaj and Jeanne Pia Mifsud Bonnici

ABSTRACT
AI systems to be used in migration, asylum and border control management are qualified as high-risk AI under the current draft AI Act in the EU. The draft Act introduces strict requirements for the development and use of these systems, including the requirement of high-quality data to be used for training algorithms in order to mitigate the risks to fundamental rights and safety. Based on research conducted in the framework of the H2020 CRiTERIA project,[1] this study analyses from a legal doctrinal approach the compliance of open-source data from Social Media platforms with the requirement of high-quality data and the present challenges for the transparency requirement. Following all the requirements introduced for mitigating the risks posed to fundamental rights and safety from high-risk AI, the compliance of open-source data from Social Media with the high-quality data requirement is put into doubt. As transparency is found to be the defining line between high-risk and unacceptable-risk AI, it is argued that the use of open data from Social Media for risk assessment border control AI systems might present an unacceptable risk for the protection of fundamental rights, if proper safeguards are not followed.

1. Introduction

A large amount of data without any privacy filters or, said differently, open-source data is available on Social Media platforms. The availability, as well as the easiness to access these data, makes them attractive to be used for training algorithms and for developing new Artificial Intelligence (AI) solutions. While clear benefits are identified for the use of risk assessment AI for border control (Dumbrava 2021, 4), legal and ethical concerns, especially linked to the protection of the fundamental rights to privacy and data protection as well as human dignity, arise when open-source data from Social Media are used for training AI systems.

In the current draft of the AI Act (2021) proposed by the European Commission (Art 6),[2] the high-risk qualification of AI refers to those systems that present potential risks for individuals for the enjoyment of their fundamental rights and for safety. AI systems to be used in the area of migration, asylum and border control fall under this category. The reason for this qualification is that AI systems for border control affect people who are often in a particularly vulnerable position and who are dependent on the outcome of the actions of the border authorities (draft AI Act (2021), Recital 39). The accuracy, non-discriminatory nature and transparency of the AI systems used in this context are particularly important to guarantee the respect of the fundamental rights of the affected individuals, for example, the rights to non-discrimination, the protection of private life and personal data, etc. These identified challenges have been at the bases of a vivid debate about qualifying AI used for border control and migration as presenting unacceptable risks and thus, banning its use.[3] The line between high-risk AI and unacceptable risk AI is a very fine one, and transparency compliance plays a crucial role for establishing this line.

In the European Union (EU), the use of open data from the public sector for training AI is currently encouraged and supported in the framework of the Digital Single Market Strategy (2015). Closely linked to this, the Data Governance Act aims to further facilitate the reuse of public sector data as well as to facilitate and encourage data sharing for individuals as well as for private businesses, based on the data altruism concept (Data Governance Act 2020, Art 2(16)). In the area of border control, monitoring, analysis and open-source intelligence based on internet activities, including Social Media platforms, is legally prescribed under the services that the European Border Surveillance System (EUROSUR 2019, Art 28(2)(h)) offers. As a result, there are current initiatives (Frontex 2020; and European Commission 2023) to assess the potential inclusion of these data in border control systems for closing the gaps that are often created by the exclusive use of official databases (COM 2016, 12). One can notice, though, that AI systems are not explicitly mentioned in the EUROSUR regulation, and open data from Social Media are not mentioned as such in the draft AI Act. As a result, practices of employing open-source data from Social Media for training algorithms might flourish following the legal maxim: 'Everything which is not prohibited is allowed'. Thus, a legal and ethical analysis of the use of open-source data for training risk assessment AI for border control is needed to assess the lawfulness of such practices.

This study analyses the legal and ethical challenges that the use of open data from Social Media for training AI systems for border control creates for the protection of the rights of individuals as well as analyses the safeguards for introducing trustworthy AI. The findings are based, but not limited, on research conducted in the framework of the H2020 CRiTERIA project. The scope of this project is to create a novel, comprehensive as well as feasible and human-rights sensitive risk and vulnerability analysis framework that will assist border agencies in better understanding contemporary security threats, connected but not restricted, to migration and to predict and detect risks from both controlled and uncontrolled border crossings. In this framework, the use of open-source data from Social Media is envisaged to fill in any information gaps and to be used for the development of innovative and effective information technology and AI methods in support of the approach for risk, vulnerability and threat analysis.

After this introduction, Section 2 identifies and analyses the legal and ethical challenges that the use of open-source data from Social Media presents. Section 3 focuses on the transparency requirement for AI. The draft AI Act is analysed with an emphasis on the transparency requirements for high-risk AI. Section 4 distinguishes between risk assessment AI systems for border control that directly affect natural persons and the ones that do not. It reflects upon the transparency requirements and open data from Social Media and projects the findings into both types of systems, the ones that directly affect natural persons and the ones that do not. The concluding remarks are presented in the final Section 5.

2. Legal and ethical challenges created by the use of open-source data from Social Media

This section focuses on the legal and ethical challenges that derive from the use of open-source data from Social Media for training AI technology to be used for risk assessment purposes. For understanding the legal challenges, the emphasis is put on the EU data protection framework as well as on studies conducted by various EU bodies with regards to the use of these data for border-crossing purposes. However, since, for the proper protection of natural persons at times of quick technology innovation, the law is only the lowest standard, attention will also be paid to ethical concerns that often escape legal protection. Identifying these challenges is very important since they enable the protection of the fundamental rights of natural persons even beyond the legal requirements.

2.1. Legal challenges

The use of open-source data from social media for risk analyses in border control has been considered for a long time by various EU institutions, as, for example, in the case of Frontex.[4] Warning about the use of this data and data protection issues have been identified by the European Data Protection Supervisor that qualifies social media users monitoring as a personal data processing activity that creates a high risk for individuals' rights and freedoms (EDPS 2019, 3). The main concern is that the use of these data is done beyond any reasonable expectations from data subjects. While individuals use Social Media services for their own purposes, as it is communication, the further use of the data goes beyond their initial purpose and context. Moreover, such processing of data is done in ways that the individual could not reasonably anticipate when making the data available (Edwards and Urquhart 2016). Especially, if the data are used for profiling data subjects, this may imply interference of interests or other characteristics in which the data subject had not actively disclosed, thereby undermining the data subject's ability to exercise control over his or her personal sphere.

The potential legal issues that the EDPS (2019) identified from the use of open-source data from Social Media in a proposal for their use from the European Union Agency for Asylum are:

- Potential high risks to the fundamental rights of data subjects and groups concerned;
- Infringement of the principles of purpose limitation and data minimisation (GDPR (2016), Art 5(1)(b)–(c));
- Infringement of the principles of fairness and transparency (GDPR, Art 5(1)(a));
- Risks in processing special categories of personal data with the result of discriminating data subjects (GDPR, Art 9(1));
- Difficulty in complying with data subjects' rights, especially the right to information, access to data and to object to data processing activities (GDPR, Chapter 3);

- Challenges to data quality since what it is posted on Social Media is not necessarily true or accurate (GDPR, Art 5(1)(d));
- Security concerns related to potential misuse of the data collected (GDPR, Arts 32–34).

Thus, any uses of open-source data from Social Media for profiling purposes must be assessed and must follow strong safeguards for the protection of data subjects' rights and freedoms. Furthermore, these uses must strictly comply with the applicable data protection framework.

Legal concerns have also been identified with regards to the use of open-source aggregate data from Social Media. These have the potential of creating a high risk of using unreliable information, and as a result, any profiling based on inaccurate data would compromise the effectiveness of border control due to incorrect correlations and data distortions (FRA 2018, 119). There are different causes for potential bias results when aggregated data are used, including issues with the training datasets (skewed, incomplete, outdated or disproportionate data) and the algorithms (poorly designed, reflecting biased norms and prejudices, poorly implemented). According to a report from eu-LISA, the problem can be addressed either by using representative data sets for training algorithms or by creating synthetic data sets with characteristics that are representative of the population (eu-LISA 2020). In contrast, the former solution could still pose data protection risks, the latter could lead to higher error rates associated with the use of synthetic data (Dumbrava 2021, 27).

The above discussion shows that there are potential legal concerns for the use of open-source data from Social Media, even at an aggregated form. The data quality is one of these concerns that have implications for the quality of the results of any analyses, even after fulfilling all the data protection standards. However, it needs to be pointed out also that these concerns are identified with regards to use of data for individual profiling or for the projection of the results of data analysis in individual cases. General data analyses that do not affect natural persons are not included in the discussion of the legal concerns thus far.

2.2 Ethical challenges

Issues such as potential discrimination, bias evaluations, potential errors or misuses of the system and data may come at a high price not only from a legal perspective but also from an ethical one (Centre for the study of Global Ethics 2010). The legal challenges identified in the previous section project themselves often also into ethical concerns. The latter might go even beyond the legal regulation and thus be present even if all the processing activity is done in compliance with the existing legal framework (Berry 2004).

Many ethical concerns are already codified. The Ethics Guidelines for Trustworthy Artificial Intelligence, for example, emphasise the need for transparency and accountability, also present in article 5(1)(a) and (2) GDPR, as well as the requirements for consent, information, diversity, and non-discrimination included in the GDPR provisions (AI HLEG 2019). Thus, observing the legal framework would already serve to comply with these challenges. However, not all ethical concerns are codified. Considering all ethical challenges, codified and not codified contributes to a better protection of the rights of natural persons, to a better acceptance of the use of new technological methods in the society, as well as it assists in pacifying relations between various actors in the process.

Thus, the ethical challenges that derive from the use of open-source data from Social Media can be linked to legal challenges or can be distinct from those. For example, the accuracy and reliability of the data, together with the change in the purpose of processing and the reliance on adequate, relevant and proportionate personal data are closely linked to the data protection legal framework. Other challenges, like self-selecting nature of Social Media users; inequalities in access to Social Media platforms; unclear boundaries between public and private spaces for Social Media users; difficulty in obtaining meaning from heterogeneous data for analysts; and difficulty in ensuring anonymity and preserving privacy of natural persons using Social Media are directly linked to the nature of the data and reinforce the data quality concern. Furthermore, one could also identify challenges deriving from the vulnerability of the natural persons crossing a border. While not everyone crossing a border would qualify as vulnerable, many are and risks can be identified for potential misuse and harm caused by the findings of the data analyses; potential harm caused by profiling; and adverse effects, like pushing potential migrants into more dangerous migration routes (Bloemraad and Menjívar 2022).

The identified challenges can be projected as falling under the following meta categories of ethical concerns:

a) Protection of the autonomy and dignity of data subjects – individuals are considered on the basis of their data and their behaviour in social media and not on the basis of their actions in the physical world. Understanding and qualifying information might require understanding the context and mental framework in which certain data were published, and it is difficult to reflect on any changes of mind or *ex post* data deletions or modifications. Furthermore, untrue information or fake data might influence the results of research.
b) Discrimination – possibility for profiling and for personal and sensitive data identification might potentially create situations of discrimination and biased data processing. Stereotypes may be reproduced even unintentionally. This might be augmented by the fact that users of social media platforms are self-selected and inequalities exist in accessing the services. The bias effect might be even the result of the way data are scraped from Social Media, thus might be inherent of another independent existing system.
c) Chilling effects in society – learning about the ways Social Media data are used, might have as a consequence that individuals use the platforms less, are not expressing their opinions freely or are using coded language. They might even be inclined to use different, and often, more dangerous migration routes (Dimitriadi et al. 2021).

2.3 Reflection on the identified legal and ethical challenges with regards to risk assessment systems

The legal and ethical challenges identified make it difficult to justify the necessity and proportionality of the use of open-source data from Social Media for training algorithms and for building any IT or AI systems to be used in individual cases of border control. While the data might fill in informational gaps, legal and ethical concerns about the reliability of the data need to be taken into account and very robust data protection standards need to be introduced in order to comply with the data protection principles of fairness and transparency, with the purpose limitation and data minimisation, with data security, data protection by design and default and with all the data subject rights.

However, one can also argue that even though there are concerns about the use of open-source data from Social Media, at the aggregated level the legal and ethical challenges are less prominent in a risk assessment tool the results of which do not target directly natural persons (Mahoney 2022). The CRiTERIA tool, for example, takes as a starting point existing methodologies used for border control, such as CIRAM,[5] which are recognised to present limitations in terms of scope, data sources, methodology and overall use. To overcome these limitations, the CRiTERIA tool proposes a multi-perspective risk and vulnerability analysis methodology with multi-source, multi-lingual analysis for serving the complex indicators of the threat and risk assessment methodology as well as for making the analysis accessible in a verifiable and understandable way. This proposed tool makes use of open-source data from Social Media to close the information gaps, but it is not used for data subject profiling or for projecting results of data analyses to individual cases. The proposed tool is designed with the scope of understanding general trends and risks at EU borders and to serve border authorities towards a complete risk assessment analyses. As such, the tool aims to be one of the various indicators to be considered during a risk and threat analyses process. As such, it provides some form of strategic intelligence instead of an operational one.

Thus, while the risks for natural persons would be minimised if they are not directly affected, the reliability of the data used for training the system still remains a point of concern. Unreliable data, at personal or aggregated level, will have as consequence unreliable results and, even if not directly, they might indirectly affect data subjects crossing a border. Furthermore, concerns about data security would continue to be present together with the difficulty of ensuring that the data minimisation principle is complied with. Thus, despite the lack of direct data subject concerns, compliance with the transparency requirements remains crucial not only from data protection but also from a technology design perspective. Since from an AI perspective non-compliance with the transparency requirements would qualify the risk to data subjects as unacceptable, the understanding and regulation of transparency in the AI draft Act is discussed in the following section.

3. Transparency and AI

AI is not yet regulated at the European level. In April 2021, a draft regulation on AI was proposed by the European Commission. In December 2023 a political agreement was reached after a trialogue procedure between the European Parliament, the Council and the European Commission. With the future introduction of this legislation, the EU aims to address the risks generated by specific uses of AI through a set of complementary, proportionate and flexible rules, which aim to provide the Union with a leading role in setting the global gold standard for AI.

In Annexe III of the draft Act, AI systems to be used in migration, asylum and border control management are considered as systems of high-risk, when they are intended to:

a) be used by competent public authorities as polygraphs and similar tools or to detect the emotional state of a natural person;
b) be used by competent public authorities to assess a risk, including a security risk, a risk of irregular immigration, or a health risk, posed by a natural person who intends to enter or has entered into the territory of a member state;
c) be used by competent public authorities for the verification of the authenticity of travel documents and supporting documentation of natural persons and detect non-authentic documents by checking their security features;
d) to assist competent public authorities for the examination of applications for asylum, visa and residence permits and associated complaints with regard to the eligibility of the natural persons applying for a status.

There are two important considerations linked to the above-listed situations. Firstly, all situations refer to cases in which the use of AI technology for border control directly affects a natural person – or, said differently, in operational intelligence. Thus, a risk assessment AI tool that is not intended for use in individual cases or, said differently, a system used for strategic intelligence, is not listed as high-risk AI.

Secondly, being qualified as a high-risk does not mean that an AI system cannot be developed or used in the future. It only means that the risks that the use of these tools might present are high for the safety and the protection of fundamental rights of natural persons. Thus, a number of checks and safeguards need to be in place as well as specific requirements enshrined in the articles 8–29 of the current AI draft Act. Although these provisions are not yet law at the time of writing, it is important to already reflect upon them. This section presents a reflection on the general and specific requirements that high-risk AI systems need to comply with and it emphasises on the transparency requirement.

The proposed AI Act is based on article 114 TFEU as its legal basis. Thus, keeping in mind the economic nature of the EU as a regional organisation, one can clearly identify that the focus of the legislation is on the AI product itself and its free movement in the internal market. Because of the economic-driven focus, the draft has an emphasis on the behaviour of the economic operators on the market (Busuioc et al. 2023). The fundamental rights' concerns come as a secondary aim of the legislation but not high enough to justify the use of a more specific legal basis. This conclusion can be identified through the general requirements and safeguards for the design of AI systems. The main focus is on the risk management, on the use of data and on data governance, the technical documentation, record-keeping, human oversight, accuracy, robustness and cybersecurity, without undermining the transparency principle. Furthermore, from a users' perspective, the draft AI Act focuses on the quality of the management system, the technical documentation, conformity assessment, the automatically generated logs, corrective actions, duty of information, as well as cooperation with competent authorities.

Thus, for safeguarding the rights of natural persons, apart from the understanding that the fulfilment of the requirements for transparency and explainability of the AI system are crucial for the use of high-risk AI, it is important to also assess these requirements in light of other legal sources. In the GDPR, the transparency principle (Art 5(1)(a)) is closely linked to the principle of accountability (Art 5(2)) and it even helps for the explainability of a data processing activity (Varošanec 2022). While arts 13–15 GDPR refer to information and explanation duties of controllers of personal data, the law is mute on the level of detail needed for fulfilling these duties. In the draft AI Act, the transparency requirement seems more developed than in the GDPR, even though it is not yet fully understood what this requirement entails. Article 10(2–4) of the draft AI Act seems to link transparency to the quality of the data used for training the AI tools, for their validation and testing. The data must be relevant, representative, free of errors and relevant. These obligations are imposed on AI providers in art 13 of the draft AI Act.

These legal requirements are very relevant as transparency is the necessary condition for trust and it is very closely linked to this concept (Larsson and Heintz 2020). Transparency is also seen as a pre-condition for accountability and as such, transparency in AI is not just understood as visibility but it also refers to the explainaibility of a process (Busuioc et al. 2023). While the use of AI for low-risk decisions carries little, if any, moral hazard and might not require a detailed explanation, the situation becomes problematic when decisions that directly affect natural persons are taken (Enschenbach 2021). Fulfilment of the transparency requirement in these cases is very important since failure would require the AI tool to qualify as falling under the category of unacceptable risk, and thus not be used.

4. Open-source data from Social Media and transparent AI for border control

A 2020 study done for the European Commission (Deloitte 2020) identified five clusters of opportunities for the use of AI in border control, migration and security. These are chatbots and virtual assistants; risk assessment and application triaging in the context of the visa process; knowledge management tools; policy insight and analytics tools; and computer vision applications 'to gain insights from image processing of individuals (faces, fingerprints, etc.) and objects'.

Furthermore, Frontex (the European Border and Coast Guard Agency) has argued for the use of more open data from Social Media in the framework of democratisation of AI (Frontex 2020, 26). Currently, in a recent draft Regulation from the European Commission (European Commission 2023), it is required to increase the number of open-source and Social Media monitoring specialists to support Member States' investigations and preventive measures concerning organised migrant smuggling and trafficking in human beings. In relation to AI, this encompasses the proliferation of open-source, low-cost technological solutions, enabling easier access for a greater number and variety of stakeholders, including border security agencies. However, when considering the use of open data from Social Media, it is important to distinguish between AI systems that affect natural persons and AI systems that do not directly affect natural persons. This distinction is important for being able to weigh the risks that the use of these systems would present.

From Annexe III of the current draft AI Act, it is clear that the high-risk qualification is reserved for these systems that directly affect the situation of a natural person. Thus, AI risk assessment systems to be used for regular and irregular border crossing for understanding general risks and threats, as in the case of the CRiTERIA system, would escape such qualification.

For high-risk systems, the compliance with the transparency requirement and especially with the data quality standard is crucial for justifying the lawful use of such systems. As clearly stated in recital 44 of the draft AI Act, high data quality is essential for the performance of many AI systems, especially when techniques involving the training of models are used, with a view to ensure that the high-risk AI system performs as intended and safely, and it does not become the source of any discrimination that is prohibited by Union law. The legal and ethical challenges of open-source data from Social Media discussed in Section 2 have shown that it is impossible to ensure that these data are free from errors and complete in order to ensure a proper training of the algorithms. From an accountability consideration, the nature of the data and of the Social Media environment makes it impossible to prove that the databases used for training the systems are unbiased by nature or that will provide unbiased output. Thus, it is impossible to prove the severity of risks linked to biased data and presented to the safety and security of natural persons. A proper reliance on the legal rules and ethical concerns would qualify such AI tools as presenting unacceptable risks.

The situation is different when the risk assessment system does not affect natural persons directly as in the example of CRiTERIA. Such a system escapes the high-risk qualification and it is thus presenting low-risk concerns for the safety of natural persons. Thus, the use of open data from Social Media would be justified for these systems. However, it must be ensured that the proper security measures are in place and that the systems as well as the created databases are not used for any other purposes than the ones that justify their use. For example, a system and database created for a general risk assessment (strategic intelligence), is not used for profiling natural persons (operational intelligence).

5. Conclusion and reflections

The use of open-source data from Social Media for training AI technology is encouraged not only because these data are easily accessible and available but also because of the silence of the current legal framework on the use of these data. The AI democratisation argument encourages their use in order to make AI more accessible and to provide low-cost solutions. In this paper, it was argued that the use of open-source data from Social Media for training AI for border control needs to be evaluated in light of the data quality and it presents problems in the framework of the transparency principle.

From a legal perspective, the use of open-source data from Social Media creates potential risks to the fundamental right to data protection of data subjects because of the potential infringement of the principles of purpose limitation and data minimisation as well as of the principles of fairness and transparency. Furthermore, it creates situations of potential discrimination of data subjects based on processing special categories of personal data, difficulties in complying with their data subjects' rights, and challenges for ensuring the quality of data and the security of the databases. From an ethical perspective, three main categories of potential concerns were identified: (i) difficulties in protecting the autonomy and dignity of data subjects; (ii) potential discrimination based on sensitive information, as well as (iii) chilling effects on society.

While the development of AI technology is advancing with tremendous speed, it is crucial for the protection of the rights of natural persons to ensure that the technology does not interfere unjustly with their fundamental rights. The draft AI Act introduces a qualification of AI technology on the basis of the risks that the use of the technology presents for the enjoyment of fundamental rights and for the safety of natural persons. Transparency, closely linked to the explainability of the technology, serves as the dividing line between high-risk and unacceptable-risk technology.

AI systems to be used for border control are qualified as high-risk in the draft AI Act. A close look to the letter of the law, however, shows that this qualification embraces only those systems that affect directly natural persons. AI used for general risk assessment systems that do not affect natural persons escapes such qualification.

A legal and ethical analysis of open-source data from Social Media has shown that they do not pass the data quality requirement. Thus, these data cannot be used for training high-risk AI. However, the data can be used for training minimal or limited risk AI. General risk assessment systems would not fall under the high-risk qualification making it possible for such systems to have less strict requirements with regards to the quality of the data used. However, these systems must ensure that the data quality would not undermine the overall results as well as they need to apply very strict data protection standards. Since it currently appears that the AI regulation in the EU will have at the basis of its existence the aim of fulfilling economic interests in the internal market, it is essential to look for safeguards for the protection of the rights of natural persons and their safety beyond the letter of this law. Only in this way, one could benefit from the advantages of technology while ensuring the protection of the rights of natural persons.

Notes

1. H2020 CRiTERIA project (Comprehensive data-driven Risk and Threat Assessment Methods for the Early and Reliable Identification, Validation and Analysis of migration-related risks) has received funding from the European Union's Horizon 2020 research and innovation action program under grant agreement No 101021866.
2. At the time of writing and of the revision of this article (January 2024), the official draft of the AI Act available does not reflect on the trialogue agreement reached between the Commission, The European Parliament and the Council on the 9th of December 2023. This agreement does not change the core of our discussion. The main outcomes of the political deal can be found here: https://www.europarl.europa.eu/news/en/press-room/20231206IPR15699/artificial-intelligence-act-deal-on-comprehensive-rules-for-trustworthy-ai accessed 30 January 2024.
3. See the open letter by 195 organisations and individuals, led by EDRi, Access Now, Refugee Law Lab and PICUM 'Civil society calls for the EU AI Act to better protect people on the move', available at: https://edri.org/our-work/civil-society-calls-for-the-eu-ai-act-to-better-protect-people-on-the-move/ accessed 14 June 2023.
4. In 2019, Frontex opened a call for tender on provision of services related to social media analysis and monitoring for the purpose of improved risk analysis regarding future irregular migratory movements impacting external borders of the European Union (EU) and Schengen Associated Countries (SAC) and to support of planning, conduct and evaluation of joint operations coordinated by Frontex, as described in terms of reference (Annex II). The call was cancelled quickly after the publication. Please check: https://etendering.ted.europa.eu/cft/cft-display.html?cftId=5471 accessed 14 June 2023.
5. A short overview of CIRAM (Common Integrated Risk Analysis Model) can be found online at: https://frontex.europa.eu/we-know/situational-awareness-and-monitoring/ciram/ accessed 14 June 2023.

Disclosure statement

No potential conflict of interest was reported by the author(s).

References

AI HLEG. 2019. "Ethics guidelines for trustworthy AI" Accessed June 14, 2023 https://ec.europa.eu/digital-single-market/en/news/ethicsguidelines-trustworthy-ai.

Berry, D. M. 2004. "Internet Research: Privacy, Ethics and Alienation: An Open Source Approach." *Internet Research* 14 (4): 323–332. https://doi.org/10.1108/10662240410555333.

Bloemraad, I., and C. Menjívar. 2022. "Precarious Times, Professional Tensions: The Ethics of Migration Research and the Drive for Scientific Accountability." *International Migration Review* 56 (1): 4–32. https://doi.org/10.1177/01979183211014455.

Busuioc, M., et al. 2023. "Reclaiming Transparency: Contesting the Logics of Secrecy Within the AI Act." *European Law Open* 2 (1): 79–105. https://doi.org/10.1017/elo.2022.47.

Centre for the Study of Global Ethics. 2010. "Ethics of Border Security" Accessed June 14, 2023 https://frontex.europa.eu/assets/Publications/Research/Ethics_of_Border_Security_Report.pdf.

COM. 2016. Communication from the Commission to the European Parliament and the Council Stronger and Smarter Information Systems for Borders and Security COM/2016/0205 final" Accessed June 14, 2023 https://eur-lex.europa.eu/legal-content/EN/TXT/?uri=COM%3A2016%3A205%3AFIN.

Data Governance Act. 2020. Regulation (EU) 2022/868 of the European Parliament and of the Council of 30 May 2022 on European data governance and amending Regulation (EU) 2018/1724 [2020] OJ L152/1.

Deloitte. 2020. "Opportunities and challenges for the use of artificial intelligence in border control, migration and security" Accessed June 14, 2023 https://op.europa.eu/en/publication-detail/-/publication/c8823cd1-a152-11ea-9d2d-01aa75ed71a1/language-en.

Digital Single Market Strategy. 2015. Communication from the Commission to the European Parliament, the Council, the European Economic and Social Committee and the Committee of the Regions: A Digital Single Market Strategy for Europe [2015] COM/2015/0192 final.

Dimitriadi, A., et al. 2021. "Countering Smuggling of Migrants Through Social Media Monitoring: Looking for a Needle in a Digital Haystack." In *'Beyond Networks, Militias and Tribes: Rethinking EU Counter-Smuggling Policy and Response' 19 EuroMesCo Policy Study*, edited by G. Sanchez, 34–51. https://www.euromesco.net/wpcontent/uploads/2021/05/RETHINKING-EU-COUNTER-SMUGGLING-POLICY-AND-RESPONSE-1.pdf.

Draft AI Act. 2021. European Commission, Proposal for a Regulation of the European Parliament and of the Council laying down harmonised rules on artificial intelligence (Artificial Intelligence Act) and amending certain Union legislative acts (21 April 2021) COM(2021) 206 final.

Dumbrava, C. 2021. "Artificial intelligence at EU borders" Accessed June 14, 2023 https://www.europarl.europa.eu/RegData/etudes/IDAN/2021/690706/EPRS_IDA(2021)690706_EN.pdf.

EDPS. 2019. "Formal consultation on EASO's social media monitoring reports (case 2018-1083)" Accessed June 14, 2023 https://edps.europa.eu/sites/default/files/publication/19-11-12_reply_easo_ssm_final_reply_en.pdf.

Edwards, L., and L. Urquhart. 2016. "Privacy in Public Spaces: What Expectations of Privacy Do We Have in Social Media Intelligence?" *International Journal of Law and Information Technology* 24: 279.

Enschenbach, W. J. 2021. "Transparency and the Black box Problem: Why we do not Trust AI." *Philos. Technol* 34: 1607–1622. https://doi.org/10.1007/s13347-021-00477-0.

eu-LISA. 2020. "Artificial Intelligence in the Operational Management of Large-scale IT Systems" Accessed June 14, 2023 https://www.eulisa.europa.eu/Publications/Reports/AI%20in%20the%20OM%20of%20Large-scale%20IT%20Systems.pdf.

European Commission. 2023. Proposal for a REGULATION OF THE EUROPEAN PARLIAMENT AND OF THE COUNCIL on enhancing police cooperation in relation to the prevention, detection and investigation of migrant smuggling and trafficking in human beings, and on enhancing

Europol's support to preventing and combating such crimes and amending Regulation (EU) 2016/794, COM/2023/754 final.

EUROSUR. 2019. Regulation (EU) 2019/1896 of the European Parliament and of the Council of 13 November 2019 on the European Border and Coast Guard and repealing Regulations (EU) No 1052/2013 and (EU) 2016/1624 [2019] OJ L295/1.

FRA. 2018. "Preventing unlawful profiling today and in the future: a guide" Accessed June 14, 2023 https://fra.europa.eu/sites/default/files/fra_uploads/fra-2018-preventing-unlawful-profiling-guide_en.pdf.

Frontex. 2020. "Artificial Intelligence – based capabilities for the European Border and Coast Guard" Accessed June 14, 2023 https://frontex.europa.eu/assets/Publications/Research/Frontex_AI_Research_Study_2020_final_report.pdf.

GDPR. 2016. Regulation (EU) 2016/679 0f the European Parliament and of the Council of 27 April 2016 on the protection of natural persons with regard to the processing of personal data and the free movement of such data, and repealing Directive 95/46/EC (GDPR) [2016] OJ L119/1.

Larsson, S., and F. Heintz. 2020. "Transparency in Artificial Intelligence." *Internet Policy Review* 9 (2): 1–16. https://doi.org/10.14763/2020.2.1469.

Mahoney, J., et al. 2022. "Ethical Considerations in Social Media Analytics in the Context of Migration: Lessons Learned from a Horizon 2020 Project." *Research Ethics* 18 (3): 226–240. https://doi.org/10.1177/17470161221087542.

Varošanec, I. 2022. "On the Path to the Future: Mapping the Notion of Transparency in the EU Regulatory Framework for AI." *International Review of Law, Computers & Technology* 36 (2): 95–117. https://doi.org/10.1080/13600869.2022.2060471.

ChatGPT for good? Taking 'beneficence' seriously in the regulation of generative artificial intelligence

Krishna Deo Singh Chauhan

ABSTRACT
Generative AI platforms such as ChatGPT have found prominence in recent times with their ability to generate texts, images, etc. Several questions pertaining to ethical and legal issues surrounding ChatGPT have arisen. In this paper, I discuss the nature and background of generative AI, situating its development in the historical context of AI. I then discuss my primary research questions: is sufficient attention paid in the literature on ethics of AI to the principle of beneficence and is there theoretical clarity on its meaning? I highlight that while there is great deal of discussion on what harms can arise from generative AI and how to stop them, there is very little discussion on what amounts to AI-for-good, particularly in the literature of AI ethics and regulation. To the extent that such discussion exists, it pushes ahead with suggesting specific solutions, without fully addressing the underlying question of what makes their prescriptions beneficent. I demonstrate that the principle of beneficence as understood in biomedical ethics and human rights frameworks has limited utility for the ethics of generative AI. These gaps in the AI regulation are prominent, as they can derail long term progress of generative AI and the realization of its full potential.

Introduction

Artificial Intelligence (AI) has emerged as a transformative force, revolutionizing various aspects of our lives and promising unprecedented opportunities for global good. Among the remarkable advancements within the AI landscape, generative AI stands out as a technological marvel, offering immense potential to shape a brighter future for humanity. By enabling machines to 'infer, from the input they receive, how to generate outputs' (OECD 2019), that include content such as text, images and even videos, generative AI opens new frontiers of innovation, creativity, and problem-solving.

The promises of generative AI straddle a wide range of applications, spanning multiple industries and sectors. At the highest level, Generative AI has the potential to boost productivity growth globally and open up new opportunities for growth across various sectors and regions. According to Goldman Sachs, generative AI could increase global GDP by nearly 7% and create markets for suppliers of technology and services worth hundreds of billions of dollars (Goldman Sachs 2023). In addition, there are a number of sector specific applications that build upon these 'foundation models' (Bommasani et al. 2021). Already, extensive integration of AI systems such as ChatGPT with other apps and services is underway (Esther 2023). Another report by Bloomberg projects an AI market worth 1.3 Trillion Dollars by 2032, fueled by ChatGPT (Rudnitsky 2023). It is clear that generative AI is here to stay.

Indeed, there is already much discussion on the tantalizing yet uncertain path towards achieving Artificial General Intelligence (AGI) that we seem to have already tread on. AGI refers to highly autonomous systems capable of outperforming humans across a wide range of intellectual tasks. Although the views on the path from generative AI to AGI are not unanimous, many experts believe that there is a clear path from generative AI to AGI, and that generative AI is a stepping stone towards achieving AGI (Bubeck et al. 2023; Rosenberg 2023; Zhang et al. 2023). They argue that generative AI can demonstrate some aspects of human intelligence, such as creativity, communication and knowledge synthesis. They also claim that generative AI can become more context-aware, adaptable and generalizable as the foundation models become larger and more diverse. They expect that generative AI will eventually reach a level of performance and complexity that will enable it to achieve AGI. While AGI poses complex ethical, social, and safety challenges, it also holds the promise of revolutionizing society and unlocking unforeseen advancements.

On this journey, do law and regulation have a role? Particularly, do they have a role in ensuring that the technology delivers on all its promises, and delivers well?

Historian Yuval Noah Harari, writing on the promises and perils of generative language models, made the following observation:

> Of course, the new power of AI could be used for good purposes as well. I won't dwell on this, because the people who develop AI talk about it enough. The job of historians and philosophers like myself is to point out the dangers (Harari 2023).

As will be shown in this paper, it appears that regulators as well as legal and regulatory scholars believe themselves to be in the same category as historians and philosophers, if not even more reluctant to talk about the 'good purposes'. 'The promises will be taken care by others, let's focus on the perils', seems to be the prevailing wisdom.

Taking a critical stance towards this notion, this paper asks two questions. First, whether sufficient attention is paid in the literature on ethics of AI to the principle of beneficence, which underlies the notion of AI-for-good? Generally, the concept of beneficence encompasses actions or individual attributes characterized by mercy, kindness, generosity, and charity. It implies altruism, love, humanity, and the advancement of the well-being of others (Beauchamp 2019). But beyond this general description, in my second research question, I ask whether as a normative principle of AI ethics, there is theoretical clarity on its meaning? Firstly, this part argues that insufficient attention is paid to the principle of beneficence, and that there are good reasons for striking a balance between 'AI-for-good' approach to AI regulation along with the 'AI-as-Wrongs' approach, which holds nearly universal sway in legal and regulatory scholarship concerning AI (Lobel 2023). To this end, it draws extensively from the work of Orly Lobel, among others. However, in the second subpart, it also puts Lobel's work along with the existing AI-for-good literature under the scrutinizing lens and demonstrates that the movement lacks a clear and theoretically rigorous notion of what it means for AI to be good. To this end, it studies the theoretical foundations of 'beneficence' as an ethical principle and maps its meaning and scope by discussing what it entails under some prominent literature that deals with beneficence. In the ethics of AI, the imperative to use AI for good has come to be represented by this principle. It has principally been borrowed from the domain of bioethics. However, this paper demonstrates that existing theoretical foundations of this principle in bioethics, and even in human rights are not suitable for its application to AI. It concludes by suggesting possible paths for further scholarship to explore for founding this principle in a more tenable manner.

In line with the above, Part I introduces AI as well as generative AI, along with the existing views on the regulation of generative AI. Part II focuses on the need for the AI-for-good approach and 'beneficence' in such regulation, in addition to the AI-as-wrongs approach. Part III critiques the existing understanding of beneficence.

Part I – generative AI and its regulation

Generative AI – meaning

What is 'generative AI'? In order to answer this question, we must first answer: what is AI?

Artificial Intelligence is a field of inquiry that aims to create machines and systems that can display intelligent behavior. What constitutes intelligent behavior and how should it be built, have however been a subject of intense disagreement and debate over the decades since the birth of this field around the middle of the last century (Wooldridge 2021). It has not even been limited to computer science, but has been explored by several fields, both in isolation, and in conjunction with each other (Russell and Norvig 2010).

For the present purposes, it suffices to say that the dominant approach in AI today is based on allowing computers to learn sub-symbolically. This can be understood best in contradistinction to an opposing approach – the symbolic approach. Under the latter, building AI systems includes providing step by step instructions to computers, the logic of which is understandable to humans. Much AI, historically, pertained to this approach. However, since around early 2010s, AI has been dominated by Machine Learning (ML), that allows AI to learn how to achieve a given outcome on its own, without humans providing the instructions to that end. This is sub-symbolic, because the logic of how the outcome is achieved is intrinsically not understandable for a human (Mitchell 2019).

AI has seen very strong growth in applicability and utility over the past decade. It has found applications everywhere, from internet-based platforms to policy making and law enforcement, from scientific research to games such as Go (Deepmind 2017; Jumper et al. 2021). Three factors are often credited with this exponential surge. First, the innovations in the underlying algorithms that make ML possible, primarily Artificial Neural Networks (ANNs), a type of algorithms that are modeled on human brain cells, or neurons. Second, the availability of vast swathes of data, which provide the input necessary to learn from. Third, advances in computing architecture and particularly, Graphic Processing Units (GPUs) (Janakiram 2018).

However, many of the initially successful applications of AI were 'discriminative', and not generative. This means that these systems could classify and predict, but not generate. For instance, consider facial recognition systems and recommendation systems.

These AI systems do not produce content, but classify which face belongs to which person or predict which content is likely to garner higher user attention. Generative AI on the other hand, such as ChatGPT or Dall.E, produces new content (Goled 2021). In other words, discriminative AI can tell you whether the animal in a picture is a cat; generative AI can actually draw you a picture of a cat (Hacker, Engel, and Mauer 2023, 3).

Generative AI – history

The origins of generative AI are often traced back to 1966, when MIT professor Joseph Weizenbaum created the first chatbot, Eliza (Fruhlinger 2023). Eliza was designed to simulate a therapist and engage in conversations with users. Even though Eliza's responses were quite simple and rule-based, it generated a lot of excitement at the time and paved the way for future developments in generative AI and chatbots (Salecha 2016).

Generally, the interest in generative AI waned and waxed in parallel with AI winters and springs. In addition to innovations in ANNs generally, two more significant advances had to happen before the current generation of generative AI could emerge. First, Generative Adversarial Networks (GANs), proposed by Ian Goodfellow and his colleagues in 2014, revolutionized the field of generative AI (Goodfellow et al. 2014). GANs consisted of two neural networks: a generator and a discriminator. The generator network created new samples, while the discriminator network tried to distinguish between real and generated samples. Through an adversarial training process, the generator gradually improved its ability to produce realistic data, while the discriminator became better at detecting fake data. GANs are the technology behind deepfakes, but have been successfully applied to numerous useful domains as well, including image synthesis for medical purposes, text generation, and music composition (McNemar 2022).

Second, introduced in 2017, Transformer models marked another significant milestone in generative AI, particularly in text generation. The key innovation of transformer models was their ability to capture the relationships and dependencies between words in a piece of text. Using a technique called 'attention', these models learned how to assign different importance to different words and phrases based on their relevance to the overall meaning of the text, or the 'context'. This proved critical, as it leapfrogged text generation much closer to human-like text, as humans also pay attention to different parts language when conversing with others, and similarly assign more importance to certain words and phrases than others (Merritt 2022).

Building on these advances, the Generative Pre-trained Transformer (GPT) models were introduced in 2018 (VanBuskirk 2023), which has led to the creation of ChatGPT et al. These models have pushed the boundaries of generative AI, enabling the generation of highly original text. Today, it would not be an exaggeration to say that generative AI is the most talked about technology. Literature discussing every aspect of generative AI, from its promises to perils, and capabilities to limitations continues to emerge profusely.

Even beyond the hype, some real-world changes are clearly on the horizon. Generative AI is expected to transform business. For instance, through generative AI, IT industry can produce and review code, marketing may use personalized marketing and virtual sales assistants, and even legal services may use it to draft and review legal documents (Chui, Roberts, and Yee 2022). In customer service, it can provide instant and accurate responses, improving user satisfaction and reducing the workload of human agents.

Clearly, it can also transform the creative industry, by bringing such features as automated and personalized content generation and increasing the variety and quality of content (Davenport and Mittal 2022). The Governments have already started studying how to use this technology to maximize economic and social gains for its citizens (Elias and Raja 2023).

The evolution of generative AI discussed above throws light on several aspects. First, despite their recent success, this technology has historical roots that goes back several decades. It also shows that the current capabilities have emerged from several generations of technologies built on top of another.

Risks of generative AI

But just like discriminative AI, and perhaps even more inconspicuous than the former, generative AI brings with a set of risks and harms. Some important examples are (Gow 2023; Ortiz 2023):

(1) Hallucinations: Generative AI models may produce outputs that are not accurate or realistic, but rather based on patterns or biases in the data. This could lead to false or misleading information, such as fake news, distorted statistics, or inaccurate predictions.
(2) Misinformation: Generative AI models may be used to manipulate images, videos, audio, or text to create realistic but fake representations of people or events. This could be used for malicious purposes, such as impersonation, fraud, blackmail, defamation, or propaganda.
(3) Data privacy: Generative AI models may inadvertently reveal sensitive or personal information about individuals or organizations that are present in the data. This could violate data protection laws and ethical principles, as well as expose people to identity theft, discrimination, or harassment.
(4) Copyright issues: Generative AI models may generate outputs that infringe on the intellectual property rights of others. Also, the training process may use copyrighted material, which also arguably counts as copyright infringement.[1]
(5) Cybersecurity problems: Since generative AI models can be used to produce innovative code, and faster than ever before, malicious actors may use it to produce novel and potentially more pernicious code to be used for cyberattacks.

But these are not all of it. On 22 March 2023, a call for pausing development of AI further was made by the Future of Life Institute, a nonprofit organization that aims to reduce existential risks from advanced technologies. The call was made in an open letter titled 'Pause Giant AI Experiments: An Open Letter' that was signed by more than 20,000 people, including Elon Musk, the CEO of Tesla and SpaceX, Steve Wozniak, the co-founder of Apple, and Andrew Yang, an entrepreneur and a former presidential candidate ("Pause Giant AI Experiments: An Open Letter" 2023).

The letter urged AI labs to pause development of AI systems more powerful than ChatGPT. The letter cited 'profound risks to society and humanity' from such AI systems, including, but not limited to the ones noted above (Kelly 2023; Rash 2023). Another paper by the CEO of OpenAI along with leading scientists made the case for

Governance of Artificial Super Intelligence, which they define as 'future AI systems dramatically more capable than even AGI' (Altman, Brockman, and Sutskever 2023).

In short, the fears from generative AI have crossed the bridge from near-term harms to existential harms. In response to both types of harms, several proposals have been made. In the next section, we discuss these proposals.

Regulating generative AI – the state of affairs

The EU AI act

A draft 'AI Act' was released by the European Union in April 2021 (European Commission 2021). The Act classified AI into different tiers based on the risks it poses. These tiers included unacceptable risk (prohibited), high risk (heavily regulated), low risk (transparency obligations), and minimal risk (voluntary codes of conduct). The primary objective behind this categorization was to safeguard the safety and fundamental rights of EU citizens.

Initially, this approach was justified as it addressed the pressing issue of discriminative AI, which was a prominent concern during the Act's drafting. However, as the focus shifted to the risks associated with generative AI, the effectiveness of this approach became questionable (Coulter and Mukherjee 2023). Applications such as ChatGPT, for example, may not directly violate safety or human rights in an obvious manner. Instead, they present risks that are more subtle and impact not only the fundamental rights of individuals but also the overall societal fabric (Chauhan 2023). The advent of generative AI thus posed challenges and complexities, necessitating further deliberation and adjustments during the negotiation process surrounding the AI Act, even while it was nearing the voting stage.

Nonetheless, certain provisions addressing the risks associated with such AI have been incorporated into the draft AI Act (Bertuzzi 2023). In a later draft,[2] the Act proposed a separate category of 'foundation models'. A foundation model has been defined as 'an AI model that is trained on broad data at scale, is designed for generality of output, and can be adapted to a wide range of distinctive tasks'.[3]

The rationale for including foundation models into the draft is clarified in Recital 60e, which notes:

> Foundation models are a recent development, in which AI models are developed from algorithms designed to optimize for *generality and versatility* of output. Those models are often trained on a broad range of data sources and large amounts of data to accomplish a wide range of downstream tasks, *including some for which they were not specifically developed and trained.* Those systems can be unimodal or multimodal, trained through various methods such as supervised learning or reinforced learning. AI systems with specific intended purpose or general purpose AI systems can be an implementation of a foundation model, which means that each foundation model can be reused in countless downstream AI or general purpose AI systems. *These models hold growing importance to many downstream applications and systems* (emphasis added).

This recital demonstrates the realization of the legislators that these technologies are not only powerful, but they will also have many more applications in the future with emergent characteristics that cannot be foreseen in advance.

Foundation models carry several regulatory requirements. Most important of these are listed in Article 28b (4) of the draft. This provision requires providers of foundation models used in AI systems designed for generative purposes to adhere to certain obligations. Firstly, they must comply with the transparency requirements outlined in Article 52 (1). This means they need to ensure that it is clear to users that the content generated by the AI system is produced by an automated process, not by humans. Secondly, these providers are responsible for training, and if applicable, designing and developing the foundation model in a manner that incorporates adequate safeguards to prevent the generation of content that violates Union law, such as infringement of fundamental rights, including the freedom of expression. Lastly, while respecting national and Union legislation on copyright, these providers are required to document and publicly share a sufficiently detailed summary of the use of training data that is protected under copyright law.

Many other obligations have been created for such systems. For instance, along with High-Risk systems, they should be registered in a database managed by the European Commission.[4] The draft Act also creates a framework for ongoing regulation. It notes that given the novel and rapidly advancing progress of foundation models, it is fitting for the Commission and the AI Office to actively oversee and periodically evaluate the legal and regulatory framework concerning these models. This is particularly crucial for generative AI systems that rely on such models, as they give rise to substantial concerns regarding the production of unlawful content, infringement of copyright rules, and the potential for misuse.[5]

Other proposals

More and diverse proposals to regulate generative AI are emerging from scholarly literature, that add to the discourse on this issue. We will consider two of these here.

First, Hacker et al. present a proposal for regulation of what they call Large generative AI models (LGAIMs) (Hacker, Engel, and Mauer 2023).

First of all, they suggest that obligations can no longer be applied only to developers, but must extend to deployers, who provide specific applications built on the AI system created by developers, and even to users, who finally use the applications to generate content. Further, they propose that regulation of LGAIMs is to be done via fulfilling three layers of obligations.

First set includes minimum standards that are required to be fulfilled for all LGAIMs. Second set includes specific high-risk rules that are applied only to LGAIMS used in concrete high-risk cases. Third set that governs collaboration along the AI value chain to enable effective compliance of (i) & (ii).

Further recommendations are categorized into four categories:

- The obligation of transparency entails the requirement to provide information about the origin and curation of training data, as well as strategies to mitigate harmful content. Professional users, particularly in journalism, academic research, or education, will be obligated to disclose which parts of their publicly available content were generated or adapted by LGAIMs.
- Mandatory risk management, although limited in scope, applies specifically to high-risk purposes. This includes implementing measures such as staged release and restricting access to security researchers and stakeholders, thereby promoting a form of 'regulated self-regulation'.

- Non-discrimination data audits are proposed to address AI-driven discrimination. This involves actions like supplementing real-world training data with synthetic data to counterbalance historical and societal biases.
- Lastly, an expansion of content moderation is recommended to address potential misuse of AI for disinformation, manipulation, and harmful speech. This aims to enhance the ability to monitor and regulate such content.

Secondly, a very interesting approach is presented by Schmit et al. They suggest a novel approach to controlling the use of AI by private entities through the application of copyleft licensing and the creation of an enforcement entity. Copyleft licenses, commonly used in open-source software, enable the use, modification, and reuse of content under specific license terms. This model proposes the use of copyleft licenses to impose ethical guidelines on AI users, such as ensuring transparent assessments of bias impact. Additionally, these licenses transfer the legal right to enforce violations to a trusted third party.

By establishing an enforcement entity, which operates similarly to a patent troll, the model creates a private entity dedicated to enforcing ethical AI standards. This entity is funded partly through fines imposed for unethical conduct. However, instead of enforcing intellectual property rights for profit, this entity's objective is to enforce the rights towards ethical ends, which have been outlined in the licenses *ex ante*. This approach allows private parties to leverage copyright law to protect ethical imperatives associated with AI use and ensure compliance with specified ethical guidelines (Schmit, Doerr, and Wagner 2023).

Without going into the merits of these proposals, it is conspicuous that their primary mandate is harm avoidance. This applies to the scholarly proposals discussed above, but also to the EU AI Act. Article 28b (4) provides for rules that *prevent harm* arising out of opacity, copyright violation, and other content generation that violates the extant law. Recital 60e notes that 'such models should be subject to proportionate and more specific requirements and obligations under this Regulation, namely foundation models should *assess and mitigate possible risks and harms …* ' (emphasis added). However, the Act does not deal with the possible goods and benefits, what such goods and benefits entail, or mechanisms to ensure that maximum benefit is derived out of the technology.

This can be further witnessed in the overarching principles laid down in the draft Act that governs AI regulation. Article 4a lays down 'General principles applicable to all AI systems', and it lays down six principles:

(1) human agency and oversight
(2) technical robustness and safety
(3) privacy and data governance
(4) transparency
(5) diversity, non-discrimination and fairness
(6) social and environmental well-being

Only one, and the last one, deals with beneficial outcomes directly: 'social and environmental well-being'. It is defined as meaning 'that AI systems shall be developed and used in a sustainable and environmentally friendly manner as well as *in a way to benefit all human beings*, while monitoring and assessing the long-term impacts on the individual, society and democracy'[6] (emphasis added). What is the way to benefit all human beings? Are sustainability and environmentally friendly development of AI necessary and sufficient conditions of beneficial AI? To what end would long-term impacts be monitored? Which kind of impacts would be considered beneficial, and which would be considered harmful? These questions are not answered.

Why is this problematic? Let's explore it in the next section.

Part II – law of AI-for-good v. law of AI-as-wrongs

This part presents two arguments: that policy and regulatory thinking around AI has a negativity bias, and that this negativity bias has undesirable consequences.

The skewed focus on non-maleficence as against beneficence

The principles of AI ethics provide guidelines and standards for the responsible development, deployment, and use of AI systems. Such principles are useful because they provide a flexible and adaptable framework that can address ethical concerns and promote responsible behavior, even in the absence of specific regulations. But importantly, even when regulation is created, they form the normative undergirding thereof.

In a study published by Jobin et al, the authors found that as many as 84 guidelines had been published by private companies, research institutions, industry organizations and governmental and inter-governmental organizations containing ethical principles or guidelines for AI. They found that 11 common ethical principles could be identified after studying and classifying the 84 documents. These were, transparency, justice and fairness, non-maleficence, responsibility, privacy, beneficence, freedom and autonomy, trust, dignity, sustainability, and solidarity (Jobin, Ienca, and Vayena 2019).

However, one observation by the authors of this study is particularly illuminating. After finding that broadly, 11 such principles could be identified, they noted: '[b]ecause references to non-maleficence outnumber those related to beneficence, it appears that issuers of guidelines are preoccupied with the moral obligation to prevent harm'(Jobin, Ienca, and Vayena 2019, 396). They also noted that consensus seemed to be emerging around five of these principles: transparency, justice and fairness, non-maleficence, responsibility and privacy. Beneficence was not one of them. The paper reveals that beneficence was found in 41 of the Guidelines, as against non-maleficence, which was found in 60 of the studied documents. This means that more than 50% of the ethical guidelines released on AI, which were also prominent enough to feature in a leading study, did not consider it necessary to lay down beneficence (or its equivalent) as an ethical principle that concerns AI (Jobin, Ienca, and Vayena 2019, 395).

This argument concerning the negativity bias has been presented most extensively by Lobel (2023). In order to fully explain it, she describes the phenomenon of 'techlash' – 'a mindset and regulatory framework that regards new technological capabilities as presumptively and primarily harmful' (Lobel 2023, 8). She argues that the near-exclusive focus on harms in the scholarship as well as in the policy making and regulation leads to a distorted discourse and 'to limited, and even wrong, policy conclusions' (Lobel 2023, 9).

The techlash reflects the shortcomings of liberal democracies, with their emphasis on law as negative constraints rather than a comprehensive approach to governance. This means that the primary focus is on limiting the power of the government and protecting individual rights, often neglecting the broader aspects of effective governance and social well-being. This has several undesirable consequences.

Undesirable consequences of the skewed focus

The negativity bias has several implications. One is that while governments can encourage innovation generally, they do not have the mandate to either determine what positive outcomes should technological innovations lead to, nor to take *any* action to ensure such ends. This implication is not only at odds with the *guardianship liberalism* required of the government (Lobel 2023, 56), but also discourages patient and thorough inquiry into the nature of beneficence, as we will discover in the next part.

Secondly, as Lobel notes, techlash based arguments suffer from a number of contradictions and fallacies. Lobel outlines six such fallacies: Let's look at the first three of these in detail to gauge the gist of her arguments[7]:

(1) The Human/Machine Double Standard – The first fallacy identified is the demand for AI perfection rather than recognizing its comparative advantage over human decision-making and the existing status quo. The author suggests that policymakers should engage in a comparative advantage analysis, comparing the performance of AI systems to what is currently achievable by humans or machines, rather than an unattainable ideal. For instance, instead of expecting autonomous vehicles to drive without any crashes, it is more meaningful to compare their performance with human-driven vehicles to determine their relative benefits.

    Not taking such comparative perspective threatens to deprive us of the benefits of automation, that might not only include, for instance, less road accidents and better safety, but also more time available for other pursuits of choice (Lobel 2023, 14).

(2) AI as Static & Fixed – The techlash discourse often exhibits a recurring pattern of labeling an entire technology as a failure based on isolated instances of automated systems that have failed or shown limitations or biases. However, it is important to recognize that AI, particularly machine learning, is an evolving technology designed to improve over time. While some notable examples of AI failures, such as facial recognition systems exhibiting lower accuracy with darker-skinned women or Amazon's biased hiring algorithm, are frequently highlighted, crucial details are often omitted. For instance, Amazon never deployed the biased hiring system, and automated screening in the job market is often more predictive and inclusive than human screening. It is essential to embed ethical choices into the initial design of AI systems, address biases in training data, and learn from past inequities. However, it is also crucial to acknowledge that technology allows for learning and improvement over time (Lobel 2023, 15).

    Once again, by not incorporating the aspects of improved efficacy, a focus on harms, without a complementing focus on benefits can lead to putting many technologies out of the market before they become so much better as to confer exceeding benefits upon the society.

(3) Ignoring Scarcity – Comparisons between AI and human specialists often overlook the scarcity and accessibility of human expertise, leading to an inaccurate assessment. For instance, in the field of medicine, headlines may highlight how an AI radiology screening algorithm performs slightly worse or similar to two highly trained human radiologists working together. However, this comparison does not reflect the realistic healthcare options most patients encounter. It fails to consider the scarcity of human specialists, including challenges related to global aging, elderly care, illiteracy, hunger, access to education and professional advice, and the vast amounts of data that need to be collected, analyzed, and moderated by public and private entities. Therefore, any comprehensive analysis of the costs and benefits of automation must incorporate these factors.

The current discourse surrounding AI often underestimates its potential to address social issues where there is a shortage of human resources. To the extent that this discourse dominates the regulatory thinking, it can undermine a great degree of social benefit (Lobel 2023, 17).

To be clear, Lobel is not arguing that the risks and harms from technologies such as generative AI are not real or do not require attention of the policy makers. They do, but the policy making at large must also deal with how to reform and guide the technology 'for good', and laws should be such so as to support the same. How this plays out is made clear by Lobel by two of her specific recommendations – right to data maximization and right to automated decision making.

Under the right to data maximization, Lobel argues that a right to complete and connected datasets can not only prevent bias by bringing everyone's data into the training data sets in a proportionate fashion, more importantly, it can promote actively good and valuable social outcomes, including the prevention of violence, trafficking, and hate crimes, promoting equality, diversity, and inclusion in workplaces, products, and service markets, etc.

Secondly, the right to automated decision making pertains to the ongoing discourse on the involvement of humans in decision-making processes that are increasingly being taken over by AI systems. Lobel notes that as AI becomes more prevalent across various sectors, concerns about algorithmic flaws and biases have sparked a demand for human oversight and control. A prevailing solution is to grant individuals either the final say in decisions or to provide human alternatives to automated processes. Numerous laws and regulations have emerged to ensure individuals have access to a human decision-maker, including the first principle enshrined in the EU AI Act. However, it is essential to consider that humans themselves can introduce biases and errors into decision-making, often unconsciously. Research has shown that AI algorithms can be less biased than humans when applied to certain tasks.

Further, questions have been raised about humans-in-the-loop. It has been argued that instead of achieving the optimal blend of strengths, hybrid systems can amplify the drawbacks of each component, leading to additional errors as information gets distorted during the transition. For instance, when developing autonomous vehicles, mechanisms that transfer control to the driver must address the fact that individuals may lose concentration and become inattentive. In such cases, the systems might need to incorporate alerts and allow sufficient time for the operator to regain control effectively, or else ensure a reliable automated decision.

Lobel argues that this has a significant implication – in specific situations, it is essential to recognize a right to an artificial decision-maker, accompanied by a corresponding obligation to automate. In other words, there should be a prohibition on human involvement when it would reduce the advantages of automation and introduce errors and biases. For instance, in the case of autonomous vehicles (AVs), there will inevitably be a point in time, (even though the exact timing may be subject to debate), when AVs will surpass human drivers in terms of safety. At this point, this right would come into existence.

Both these rights are (by their very names) an antithesis to the much more well-established principle of data minimization and the right against solely automated decision making.[8] Lobel's two rights are however not meant to cancel either of these rights, but instead, to complement them. Regulatory thinking needs more nuance, and both sets of opposing rights have their own place, depending on the requirements of the individuals and the society. But without these complementing rights, the negativity bias takes over and imperils significant good that can come of the technology.

Lobel, thus lays the groundwork for giving beneficence its due in regulatory thinking concerning generative AI. Her work does not pertain to generative AI *per se*, but as can be seen from the discussion concerning existing approaches to regulating generative AI, which is heavily dominated by AI-as-Wrongs approach, there is a clear need for balancing with AI-for-good. Perhaps there could be a 'right to beneficial automation' in generative tasks. The scope of such a right is not as crucial at the moment as the very acknowledgement that thinking towards proactively beneficial regulation is required in the case of generative AI, as much as in AI generally.

However, the paper will now turn its attention to a different, even more foundational issue – that despite the right approach as well as the best intentions, Lobel's work as much as other the current literature on the AI-for-good approach is lacking a stable theoretical foundation.

Part III – theoretical poverty of AI-for-good approach

In her paper, Lobel extensively discusses what AI-for-good would look like. She focuses on six fields of application: Environmental/Climate Applications, Food Scarcity and Poverty Alleviation, Health & Medicine, Accessibility & Accommodation, Education, Agency Compliance & Law Enforcement. However, what makes these applications good? She addresses these questions in the following words:

> What is AI-for-Good? The answer depends of course on our definition of 'good,' but there are social values and goals that are likely to garner a broad consensus: protecting the environment, combatting hunger and illiteracy, advancing medicine and healthcare, and supporting education and accessibility. And of course, tackling all these social goals with increased speed, efficiency, and consistency.

But why should values and goals that are 'likely to garner broad consensus' be the definition of good? There can be several instances where broad consensus can emerge around morally reprehensible goals, such as in Nazi Germany. These issues are not addressed. This is not to say that the goals outlined by Lobel are not beneficial goals or do not deserve protection. However, what amount to being beneficial, or in other words, fulfills the ethical requirement of 'beneficence', needs better grounding, such that penumbral cases can be dealt with in an acceptable and stable fashion. Much like Lobel, other works on AI-for-good treat the notion of beneficence as 'obvious', which stops from such a theoretical framework from being constructed.

Let's look at this problem in greater detail.

Beneficence not obvious

In order to understand why beneficence is not obvious, let's argue from the converse. Consider the following: The quickest way to solve the problem of road accidents would be to ban all the cars. No cars, no accidents. But this measure would be wrong. Because cars provide beneficence. They make lives easier, open up employment opportunities, allow for quicker access to emergency services, and so on, thus enhancing the well-being of the users. Beneficence thus underpins the very use of cars. Any curbs on their use have to be justified in the light of overriding need to prevent maleficence, or harm. Traffic rules, insurance mandates and criminalization of rash driving are well known examples.

In the same vein as above, the quickest way to prevent all the potential harms from AI is to ban all AI. If there is no AI, there will be no fear of superintelligent-AI-gone-wild (Bostrom 2014; Rash 2023). There would be no powerful chatbot that can supercharge threats of misinformation, cybersecurity, privacy violations and so on. But this would arguably not be an acceptable solution.

Beneficence is the *raison d'etre* of cars as much as of AI. Such *raison d'etre* must be understood in detail. But instead, it is considered obvious. The 'obviousness' of it stands in the way of greater attention and deeper scrutiny of the nature of beneficence. Further scrutiny of literature on AI-for-good reveals the same problem.

Floridi and others for instance, have discussed the idea of 'Artificial Intelligence for Social Good', or AI4SG at length (Floridi et al. 2020). AI4SG has gained significant prominence in the AI community, which can also be seen through significant scholarly interest in the field (Cowls et al. 2021; Umbrello and van de Poel 2021), and also from a number of workshops and conferences (Tomašev et al. 2020).

Floridi et al. (2020) argue that unless the essential factors that underpin the AI4SG movement are identified, the movement will not be able to avoid two important pitfalls: instances of good AI failing due to avoidable mistakes, and ensuring that instances of successful AI, even those which are accidental success, are replicable. In this context, the authors once again make explicit the significance of beneficence in unequivocal terms:

> The factors described in this article have been identified in coherence with more general work in the field of AI ethics. Each factor relates to at least one of five ethical principles of AI—beneficence, nonmaleficence, justice, autonomy, and explicability … This coherence is crucial: AI4SG cannot be inconsistent with the ethical framework guiding the design and evaluation of AI in general. *The principle of beneficence is of particular relevance.* It states that the use of AI should provide benefit to people and the natural world, and indeed AI4SG projects should not just comply with but reify this principle … *Beneficence is thus a necessary condition of AI4SG, yet it is insufficient, not least because the beneficent impact of an AI4SG project may be 'offset' by the creation or amplification of other risks or harms* (emphasis supplied).(Floridi et al. 2020, 1774)

But in this context, several interesting observations emerge. First comes as a footnote to the statements above. The authors state:

> This should not be taken as necessitating a utilitarian calculation: the beneficial impact of a given project may be 'offset' by the violation of some categorical imperative. Therefore even if an AI4SG project would do 'more good than harm', the harm may be ethically intolerable (Floridi et al. 2020, 1774).

This is a very significant remark. It identifies that there are certain 'red lines', which cannot be crossed, and these red lines, as per the authors, are essentially deontic. They prohibit violating something very akin to the categorical imperative. Categorical imperative provides *what must not be done*. But by its very nature, it does not provide what must be done. In other words, it's a principle of non-maleficence, and not beneficence. To this extent, no clarification emerges, at least here, as to how beneficence must be understood.

Second comes along with the definition of AI4SG, which does provide some elaboration, but not exactly on the principle of beneficence, rather on the larger project of AI4SG, which by authors' own admission, is premised upon something more than beneficence. AI4SG is defined as 'the design, development, and deployment of AI systems in ways that (i) prevent, mitigate or resolve problems adversely affecting human life and/or the wellbeing of the natural world, and/or (ii) enable socially preferable and/or environmentally sustainable developments'. But the authors state as a disclaimer to the definition that 'there is likely to be considerable disagreement and contention regarding what would constitute a socially good outcome'[9]

That might well be the case. It is also well recognized that the meaning and scope of terms such 'socially good outcomes', 'beneficence', and 'common good' are contested and unclear, as much as the need for beneficence itself is obvious. But this does not deter from the fact that if a significant aspect of this domain is not thoroughly scrutinized, much less understood, it is important to engage with it, whether it is contested or not. A theoretical framework that systematically ignores one of its important pillars risks being piecemeal and incomplete. The literature on beneficence in AI ethics seems to blissfully suffer from this blind spot.

Similar phenomenon is observed in Floridi and Cowls (2019). This work identifies a unified framework consisting of five ethical principles for AI. They note that while there is a proliferation of AI ethics principles, it is important to distill a number of guidelines, and the principles contained therein, so as to avoid several undesirable fallouts. First, if they are all nearly the same, there could be redundancy. Even worse would be the case if there are significant divergences, which could lead to ambiguity as to their scope and confusion as to their relevance. Lastly, the most harmful would be the creation of a 'market for principles', one that allows stakeholders to pick and choose principles that they find convenient.

In order to avoid these fallouts, they propose that the entire gamut of AI ethics principles can be summed up in five principles: beneficence, non-maleficence, autonomy, justice and explicability. The first four are coextensive with the literature on Bioethics and Floridi and Cowls explicitly note this. They observe that '[o]f all areas of applied ethics, biomedical ethics is the one that most closely resembles digital ethics in dealing ecologically with new forms of agents, patients, and environments' (Floridi and Cowls 2019, 5).

Beneficence, thus, is a central principle in this discussion. But what does it mean? This is an area in which the literature does not provide sufficient clarity, despite the initial call to avoid significant divergences and ambiguities in the meaning of ethical principles for AI, and which can actually lead to problematic outcomes.

In this paper, the authors note that different sets of ethical principles use different terms for the larger idea of beneficence. Some invoke the term 'well-being'. Others call it 'common good', or something on these lines such as Partnership on AI's resolve to 'ensure that AI technologies benefit and empower as many people as possible'.

But replacing beneficence with other terms does not really elaborate on its meaning. Other guidelines use yet more confounding terms, such as 'human dignity' and 'sustainability'. The former is extensively used in the context of literally all other principles of biomedical ethics (and in the context of this article, by extension, AI ethics) such as autonomy, non-maleficence, and justice, thereby rendering its use to define beneficence completely indeterminate and amorphous. The latter, meaning 'ensur[ing] the basic preconditions for life on our planet, continued prospering for mankind and the preservation of a good environment for future generations' replaces beneficence with other terms, primarily, 'prospering', which does not shed any more light on its meaning than beneficence itself.

Another telling sign that beneficence does not get a deeper scrutiny is straightaway observable in the treatment meted out to this topic by Floridi and Cowls, when they state, that in the literature on AI ethics, beneficence is 'perhaps the easiest of the four traditional biomedical ethics principles to observe'. The description that follows fails to clarify both what beneficence is and how does its meaning as understood in biomedical ethics translates to the context of AI ethics, even though the latter premise is central to this paper.

At this stage, the reader might continue to wonder why is it not obvious what beneficence means and why must we clarify it further. After all, the more deeply a presupposition (in this case, about what constitutes as beneficent) is ingrained, the harder it is to question it. The reader might continue to treat all the terms above as self-evident.

They are not. As an epilogue to the discussion above, let me reach back to the very technology under discussion – generative AI – and provide a concrete example.

Let's ask a simple question: In what way does ChatGPT 'benefit' people? Or to put this in ethical terms, how can we understand what the ethical principle of beneficence implies in its context? Have the people at OpenAI stayed true to the principle of beneficence that AI ethics requires them to?

At first glance, it may look exceedingly obvious that they have. ChatGPT could make a wide array of professionals more productive. Already, coders and lawyers have used ChatGPT to make their outputs more efficient, by using it as an aid, a collaborator, an augmenter (Mustafa 2022; Zeeman n.d.). Haven't they made the lives of everyone (who presumably has to write something – anything) much easier, and have thus benefit them?

Perhaps they have, but even before we take a closer look, it becomes equally obvious that it is not necessarily beneficial to everyone in every case.

Consider the possibilities for students. Students around the world might be able to use the ease conferred by ChatGPT to score better marks in assignments. But it is not the ability to write more easily that benefits them. They can use the 'ease' to write assignments that they neither understand, nor can derive any value from. Does the technology, and the ease that it confers, benefit them? It appears that the answer is no. Educators and institutions everywhere are wondering how to ensure that such a world doesn't come to pass where students can write their essays and assignments using ChatGPT (Hern 2022; Weale 2023). Others worry that this would weaken the thinking and writing skills of the students, perhaps rightly so. Yet others wonder if we need to rethink the examination system altogether (Marche 2022).

Thus, it is obvious that it is beneficial and it is obvious that it is not. Which only means one thing – that nothing is obvious. And it is the job of normative theory behind AI regulation to clarify such muddled issues – that which current literature fails at, and the work that follows wishes to address.

In the next section, let us further test some of the theoretical bases upon which beneficence is grounded, whether assumed or explicit. There are two such bases: biomedical ethics and human rights.

Unsuitability of existing frameworks on beneficence

Beneficence in biomedical ethics and AI ethics

As noted above, beneficence as a notion is often seen as having primarily originated in biomedical ethics. A widely acknowledged account of the principles of biomedical ethics is provided by Beauchamp and Childress (Beauchamp and Childress 2019).

Beauchamp and Childress noted that beneficence is demanded by morality, and it constitutes of all principles and dispositions with the goal of promoting the well-being of other persons. Some philosophical theories suggest that beneficence and morality are the same, but this position is disputed by Beauchamp and Childress.

Some important characteristics of this principle emerge from the discussion by Beauchamp and Childress. Firstly, beneficence is more than merely the moral requirement of not harming others. It requires positive steps to help others. Beauchamp and Childress note that 'Rules ... of nonmaleficence (1) are negative prohibitions of action, (2) must be followed impartially, and (3) provide moral reasons for legal prohibitions of certain forms of conduct. By contrast, rules of beneficence (1) present positive requirements of action, (2) need not always be followed impartially, and (3) generally do not provide for legal punishment when agents fail to abide by them' (Beauchamp and Childress 2019, chap. 6).

Secondly, within the context of biomedical ethics, there are two types of beneficence: obligatory beneficence and nonobligatory ideals of beneficence. Their scope *inter se* is heavily disputed. Thirdly, there is also a distinction between general and specific beneficence. The question is, does a special relationship exist between the parties? If yes, then this leads to specific beneficence. This distinction is also a factor in understanding the difference between obligatory beneficence and nonobligatory ideals of beneficence. As discussed in more detail later, both these distinctions have significant implications for regulation of AI, and contribute to reasons why beneficence in healthcare ethics cannot directly be applied to AI ethics and make more salient, the need for clarity on the meaning of 'beneficence'(Beauchamp and Childress 2019, chap. 6).

This leads us to the important question – whatever beneficence means in the context of bioethics, can it mean the same thing in the context of AI ethics too, as assumed by Floridi and others in a slew of works?

There are serious doubts regarding the utility of borrowing principles of biomedical ethics in AI ethics. A fairly comprehensive elaboration of these principles is done by Mittelstadt (Mittelstadt 2019, 501).

Taking note of work by Floridi and others that brings AI ethics' principles closer of principles of biomedical ethics, he elaborates upon the reasons why the relative success of principlism in biomedical contexts is unlikely to succeed in the case of AI ethics. Mittelstadt notes four such reasons.

First, medicine has a common aim – to promote the health and well-being of the patient (this 'well-being' is to be understood as medical well-being, which is distinct from the broader 'well-being' understood in AI ethics, which is closer to 'flourishing'). This underlies the entire profession and each one of its practitioners (Mittelstadt 2019, 501).

This also results in the emergence of fiduciary duties in the medical profession. The interests of the subjects of the profession, i.e. the patients, trumps other interests and the practitioners are required to promote the best interests of the patients (Mittelstadt 2019, 501).

No similar subject of ethical primacy exists in the field of AI. There is also no fiduciary duty towards the subjects, the users of the AI systems. In most cases, where the developers of AI are corporations, their main fiduciary duty is towards the shareholders to maximize the profits, which often can and does conflict with the public interest and the users' interest (Mittelstadt 2019, 501).

Second, AI ethics does not have the same professional history and ethical norms as medical ethics. Medical ethics matured through time and also failures and ethical scandals, which shaped the understanding of medical ethics in a much more concrete fashion. The Nuremberg Code in response to the atrocities of World War II, the Belmont Report and the US National Research Act in response to the Tuskegee Syphilis study are a few notable examples. A similar maturing of AI ethics is lacking at the moment (Mittelstadt 2019, 502).

A related yet distinct issue emerges under this point: that AI, unlike medicine, is not a single profession (Mittelstadt 2019, 503). Biomedical ethics are inherently sector specific, whereas AI is a general-purpose technology, applicable in a large number of sectors, of which health care is just one. There might yet be place for biomedical ethics in AI, when AI is applied to the health care sector. Much literature covers this ground. But this makes it even clearer that biomedical ethics cannot translate to AI in general.

One might say that software engineering is one profession under which AI development might be placed. However, this puts in starker contrast the two professions. Software engineering does not have fiduciary duties, licensing schemes, as well as legal and professional accountability (see the fourth point below) systems in place, like in medical ethics. Some professional organizations such as the Institute of Electrical and Electronics Engineers (IEEE) and the Association of Computing Machinery (ACM), have codes of ethics in place, but compared to the authoritative codes in medical ethics, they are shallow and come with no real sanctions.

Further, in medicine, most interventions impact human bodies, and the impacts can therefore be visible for objective study, whereas impacts caused by AI are neither bound to a single body (or place or system) and is therefore harder to be seen and understood by AI developers. The distance between the interventions and ethically relevant impacts increases, which reduces the ethical salience of those factors.

Third, AI does not possess the same methods to translate principles to practice. In medical ethics, a wide range of institutions ensure that ethical principles are given concrete meaning and enforcement. These include professional societies and boards, ethics review committees, accreditation, licensing schemes and peer self-governance. Nothing comparable exists in AI, barring the few areas which have existing regulations, such as data protection laws.

Fourth and last, AI ethics lacks legal and professional accountability mechanisms that are present in medical ethics. These include accepted legal standards concerning malpractice, licensing and certification schemes and professional medical boards. Similar mechanisms are absent in AI ethics (Mittelstadt 2019, 504; Murphy et al. 2021).

AI ethics also suffers from a unique challenge – that ensuring that ethics is not just practiced by professionals but is embedded in the design. Ethical design is an important requirement of AI ethics, which also poses a methodological challenge – how to ensure this in the absence of strong institutions, different organizational paradigm of AI development, and the costs of designing with ethics, and not mere commerce in mind.(Mittelstadt 2019, 504)

In addition to the above, a couple of more issues emerge from Mittelstadt's work. He addresses the point that while professional norms, regulations and fiduciary duties do not exist right now, they might emerge in due course. Specifically, if fiduciary duties emerge from AI ethics, it could be evidence that the principled approach did work.(Mittelstadt 2019, 502) However, there are challenges in such emergence. One factor that contributes to this challenge is opacity. To the extent that the mechanics of the decision-making process are not visible, it is harder to understand whether the duty has been fulfilled. Another factor is the diffused nature of human actors in the context of AI, such that when problem arises, 'they can rarely be traced back to a single team member or action (Floridi 2016); responsibility must be assigned across a network of actors that influenced the system's design, training and configuration' (Mittelstadt 2019, 503).

Beneficence in human rights and AI ethics

Kriebitz and Lütge make a different argument, bringing together AI and human rights (Kriebitz and Lütge 2020). Talking specifically in the context of corporate decision makers, they note that Human rights play an important role in the context of AI regulation as they are considered the foundational norms widely. They discuss the responsibilities of corporate actors in terms of human rights standards in the context of developing and using AI. The paper also mentions the Ruggie principles, which focus on the enforcement of human rights by companies (Kriebitz and Lütge 2020, 86). The objective of the article is to establish a link between discussions on AI ethics and discussions on the human rights responsibilities of corporate decision-makers, asserting that these two discourses mutually enhance and augment one another by encompassing broader realms of business ethics and technology ethics.

Interestingly, a significant aspect of the paper deals with the role of the beneficence criterion of AI ethics and how it might be applied in human rights-related areas. But problems arise in this discussion when the authors bring into picture the Sustainable Development Goals as the proxy for Human Rights. This is despite the acknowledgement by the authors that '[U]sing the SDGs as a proxy for human rights might be somewhat problematic, as there is an ongoing debate currently about the exact relation between the two frameworks' (Kriebitz and Lütge 2020, 95). The authors choose to pick a few of the SDGs which correspond with the rights in International Covenant on Economic, Social and Cultural Rights such as the 'right to an adequate standard of living', the 'right to education' or the 'right to health'.(Kriebitz and Lütge 2020, 95)

This is a cardinal mistake. Picking a handful of SDGs works exactly because some of them neither conflict with each other nor with the larger idea of human rights. But because there is no pecking order among SDGs and all SDGs are equally important, problems arise exactly when conflicts arise among different SDGs. Human rights as a framework fails to provide any guidance as to how trade-offs between SDGs can be made and different interests and rights balanced. The failure of human rights framework towards solving other problems where different rights conflict with each other, such as the problem of content moderation, are also evidence for the unsuitability of this framework (Dvoskin 2020). This failure extends to the criteria of beneficence in AI, which is the basis for invoking AI towards the achievements of the SDGs.

It would be added briefly that the invocation of SDGs in the context of AI ethics is an important manifestation of beneficence. It serves as one of the more concrete and acceptable goals which the principle of beneficence should lead to. But Human Rights is not a suitable framework as far as interpreting the meaning of beneficence is concerned.

Conclusion

This paper makes two arguments. First, that the regulation of generative AI must focus on enhancing the positive outcomes as much as preventing the negative outcomes. Secondly, it must dig deeper into theoretical foundations of what it means for generative AI for good. In this paper, I highlighted that the commonly assumed bases for determining 'beneficence' of AI systems are not suitable. However, I do not comment upon which other frameworks might be more suitable.

However, it is clear that in the world of fast changing technology with emergent properties that disrupt the very way of life for modern human beings, shaping the use of AI is difficult without having the clearest possible conception of what we want to achieve out of these technologies. In other words, of what is 'beneficent'.

Notes

1. For instance, see the lawsuit Andersen v. Stability AI Ltd, U.S. District Court for the Northern District of California, No. 3:23-cv-00201
2. Draft Compromise Amendments on the Draft Report – Proposal for a regulation of the European Parliament and of the Council on harmonized rules on Artificial Intelligence (Artificial Intelligence Act) and amending certain Union Legislative Acts, (COM(2021)0206 – C9 0146/2021–2021/0106(COD))
3. Article 3(1c)
4. Recital 69.
5. Recital 60 (h)
6. Article 4a(1)(f)
7. The other three are, not giving underuse and the resultant loss of gains sufficient importance, thinking in binary solutions, i.e., either adopt or ban, without looking for more nuanced middle paths that enhance beneficial outcomes while also preventing harm, and

distributional assumptions, which deal with the assumption that bias caused by AI is most harmful to already marginalized people.

8. See, Article 5(1)(c) and Article 22 of General Data Protection Regulation
9. Footnote 1 in (Floridi et al. 2020).

Acknowledgements

I thank Professor Vishwas H. Devaiah for his guidance with this paper. I would also like to thank the panelists and participants at the BILETA symposium on, 'Finding an Optimal Way to Tackle Technology Maze: Mapping Law and Policy Interventions' organized by the Centre for Intellectual Property and Technology Law (CIPTEL) & Jindal Institute of Behavioral Sciences (JIBS) with The British and Irish Law Education Technology Association (BILETA) on 6th & 7th January 2023 at O. P. Jindal Global University, Sonipat, Haryana, India for their comments and suggestions. Finally, I would like to thank Gayatri Srivastava for her research assistance with this paper.

Disclosure statement

No potential conflict of interest was reported by the author(s).

References

Altman, Sam, Greg Brockman, and Ilya Sutskever. 2023. "Governance of Superintelligence." May 22, 2023. https://openai.com/blog/governance-of-superintelligence.

Beauchamp, Tom L. 2019. "The Principle of Beneficence in Applied Ethics." Stanford Encyclopedia of Philosophy. November 2, 2019. https://plato.stanford.edu/entries/principle-beneficence/#ConcBeneBene.

Beauchamp, Tom L., and James F. Childress. 2019. *Principles of Biomedical Ethics*. 8th ed. New York: Oxford University Press.

Bertuzzi, Luca. 2023. "AI Act Moves Ahead in EU Parliament with Key Committee Vote." Www.Euractiv.Com. May 11, 2023. https://www.euractiv.com/section/artificial-intelligence/news/ai-act-moves-ahead-in-eu-parliament-with-key-committee-vote/.

Bommasani, Rishi, Drew A. Hudson, Ehsan Adeli, Russ Altman, Simran Arora, Sydney von Arx, Michael S. Bernstein, et al. 2021. "On the Opportunities and Risks of Foundation Models." https://doi.org/10.48550/ARXIV.2108.07258.

Bostrom, Nick. 2014. *Superintelligence - Paths, Dangers, Strategies*. Oxford: Oxford University Press.

Bubeck, Sébastien, Varun Chandrasekaran, Ronen Eldan, Johannes Gehrke, Eric Horvitz, Ece Kamar, Peter Lee, et al. 2023. "Sparks of Artificial General Intelligence: Early Experiments with GPT-4." https://doi.org/10.48550/ARXIV.2303.12712.

Chauhan, Krishna Deo Singh. 2023. "Nurturing AI's Potential: The Need for a Soft Regulatory Approach in India." *Journal of Innovation, Competition & Information Law* (blog). May 23, 2023. https://jicil.in/blog/2023/05/23/nurturing-ais-potential-the-need-for-a-soft-regulatory-approach-in-india/.

Chui, Michael, Roger Roberts, and Lareina Yee. 2022. "Generative AI Is Here: How Tools like ChatGPT Could Change Your Business." December 20, 2022. http://ceros.mckinsey.com/quarterly-digital-promo.

Coulter, Martin, and Supantha Mukherjee. 2023. "Exclusive: Behind EU Lawmakers' Challenge to Rein in ChatGPT and Generative AI." *Reuters*, May 1, 2023, sec. Technology. https://www.reuters.com/technology/behind-eu-lawmakers-challenge-rein-chatgpt-generative-ai-2023-04-28/.

Cowls, Josh, Andreas Tsamados, Mariarosaria Taddeo, and Luciano Floridi. 2021. "A Definition, Benchmark and Database of AI for Social Good Initiatives." *Nature Machine Intelligence* 3 (2): 111–115. https://doi.org/10.1038/s42256-021-00296-0.

Davenport, Thomas H., and Nitin Mittal. 2022. "How Generative AI Is Changing Creative Work." November 14, 2022. https://buy.tinypass.com/checkout/template/cacheableShow?aid = mbs77qtzUz&templateId = OTBSP342X41S&templateVariantId = OTV3DU7DCXX1T&offerId = fakeOfferId&experienceId = EX6OE1720PPS&iframeId = offer_2abeca1b1c01117ffed3-0&display Mode = inline&widget = template&url = https%3A%2F%2Fhbr.org.

Deepmind, dir. 2017. *AlphaGo - The Movie.*

Dvoskin, Brenda. 2020. "International Human Rights Law Is Not Enough to Fix Content Moderation's Legitimacy Crisis." *Berkman Klein Center Collection* (blog). September 16, 2020. https://medium.com/berkman-klein-center/international-human-rights-law-is-not-enough-to-fix-content-moderations-legitimacy-crisis-a80e3ed9abbd.

Elias, Jibu, and Anjali Raja. 2023. "IndiaAI - Impact, Opportunity and Challenges of Generative AI." Ministry of Electronics and Information Technology, Government of India.

Esther, Ajao. 2023. "Microsoft Integrates ChatGPT into Azure; GPT-4 Expected Soon | TechTarget." Enterprise AI. March 13, 2023. https://www.techtarget.com/searchenterpriseai/news/365532417/Microsoft-integrates-ChatGPT-into-Azure-GPT-4-expected-soon.

European Commission. 2021. "Proposal for a Regulation of the European Parliament and the Council Laying down Harmonised Rules on Artificial Intelligence (Artificial Intelligence Act) and Amending Certain Union Legislative Acts.".

Floridi, Luciano. 2016. "Faultless Responsibility: On the Nature and Allocation of Moral Responsibility for Distributed Moral Actions." *Philosophical Transactions of the Royal Society A: Mathematical, Physical and Engineering Sciences* 374 (2083): 1–13. https://doi.org/10.1098/rsta.2016.0112.

Floridi, Luciano, and Josh Cowls. 2019. "A Unified Framework of Five Principles for AI in Society." *Harvard Data Science Review*, June. https://doi.org/10.1162/99608f92.8cd550d1.

Floridi, Luciano, Josh Cowls, Thomas C. King, and Mariarosaria Taddeo. 2020. "How to Design AI for Social Good: Seven Essential Factors." *Science and Engineering Ethics* 26 (3): 1771–1796. https://doi.org/10.1007/s11948-020-00213-5.

Fruhlinger, Josh. 2023. "What Is Generative AI? The Evolution of Artificial Intelligence." InfoWorld. March 10, 2023. https://www.infoworld.com/article/3689973/what-is-generative-ai-the-evolution-of-artificial-intelligence.html.

Goldman Sachs. 2023. "Generative AI Could Raise Global GDP by 7%." Goldman Sachs. April 5, 2023. https://www.goldmansachs.com/intelligence/pages/generative-ai-could-raise-global-gdp-by-7-percent.html.

Goled, Shraddha. 2021. "What Are Discriminative & Generative Models? How Do They Differ?" Analytics India Magazine. March 22, 2021. https://analyticsindiamag.com/what-are-discriminative-generative-models-how-do-they-differ/.

Goodfellow, Ian J., Jean Pouget-Abadie, Mehdi Mirza, Bing Xu, David Warde-Farley, Sherjil Ozair, Aaron Courville, and Yoshua Bengio. 2014. "Generative Adversarial Networks." arXiv. https://doi.org/10.48550/arXiv.1406.2661.

Gow, Glenn. 2023. "Top 5 AI Risks In The Era Of ChatGPT and Generative AI." Forbes. September 4, 2023. https://www.forbes.com/sites/glenngow/2023/04/09/top-5-ai-risks-in-the-era-of-chatgpt-and-generative-ai/?sh = 49a3b0531aca.

Hacker, Philipp, Andreas Engel, and Marco Mauer. 2023. "Regulating ChatGPT and Other Large Generative AI Models." arXiv. http://arxiv.org/abs/2302.02337.

Harari, Yuval Noah. 2023. "Yuval Noah Harari Argues That AI Has Hacked the Operating System of Human Civilisation." *The Economist*, April 28, 2023. https://www.economist.com/by-invitation/2023/04/28/yuval-noah-harari-argues-that-ai-has-hacked-the-operating-system-of-human-civilisation?gclid = CjwKCAjwg-GjBhBnEiwAMUvNW_r-SjI3PsoyprDkGFfjsAMEapD0Mure_7btMg3U_ubum1anNh4ZrhoCp6kQAvD_BwE&gclsrc = aw.ds.

Hern, Alex. 2022. "AI Bot ChatGPT Stuns Academics with Essay-Writing Skills and Usability." *The Guardian*, December 4, 2022, sec. Technology. https://www.theguardian.com/technology/2022/dec/04/ai-bot-chatgpt-stuns-academics-with-essay-writing-skills-and-usability.

Janakiram, MSV. 2018. "Here Are Three Factors That Accelerate The Rise Of Artificial Intelligence." Forbes. May 27, 2018. https://www.forbes.com/sites/janakirammsv/2018/05/27/here-are-three-factors-that-accelerate-the-rise-of-artificial-intelligence/.

Jobin, Anna, Marcello Ienca, and Effy Vayena. 2019. "The Global Landscape of AI Ethics Guidelines." *Nature Machine Intelligence* 1 (9): 389–399. https://doi.org/10.1038/s42256-019-0088-2.

Jumper, John, Richard Evans, Alexander Pritzel, Tim Green, Michael Figurnov, Olaf Ronneberger, Kathryn Tunyasuvunakool, et al. 2021. "Highly Accurate Protein Structure Prediction with AlphaFold." *Nature* 596 (7873): 583–589. https://doi.org/10.1038/s41586-021-03819-2.

Kelly, Samantha Murphy. 2023. "Elon Musk and Other Tech Leaders Call for Pause in 'out of Control' AI Race | CNN Business." CNN. March 29, 2023. https://www.cnn.com/2023/03/29/tech/ai-letter-elon-musk-tech-leaders/index.html.

Kriebitz, Alexander, and Christoph Lütge. 2020. "Artificial Intelligence and Human Rights: A Business Ethical Assessment." *Business and Human Rights Journal* 5 (1): 84–104. https://doi.org/10.1017/bhj.2019.28.

Lobel, Orly. 2023. "The Law of AI for Good." *SSRN Electronic Journal*, San Diego Legal Studies Paper No. 23-001. https://doi.org/10.2139/ssrn.4338862.

Marche, Stephen. 2022. "The College Essay Is Dead." The Atlantic. December 6, 2022. https://www.theatlantic.com/technology/archive/2022/12/chatgpt-ai-writing-college-student-essays/672371/.

McNemar, Erin. 2022. "How Can Artificial Intelligence Change Medical Imaging?" HealthITAnalytics. January 25, 2022. https://healthitanalytics.com/features/how-can-artificial-intelligence-change-medical-imaging.

Merritt, Rick. 2022. "What Is a Transformer Model?" NVIDIA Blog. March 25, 2022. https://blogs.nvidia.com/blog/2022/03/25/what-is-a-transformer-model/.

Mitchell, Melanie. 2019. *Artificial Intelligence: A Guide for Thinking Humans*. New York: Farrar, Straus and Giroux.

Mittelstadt, Brent. 2019. "Principles Alone Cannot Guarantee Ethical AI." *Nature Machine Intelligence* 1 (11): 501–507. https://doi.org/10.1038/s42256-019-0114-4.

Murphy, Kathleen, Erica Di Ruggiero, Ross Upshur, Donald J. Willison, Neha Malhotra, Jia Ce Cai, Nakul Malhotra, Vincci Lui, and Jennifer Gibson. 2021. "Artificial Intelligence for Good Health: A Scoping Review of the Ethics Literature." *BMC Medical Ethics* 22 (14): 1–17. https://doi.org/10.1186/s12910-021-00577-8.

Mustafa, Filiz. 2022. "How To Use Chat Gpt To Code, Build A Website And Write Social Media Posts." HITC. December 6, 2022. https://www.hitc.com/en-gb/2022/12/06/how-to-use-chatgpt-to-code-build-a-website-and-write-social-media-posts/.

OECD. 2019. "Recommendation of the Council on Artificial Intelligence.".

Ortiz, Sabrina. 2023. "The 5 Biggest Risks of Generative AI, According to an Expert." ZDNET. April 24, 2023. https://www.zdnet.com/article/the-5-biggest-risks-of-generative-ai-according-to-an-expert/.

"Pause Giant AI Experiments: An Open Letter.". 2023. *Future of Life Institute* (blog). March 22, 2023. https://futureoflife.org/open-letter/pause-giant-ai-experiments/.

Rash, Wayne. 2023. "Tech Leaders Ask For Pause In AI Development." Forbes. March 29, 2023. https://www.forbes.com/sites/waynerash/2023/03/29/tech-leaders-ask-for-pause-in-ai-development/.

Rosenberg, Scott. 2023. "Where AI Evolves from Here." Axios. May 18, 2023. https://www.axios.com/2023/05/18/ai-agi-artificial-general-intelligence.

Rudnitsky, Jake. 2023. "ChatGPT to Fuel $1.3 Trillion AI Market by 2032, New Report Says." *Bloomberg.Com*, June 1, 2023. https://www.bloomberg.com/news/articles/2023-06-01/chatgpt-to-fuel-1-3-trillion-ai-market-by-2032-bi-report-says.

Russell, Stuart, and Peter Norvig. 2010. *Artificial Intelligence: A Modern Approach*. 3rd ed. New Jersey: Pearson.

Salecha, Manisha. 2016. "Story of ELIZA, the First Chatbot Developed in 1966." Analytics India Magazine. October 5, 2016. https://analyticsindiamag.com/story-eliza-first-chatbot-developed-1966/.

Schmit, C. D., M. J. Doerr, and J. K. Wagner. 2023. "Leveraging IP for AI governance." *Science* 379 (6633): 646–648. https://doi.org/10.1126/science.add2202

Tomašev, Nenad, Julien Cornebise, Frank Hutter, Shakir Mohamed, Angela Picciariello, Bec Connelly, Danielle C. M. Belgrave, et al. 2020. "AI for Social Good: Unlocking the Opportunity for Positive Impact." *Nature Communications* 11 (2468): 1–6. https://doi.org/10.1038/s41467-020-15871-z.

Umbrello, Steven, and Ibo van de Poel. 2021. "Mapping Value Sensitive Design onto AI for Social Good Principles." *AI and Ethics* 1 (3): 283–296. https://doi.org/10.1007/s43681-021-00038-3.

VanBuskirk, Adam. 2023. "A Brief History of the Generative Pre-Trained Transformer (GPT) Language Models." *WordBot* (blog). March 31, 2023. https://blog.wordbot.io/ai-artificial-intelligence/a-brief-history-of-the-generative-pre-trained-transformer-gpt-language-models/.

Weale, Sally. 2023. "Lecturers Urged to Review Assessments in UK amid Concerns over New AI Tool." *The Guardian*, January 13, 2023, sec. Technology. https://www.theguardian.com/technology/2023/jan/13/end-of-the-essay-uk-lecturers-assessments-chatgpt-concerns-ai.

Wooldridge, Michael J. 2021. *A Brief History of Artificial Intelligence: What It Is, Where We Are, and Where We Are Going*. First U.S. ed. New York: Flatiron Books.

Zeeman, Maddy. n.d. "ChatGPT Can Supplement, Not Replace the Legal Profession." Michigan Technology Law Review. Accessed January 14, 2023. http://mttlr.org/2022/12/chatgpt-can-supplement-not-replace-the-legal-profession/.

Zhang, Chaoning, Chenshuang Zhang, Chenghao Li, Yu Qiao, Sheng Zheng, Sumit Kumar Dam, Mengchun Zhang, et al. 2023. "One Small Step for Generative AI, One Giant Leap for AGI: A Complete Survey on ChatGPT in AIGC Era." https://doi.org/10.48550/ARXIV.2304.06488.

Patents in metaverse: an analysis of scope and challenges

Prajakta Kale

ABSTRACT
'Metaverse' is set to be the disruptive technology which is about to bring an overhaul in the functioning of myriad sectors ranging from education, entertainment, health care, businesses amongst others. The key feature of this technology is the immersion of physical world into a virtual world. Metaverse in a way finds its roots on the technologies of Virtual/ Augmented Reality (VR/AR) which essentially are about simulating real world and augmenting the real – world experience in the digital world. Intellectual Property Rights which exist for protection of intangible assets, hence are vital in perspective of Metaverse. This research analyses the IP form of Patents in reference to Metaverse. Patents are an attractive choice due to the commercial advantage and the higher level of protection it offers compared to other IP forms. The trend of surge in patent applications seen with emerging technologies like AI and Blockchain is likely to be reflected with metaverse. The article views the metaverse and patent domain through an overarching lens gauging the possible scope and challenges. The analysis is based on US, EU and Indian patent laws to get a comprehensive picture across the world.

1. Introduction

Technology seldom fails to surprise us. It exists to ease, facilitate and make our working more meaningful. Intellectual Property and in particular 'patents' ensure incentive for creating or advancing technology and further encourages innovation (Suthersanan, Dutfield and Chow 2007). This ability of patent system to promote innovation has been the cornerstone of today's economy (Ouyong, Sun, and Xinzhen 2022). Technological companies therefore prefer to be at forefront in filing patents. The recent technological developments like Artificial Intelligence and even metaverse has led to a significant surge in patent applications worldwide (European Innovation Council and SMEs Executive Agency 2022; World Intellectual Property Organization 2023). A key feature of advanced technologies like AI, blockchain and even metaverse is its application in varied sectors which results in strong interconnection across different industries (Ouyong, Sun, and Xinzhen 2022; Prudy 2022). This makes it even more significant to study the impact of patenting these technologies. Any phenomenal advancement in technology does pose challenges to the existing patent laws. The laws should be such that they do not hinder the development in technology and at the same time they must ensure that they do not bestow rights for the technology which fails to meet technical, regulatory or societal standards. To ensure this balance, it is important to first understand the basics of any technology. Is it significantly different from the past technologies or a mere improvement? If patent is granted for such technology what would be the short-term and long-term ramification? The paper is an attempt to analyse the 'metaverse' technology and the scope, impediments and functioning of patents in this technology.

2. Understanding metaverse

The dictionary meaning of the term 'meta' is beyond and 'verse' means universe. In its literal sense therefore metaverse would imply something that is beyond the universe, a new world which in turn could be inferred as a virtual world. The term as such is not a recent development and had been proposed in a science fiction way back in 1990s (Gerratana and Ganguly 2023). There is no universally agreed definition of metaverse as it has several dimensions and in the present form it would mean different for varied people ("What Is the Metaverse?" 2022). But broadly, Metaverse could be understood as a digital space which combines features of virtual reality (VR), augmented reality (AR) and other advanced internet technologies that allows lifelike experiences on personal and professional front ("What Is the Metaverse?" 2022). The concepts of virtual reality and augmented reality are not new. The notion of Virtual reality emerged in 1930s where science fiction imagined a world different from the existing physical world and it was since 1970s that the presence of virtual reality devices for flight simulations, automobile industry design, virtual reality headsets was seen ("Virtual Reality," n.d.; "Demystifying the Virtual Reality Landscape," n.d.). Why then, metaverse has become a buzzword recently? The reason could be traced to rise, development and integration of technologies like Artificial Intelligence (AI), Blockchain, Internet of things, 3D computing, XR devices, digital twins and cloud computing (Glee 2022). The integration of these platforms and technologies are perhaps the basis of hope for metaverse having ability to perform phenomenal role in various sectors today. Be it education, banking, entertainment, tourism, health, commerce, finance, work – metaverse is imagined to bring effective functioning of several sectors (Prudy 2022).

2.1. Prominent features of metaverse

It is evident that revived focus on metaverse is because of certain features which did not exist before. In this section, the prominent features of metaverse are analysed along with their meaning and application. This analysis shall further aid to understand Patents in metaverse.

2.1.1. Immersion

A core feature of metaverse, is immersion. A user entering the artificial, virtual world is able to 'interact and manipulate' it i.e. the user gets the feel of physical world in the artificial world (Spring 2023; "Virtual Reality," n.d.). This immersive experience is majorly through 'extended reality' an all-encompassing term for the combined experience of physical and digital worlds. Extended reality includes virtual, augmented and mixed reality. Virtual reality offers the most immersive experience through devices like VR headset, simulation etc. A user in virtual reality feels to be like in a completely different world where he can even experience touch by movement or manipulation, known as haptic technology ("VR v. AR v. MR: What You Need to Know," n.d.; "Haptic Technology," n.d.). Playing games in a computer simulated environment or watching some live concert in the artificial world are example of virtual reality. Augmented reality adds a layer of digital world over the actual real world. For instance, the AR view of Amazon, the online shopping app, where customers can position furniture or any item of home décor in their own room or space and imagine how the object would appear in reality (Perez 2020). Augmented reality thus enhances the real-world experience and has huge commercial significance as it can be used for marketing, increasing the awareness of any brand and might as well boost sales of any product (Hayes 2023). Mixed reality is the convergence of real and virtual world where one can manipulate and interact with both the worlds ("VR v. AR v. MR: What You Need to Know," n.d.). For instance, Meta 2 is a device which through the wearable lens allows the users to manipulate and interact with holograms as if they are in real world ("Everyday Examples of Mixed Reality" 2019).

Metaverse can thus be accessed through devices like VR headset, AR glasses or wearable lenses. On a scale for immersive experience, VR offers the most immersive experience and AR the lowest. It is pertinent to note that metaverse can also be accessed through devices as common as a smartphone. For instance, the AR view on Amazon app.

2.1.2. Avatar

On social media say Facebook or WhatsApp, we often keep profile pictures to help others identify us. Similarly, in a metaverse, an avatar is used to identify us in the digitised virtual world (Ponde 2023a). An avatar mimics the real-world physical appearance of a person, even facial expression or body language ("What Is an Avatar, and How to Create a Metaverse Avatar?," n.d.). However, it is also possible to customise the avatar so that it looks like somebody else or even a hypothetical character (Perez 2023a; "What Is an Avatar, and How to Create a Metaverse Avatar?," n.d.).

2.1.3. Interoperability

"The metaverse is not a single app. It's a network of millions of virtual worlds people visit to play games, socialise and collaborate. Today, most of those worlds are closed and disconnected walled gardens" ("Break down Walls to Build a More Connected Virtual World," n.d.). However, metaverse is envisaged to be a connected network which shall ensure continuity to the user while he traverses from one virtual space to other. A user will feel continued existence when he moves between spaces (Ponde 2023b). For instance, a user has bought fancy shoes for his avatar and then wearing those he moves on to watch a musical concert. While doing so the user can be in the same avatar or can chose to be a different one. This is close to actual physical experience, unlike today's internet where you have to log in to different websites for different purposes. An analogy of the above example, for buying shoes you may need to log in to say Amazon app and then to listen to a live concert you may sign in to You tube and watch the live recording. Interoperability is thus a feature which predominantly differentiates the present-day internet and the next generation of internet. Interoperability could be understood from two dimensions. First, technical interoperability which relates with hardware and software concerns like intellectual property protection, data privacy across platforms etc. and second is usage interoperability which is concerned with making metaverse access inclusive and equitable (World Economic Forum in association with Accenture 2023).

2.1.4. Decentralisation

The internet as it stands today is a distributed network i.e. there are servers which are spread across and owned by various service providers ("What Is Metaverse?: What Decentralization Means in the Metaverse" 2023). Essentially, there are varied agencies which control, own and regulate today's internet. Metaverse is based on the idea of decentralization wherein there are multiple servers like the distributed network, however each server is independent ("What Is Metaverse?: What Decentralization Means in the Metaverse" 2023). That is the functioning of each node is independent and no node instructs the other. In a decentralised network, all nodes have the exact same data and any modification is based on consensus mechanism between the member of the group. This ensures that if the functioning of any node fails, the other have the data and there is no loss. Moreover, because same data is present on every node, it will be easy for companies in metaverse to confirm ownership of data by any particular user and to authenticate any relevant information pertaining to that user. A stronger decentralization is focused in the metaverse which means unlike a centralised system, users in the metaverse will have no need to depend on any one single authority. This eventually leads to transparency in the entire ecosystem (Jaswant and Kale 2021). Blockchain which is strongly rooted in the concept of decentralisation is thus an essential technology for metaverse.

Web 3.0, a term used to indicate the new generation of internet could play a crucial role in metaverse. An important difference between web 3.0 and today's internet or web 2, is decentralization (Terra 2023). The three generations of internet could be characterised with increasing level of participation by users. Users of web 1.0 could simply read and it was static (Sinhal 2022). Then came web 2.0, internet in present form which is more interactive with say different social media platforms. Web 3.0 would be most participatory, as because of decentralization, participation would be 'permissionless', i.e. there will not be any governing authority required to grant permission (Sinhal 2022). This is unlike web 2.0 which has control and ownership by several agencies. Further, Web 3.0 is imagined to be semantic, one with capability to understand human beings and which uses advanced technologies like Artificial Intelligence and machine learning (Sinhal 2022).

Presence of Decentralised Autonomous Organisation (DAO) is another feature of web 3.0 (Marr 2022). DAOs are organization where people come together and form rules, regulation to achieve some goals ("What Is Metaverse? : A Community Focused Economy" 2023). The functioning of DAO is democratic in the sense that there is absence of a centralised authority and collective decision making is followed. DAO is analogous to cooperative society where voting rights are proportional to the contributions made ("What Is Metaverse? : A Community Focused Economy" 2023). For instance, 'Decentraland', a metaverse which facilitates buying of virtual plots and other assets through its cryptocurrency, is a DAO where voting power is proportional to the cryptocurrency or land held (Schneider 2022b)

2.1.5. Non-fungible token (NFT)

As the name indicates, NFT is a token which is non-fungible, i.e. it cannot be replicated or replaced with an exactly same item (Berger 2023). NFT is a kind of digital receipt on a blockchain which proves ownership and authenticity of any digital art or asset (Jablonski 2021). NFTs could play a significant role in metaverse and several companies have already started to leverage it (Fonarov 2022). For instance, Nike is making NFTs for its products in its own virtual space in metaverse (Fonarov 2022). NFTs can be traded. A user buying an NFT is actually buying the ownership of that asset (Jablonski 2021). This NFT can later be resold at high price looking at demand dynamics.

2.1.6. Artificial intelligence

Alvin Graylin, China President of HTC, elaborates Metaverse as: – Metaverse = Internet + 3D + Artificial Intelligence → Extended Reality or XR (Graylin 2022). That is, AI is considered to be the power behind metaverse and gives it a distinct character. Web 3.0 is imagined to be a web that executes, understands and is semantic. AI, a technology which enables machines to emulate human brain and perform cognitive functions like thinking, memorising, reasoning; can give these characteristics to web 3.0 ("What Is AI?" 2023). The virtual space in metaverse can become more realistic, dynamic with use of AI (Salazar 2023). AI is being used to make the avatar more human like; virtual shopping stores powered by AI are giving more immersive experience to customers (Lee 2022; Salazar 2023). Apart from this, Generative AI which is trained on different data sets, has potential to generate new content and can be of immense application in metaverse (Lv 2023).

2.1.7. Digital twins

> 'A digital twin is a digital representation of a real-world entity or system. The implementation of a digital twin is an encapsulated software object or model that mirrors a unique physical object, process, organization, person or other abstraction. Data from multiple digital twins can be aggregated for a composite view across a number of real-world entities, such as a power plant or a city, and their related processes.' (Gartner n.d.)

Businesses worldwide are actively planning to utilise Digital twins of their product, factories in the metaverse to analyse and gauge the functioning before making hefty investment in any project(Bidar 2022)

3. Patents in metaverse

Metaverse, though in early stages today is predicted to turn into trillion-dollar industry and set to boost GDP of several countries (Chan 2023; Levine 2023). Many companies have begun to invest heavily in the metaverse. Companies who traditionally sold only physical goods are now entering metaverse offering immersive shopping experience to customers (Chan 2023). Thus, Intellectual Property rights which by nature protect intangible creation, invention holds tremendous significance in this intangible world of metaverse. IP rights not only would incentivise more innovation but also metaverse being amalgamation of several technologies, a robust mechanism for its protection will be required (World Intellectual Property Organization 2023). Further, if companies are investing heavily, it is natural to seek protection of its assets. Patent, an IP form protecting invention holds huge commercial significance as it gives exclusive rights to the inventors, attracts investment and is a valuable asset in itself (R K Dewan & Co 2020). There has been a remarkable growth in filing of metaverse patent applications across different countries in recent times (Glee 2022). This section of the paper provides the basics of patents vis-à-vis metaverse.

3.1. Product and process patents

The TRIPS agreement, to which majority of the countries in the world are party to, obligates its member countries to make available patents for any invention, whether a product or process in all fields of technology ("Overview: The TRIPS Agreement," n.d.).

Patents in metaverse could be product or process. For instance, patents related to hardware components of VR, AR and devices used to access them say sensors, lenses, wearable glasses can be categorised as product patents (Recktorchek 2022). Metaverse is characterised by digital products. As mentioned above, companies which functioned in the traditional market setup are utilising metaverse and coming into limelight through metaverse. 'Loreal' known for its beauty products has filed several patents in metaverse (Talon 2022). These patent applications are mostly related to virtual cosmetics and other digital products (Talon 2022). Patent law as it exists in the present form was meant for only physical products. Can these virtual goods satisfy the criteria of products? Under US Patent law a patent can be granted to an invention which is process, machine, manufacture or composition of matter. Analogous to product patent is the term 'manufacture'. The US Supreme Court has interpreted 'manufacture' as any article which is tangible, i.e. any article or product that is intangible cannot be patented (In re Petrus A.C.M. NUIJTEN 2007). In China as well, patents can only be filed for physical products. Despite latest amendment in Chinese patent law which allows products showing industrial application to be patented, whether these products can be virtual product is still not clear (Li 2022). Thus, patenting a product in metaverse could be challenging given existing laws.

Process patents in metaverse would mostly be related to software. This can be about processes within the metaverse or processes for accessing the metaverse (minesoft n.d.). Simulation of real world in the virtual world would also be a key area where patents would be sought (minesoft n.d.). Software patents is in itself a complex domain given the subject matter eligibilities of patent law in different jurisdictions and fulfilling of other patentability criteria. Further software patents related to AI, Blockchain technology come with its unique set of challenges (Xie 2022). As these technologies are prominent feature of metaverse, the software patents could be a difficult task.

3.2. Ownership

Ownership implies the entitlement of a patent, to whom the patent is granted and who can exercise the rights associated with patent. Logically, the person developing the patentable invention is the inventor of the patent (Cook 2018). It is not always the case that an inventor owns the patents. It can also be owned by businesses who employ these inventors (Abbott 2019). The question of who should be the inventor has become complex due to the nature of advanced technologies. There are instances where patent applications have named AI as an inventor. A prominent example is that of DABUS – an AI based creativity machine which was listed as inventor by Artificial Inventor Project Team (Abbott 2019). The team filed for patent in different countries. With exception of South Africa, jurisdictions like US, UK, EU have not accepted AI inventorship and conferring it with ownership rights (Basham 2021; Maura 2023). The ground for rejection has been that the tenets of patent law consider an inventor to be a natural person (Thaler v. Comptroller General of Patents Trade Marks and Designs 2021; Thaler v. Vidal 2022). AI which emulates human brain has the ability of self-learning due to which it is believed that it can create or invent. However, offering inventorship to AI for this reason seems to fundamentally contrast patent law. AI is slated to play a phenomenal role in a metaverse. The problem of inventorship will be compounded in a metaverse. For instance, in a metaverse, a company through an AI can convert 2D images into 3D models. Who should be the inventor in the metaverse platform? Is it the company, the AI responsible for conversion of images or should it be the human avatar who as part of that company, enabled or facilitated the conversion? Thus, if with AI, the confusion about inventorship was between AI and natural person behind AI; in metaverse, a further layer of confusion is added as the avatar being an inventor (European Innovation Council and SMEs Executive Agency 2022). Besides, with Generative AI, the issue of inventorship is even more challenging as there are creators of the Generative AI model and then there are users who cause output to be produced. Both these categories can claim to be an inventor (jones day 2023). With strong potential of Generative AI in metaverse, the issue of inventorship is bound to rise. Another possibility of an unusual inventor in metaverse, is the DAO. There are natural persons behind a DAO, and therefore a DAO may not face the same challenge as an AI (Katopis 2022). But can a DAO in itself be an inventor is a complex question to solve as at the end of the day it is nothing but a virtual organization not capable to be termed as 'person'.

3.2.1. Law on inventorship

US law gives scope for an individual to be termed as inventor or group of individuals be joint inventors when they invent any new machine, composition of matter, process or manufacture or a new improvement of these entities (Title 35 – Patents n.d.). An additional layer of requirement for being an inventor in US is conception i.e. a concrete and permanent idea of an operative invention (Ethicon, Inc. v. United States Surgical Corp. 1998). It needs to be analysed if an AI and DAO can conceive things. AI is widely used for prediction but can it have a definite accurate idea so as to imagine a functioning of an invention? As US law allows joint inventors, there is a silver lining for DAO but it may fall short of the requirement of conception.

In UK, an inventor is 'actual devisor of the invention' and it has been further clarified by the Courts that this actual deviser is a natural person who has contributed towards an inventive concept (Cook 2018; Patents Act 1977). Considering the word 'actual' in its literal sense itself makes it tough for AI or DAO to be classified as inventor. This is even more complex for an 'avatar'. An avatar can be considered to be digital twin of the real human being. When an avatar invents something while working in the metaverse, is it 'actually' the human being who has invented? In such a case, the natural person behind the avatar would be the inventor. In India, an inventor is a person or government organization (The Patents Act 1970). The term person does not specifically say natural person, which is a constructive sign for AI or DAO to be termed as inventor. Thus, the issue of inventorship faces unique issues in different jurisdictions.

3.3. Patentability criteria – novelty

For a patent to be granted for any invention, it has to be 'new' or 'novel'. Whether the invention is new or not is decided by examining the 'state of art' or 'prior art'. For UK,

> 'it is all matter (whether a product, a process, information about either, or anything else) which has at any time before the priority date of that invention been made available to the public (whether in the UK or elsewhere) by written or oral description, by use, or in any other way.' (The Patents Act 1977)

Basically, there is lack of novelty when the invention is already anticipated. As discussed earlier, the types of patents in metaverse are mainly hardware patents which are based on augmented reality and virtual reality. There are already patents associated with these technologies and therefore it is natural that patent applications based on these technologies would face novelty related issues ("Intellectual Property for the Metaverse" 2023).

The software patent applications in metaverse are also bound to face novelty challenges. Software patent applications in themselves have hurdles in searching for prior art. One obvious reason is significant growth of software patents being filed. Software is at the core of advanced technologies. Therefore, a rising trend in filing patent applications is manifested. Moreover, software has application in various fields unlike other technical sector specific technical inventions. Vast the prior art, difficult is the prior art search. The peculiar nature of software also gives rise to novelty related issues. Software tends to become outdated quickly due to its short life cycle (Shaikh, Khode, and Deshpande 2018). There is considerable gap between filing and granting of patents and by the time patents are granted it may happen that the software becomes outdated. This makes it difficult at times for prior art searches to depend on data from patents granted or applied. Technologies like AI, which are significant for metaverse, have the ability to self-learn and thus the software evolves at an even higher pace (Kompella 2020). Thus, the novelty problems with traditional software are sure to escalate with the advanced technologies which are at heart of metaverse.

We discussed earlier the concept of digital twins. Digital twin is also basically an encapsulated software. There have been patent applications filed in U.S. mentioning 'digital twins' but very few have been granted (Wendt 2020). A software patent application for a digital twin in a metaverse is likely to face novelty challenges. First, due to the nature of software itself and second due to the nature and features of metaverse. Suppose a company has a digital twin for one of its manufacturing units in the metaverse. A digital twin is an example of integration of virtual and physical world (Tao et al. 2019). For instance, an employee of the company may input real time data on the digital twin in metaverse and check the functioning of manufacturing unit. It might also happen that the employee or any other person who gets access to the digital twin, files patent on the manufacturing method which was under observance on the digital twin in the metaverse. But the method technically is prior art. And thus, the application might not satisfy the novelty criteria.

3.4. Patentability criteria – inventiveness

A significant criterion for patentability is the criteria of inventiveness or non-obviousness. As per the Indian Patent Act, 1970, Section 2(1) (j a) the invention to be patented should have an inventive step which is defined as 'a feature of an invention that involves technical advance as compared to the existing knowledge or have economic significance or both and makes the invention not obvious to a person skilled in the art.' The UK patent law also points out that the invention should have an inventive step and that it should not be obvious to the person skilled in the art (The Patents Act 1977). Under US law this criterion is referred to as 'non-obviousness'. US law has a concept of PHOSITA – person having ordinary skills in the art. The patentability of an invention is dependent on whether for PHOSITA the invention is non-obvious as per section 103 of the patent law (Title 35 – Patents n.d.). A broad interpretation of the three jurisdiction shows that there are two essential characteristics of this criteria. First the invention has to be an advancement over existing technology. This does not mean that it has to be new. Novelty is different than inventive step though it may seem apparently similar. For metaverse, hardware patents particularly in the VR, AR domain are likely to satisfy this criterion. It was mentioned earlier that patents in VR, AR are not a new thing. However, for metaverse which has features like interoperability, AR and VR hardware need to show some advancement over existing technology. That is unless they have an inventive step, they are hardly of any relevance for metaverse. Same goes for software patents in metaverse. AI and blockchain are advanced technologies which are at the base of metaverse. The software for these technologies differs substantially than traditional software. For instance, conventionally traditional software is designed to perform some fixed tasks (Dmitry 2023). But AI software learns continuously to give some prediction or recommendation. So certainly, this software is advanced version of traditional software and satisfying the inventive step criterion may not be a hurdle.

However, the roadblock for patents in metaverse could be person skilled in the art. Broadly this person is considered to have an ordinary skill in the related field of invention. For example, if the invention for which patent is applied relates to a method of producing a drug, then person having ordinary skills might be a chemist who has a basic knowledge of drug manufacture. Pertinent to note is that the law does not want this person to be an expert or someone who is extraordinarily skilled in the given field. But he is someone who has basic knowledge of the field and the given invention should not be obvious for such person (Bentley et al. 2022).

Looking at the advanced technologies of our concern, it is quite doubtful that a person with ordinary skill can decide about the obviousness of the invention. Assume a patent has been filed for a digital twin in metaverse by Company X. The company wants to manufacture smart refrigerator which can alter temperature depending on the food item stored. Prior to investing, the company makes a digital twin, which as discussed earlier is an encapsulated software where integration of real and virtual world takes place. Looking at the success of functioning of the smart refrigerator, they decide to file a patent on the digital twin itself before starting with the actual manufacturing in physical world. Now, to decide whether the invention is obvious, person skilled in the art should have knowledge about functioning of advanced software, knowledge about functioning of electronic devices and knowledge about advanced technology. As this digital twin is in metaverse, the person should have knowledge about its essential features like decentralisation, interoperability and so on. Now, even though the threshold of knowledge expected from this hypothetical person PHOSITA is not high, it is rather what is termed as ordinary, it is unlikely that the conventional notion of this person would be in position to decide obviousness. In the example given, the person needs to have knowledge of multiple disciplines. Thus, the conventional threshold of PHOSITA may not suffice the advances in technology (Abbot 2019). This hypothetical person could itself be based on these advanced technologies, for instance, AI based inventive machines can act as PHOSITA (Gokhale 2022).

3.5. Subject matter eligibility

This factor relates to what can be patented and what cannot be patented under a patent law of a particular jurisdiction. In this section, we discuss some facets from different jurisdictions which might be of relevance for metaverse patents in general.

3.5.1. Exclusion of abstract idea and computer programs

In U.S. as per section 101, statutory subject matter categories are process, machine, manufacture or composition of matter (Title 35 – Patents n.d.). A metaverse may fall into either of these categories and there seems to be no subject matter obstacle for it. However, what is excluded from patents in U.S. is an 'abstract idea' ("2106 Patent Subject Matter Eligibility [R-10.2019]," n.d.).

This in particular could be problematic for software patents in metaverse. A software in its basic sense, is a set of instructions which is responsible for operating a particular technology. However, when a patent is sought for any software, the inventor seeks to protect the functional aspects of a software (Teska 2008). That is, the concept behind software is protected through patents. Therefore, the protection happens at a very abstract level. Software patent applications have thus faced several hurdles in U.S. due to the 'abstract idea' exclusion in its patent laws. A prominent example is the case of *Alice Corp v CLS Bank International* (Alice Corp v CLS Bank International 2014). The invention concerned was a method of exchanging financial obligations using computer system as a third-party intermediary. The court stated that a method 'directed to an abstract idea of employing an intermediary to facilitate simultaneous exchange of obligations in order to minimize risk' is a 'basic business or financial concept,' and that a 'computer system merely "configured" to implement an abstract method is no more patentable than an abstract method that is simply "electronically" implemented' (Alice Corp v CLS Bank International 2014). If we draw an analogy of this case and metaverse, then in a crude form metaverse also consists of methods which exists on 'electronic medium'. Digital twin in a metaverse again is a prominent example. Thus, it is very likely that Metaverse software patents face hurdles in this regard. The Alice case gave rise to 'two step analysis': (1) Whether the claims in issue are directed to a patent ineligibility concept (i.e. law of nature, abstract idea or natural phenomena) and (2) If yes, then whether the claims contain an 'inventive concept.' The notion of inventive concept and its possible obstacles are already discussed in the previous section. Despite some prominent judgments related to software patents in U.S., uncertainty still lingers on about the exact components of abstract ideas. Advanced technology software further compounds the subject matter eligibility concerns. For example, in U.S. patent applications have been rejected because they have claimed protection to concept which involves emulating human activities (Decosta 2017).

This was considered 'abstract idea'. The basic idea of AI is about emulating human brain or activities. Therefore, AI based patent applications has challenges on its way.

Moreover, metaverse also emulates physical world activities. The presence of 'avatar' working in a virtual working space in a metaverse is an extension of physical world or rather more appropriately an emulation. So, patents in metaverse indeed have hurdles.

In the EU, Article 52(2) of the European Patent Convention excludes from patents – computer programs ("European Patent Convention," n.d.-a). At its core any software is computer programs and thus software as such is not patentable in EU (White and Piroozi 2019).

However, if a computer program shows some technical effect, then it is patentable (Bentley et al. 2022). Despite this stringency, there has been a trend in EU to seek patent protection for computer implemented inventions through what is known as whole content approach (Matveev and Martyanova 2022). Under this interpretation the courts focus on the invention as a whole and ignore the presence of any excluded subject matter like computer programs. This means though an invention has computer programs, the patent is not rejected merely based on this fact but is rather seen in its entirety to consider patentability. Compared to other jurisdictions, obtaining software related patents is still a tricky matter in EU. For metaverse, patents would mostly relate to computer simulation as discussed in one of the earlier sections. There was a recent decision by European Patent Office's Enlarged Board of Appeal on invention related to computer implemented simulations (minesoft n.d.). It can be inferred from the judgment that most computer simulation cannot be patented as 'most simulations as such may have few technical effects' (Mathys&Squire 2021; G 0001/19 (Pedestrian simulation) 2021). The concerned invention here was about an invention about pedestrian simulation which can be applied and implemented further in different venues. It can be gauged from the understanding of metaverse so far that patent applications would be similar to these and are likely to face impediments.

In India as well, computer programs are explicitly excluded from being patented as per section 3(k) of the Indian Patent Act, 1970 (The Patents Act 1970). It is only when they manifest a technical effect, they are patentable ("Software Patent Registration" 2023). However, there is quite a bit of subjectivity in the terms 'technical effect'. When conventional software patents face issues, it is natural that software for advanced technologies will face even more hurdles. Recently, an Indian court expressed need to update the patent manual in light of AI and machine learning technologies (AGFA NV & Anr v The Assistant Controller of Patents and Designs & Anr [2023] Delhi HC. 2023).

Patent applications in these fields have large number of claims and are interlinked to each other. Therefore, the Court stressed on clarity and succinctness in the guidelines. In another case pertaining to patent on system of gifting a media item, which was rejected considering section 3(k), the Court highlighted the need to re-visit section 3(k) in light of emerging technologies (Mandhani 2023; Opentv Inc vs The Controller Of Patents And Designs 2023). Thus, when it comes to subject matter eligibility of patent related to metaverse in India, there are hurdles but the very fact that the judiciary is acknowledging the need to change and revise the existing law certainly provides a ray of hope.

3.5.2. Inventions against public order or morality

Another prominent subject matter is of immoral inventions or those against public order. This concept finds mention in the jurisdictions we have been discussing so far.

For instance, as per article 53(a) of the European Patent Convention, if a patent is filed for an invention and such that its commercial exploitation might cause disorder in public or foster criminal, offensive behaviour, then it is denied patent (European Patent Convention n.d.-b). This category of subject matter needs to be evaluated for patents related to metaverse. Unfortunately, metaverse responsible for criminal or offensive behaviour is no longer just an assumption but the threat is for real (Cantley and Dietrich 2015). Recently, a woman was raped when she logged in metaverse space through her avatar (Diaz 2022). The experience was so horrid for the woman that her hands in real world were shaking. If a user or rather his avatar is touched in the metaverse, a vibration is felt in the controls in the hand (Diaz 2022). Not to mention the psychological distress it may have caused. Research has shown that if an avatar is slapped in metaverse, it increases the heartbeat and physically affects the real-world person behind that avatar (Cantley and Dietrich 2015).

In the instance of sexual assault discussed above, if someone is accessing the Metaverse then it is likely through some VR/ AR device and the avatar must have entered some virtual space. Both the hardware part of this scenario and the software part, are likely to have patents associated with it. For instance, an advanced VR headset by a leading company could be used to access the metaverse. The space which was visited in the metaverse, might have different AI software behind it, which again is patentable invention. Pertinent to note is the fact that these inventions may satisfy the criteria we have discussed so far – novelty, inventive step, non-obviousness and partly subject matter eligibility when it comes to hardware and software inventions. However, these inventions may be contrary to public order and morality.

Justine Pila in her article on emerging technologies and the public order, morality exception, argues why it is necessary to re-interpret this exception in light of emerging technologies (Pila 2020). Though the technology Pila refers is related to biotechnology, the same analogy can be drawn for metaverse as well. It is required that those opposing the patent with regards to this article, have to come with strong evidence that the patent poses a risk to public policy. Coming up with evidence for a metaverse related patent would be difficult for multiple reasons, for instance, the technology being in nascent stage, the consequences are not well established and can be only predicted. Thus, presenting strong evidence would be a task. Another factor be considered is the narrow interpretation of *ordre public* which covers protection of physical integrity of individuals (Pila 2020). However, the aspect of psychological distress discussed above, may not come under the purview of this interpretation. The consequences from metaverse are indeed unpredictable and uncertain. Thus, while a patent application concerning metaverse is being considered, the aspect of morality and public order can be ignored only at its own peril.

3.6. Infringement of patents

A patent gives exclusive set of rights to patentees to make, sell, use or import the invention. When these rights are exercised without the consent of the owner of the patent, infringement takes place (Cook 2018). This section shall analyse infringement of patents in metaverse with broad interpretation of infringement in the jurisdictions we have considered so far.

Infringement can be direct or indirect. Direct infringement takes place when the infringer has performed some activity which only owner could have performed (TedKBL 2021). This is quite straightforward involvement by the infringer.

Indirect infringement, on the other hand takes place when a person contributes or induces infringement but does not directly take part in it (TedKBL 2021).

To determine patent infringement, it is vital to know the scope of protection for the patent. This can be done literally i.e. when every claim of the patent is able to describe the accused product or process literally, as it is. In circumstances where the accused product or process is not reflected through strict or literal interpretation of claims, several jurisdiction resort to Doctrine of equivalents (Pumfrey et al. 2009). According to this doctrine, infringement takes place when the accused device or product performs substantially the same function in substantially the same way to obtain the same result ("2186 Relationship to the Doctrine of Equivalents [R-07.2022]," n.d.). Another approach which is adopted in claim interpretation is the purposive construction where claims are understood from the eyes of person skilled in the art and the purpose of the invention remains the focal point of interpretation (Bentley et al. 2022). The jurisdictions in our consideration apply these approaches, however it is beyond the scope of this paper to discuss application of these approaches in these jurisdictions. For the purpose of this paper, I stick to how these approaches will see its application in metaverse related patents.

Revisiting the basics of what is metaverse, we have discussed that it is designed to immerse physical world into virtual world. This very basic fact increases the probability of infringement of patents in metaverse particularly in light of Doctrine of equivalents (Schneider 2022a). Assume that company A is impressed by a particular manufacturing method of Company B. This method of Company A is already patented. Company B, to check the feasibility of the manufacturing method of Company A for its own company, creates a digital twin of that method in the metaverse. Now here, the data which Company B would enter into their encapsulated software on the metaverse, the environment of their Company will surely differ from that of Company A. However, the digital twin will be performing substantially the same function to obtain substantially the same result as that of company A. Will Company 'B' be liable for infringement under Doctrine of equivalents? It is important to note that the Company B has not come up with any real-life manufacturing method which is substantially similar to that of Company A. So technically they have not done anything which only the owner is authorised to do with his invention, specifically, 'make' the invention. But it can also be argued that an attempt was made to make it through metaverse. Whether or not this situation will amount to infringement, needs further careful analysis and is certain to be challenging. Further, for metaverse patents which need to be interpreted through purposive construction, viewing it through lens of person skilled in the art is bound to be challenging for the reasons discussed in the section on inventiveness. A higher and not ordinary standard of this person would be required and this will be problematic for interpretation.

The European Patent Office, predicts global accessibility of metaverse in coming times (Wessing 2022). In the initial sections we discussed that metaverse can be accessed through devices which are commonly available, say a smartphone. This essentially indicates that there are chances of unauthorised access to patented inventions in metaverse and thereby cause infringement. In the example discussed above, assume that Company B has taken permission from the owner of Company A. But someone in metaverse may get unauthorised access to the digital twin, understand the entire method and manufacture it in real world. This is infringement of A's method but who can be held liable in this case, is a tough question to answer. It might be the case that some rival competitor has influenced the unauthorised accessor and hence it can also be a case of indirect infringement.

An avatar may infringe a patent in the metaverse space. In that case, it is still possible to determine and trace the identity of the real person behind the avatar. However, technology has become so advanced that there is software which can customise the avatar in such a manner that it is different than the real person. An avatar of a person can even look like some celebrity (Boreham 2022). Or, the person who wants to infringe may take an avatar of someone else so that the other person is considered the infringer.

Now, if this customised avatar infringes a patent in metaverse, it will be very difficult to trace the identity of real infringer. Further, AI is used to create what is called as deepfake images, video or audio (Sample 2020). Through this technology, original images, video or audio are modified so that fake versions of the same are created. There have been instances of deepfake videos of national leaders speaking irrelevant stuff. This technology thus can have serious negative ramifications. If these deepfakes are used in metaverse, it will magnify the complexities of patent infringement. A persistent problem with regards to infringement in metaverse would be where to sue the infringer? Laws of which jurisdiction would be applicable is questionable (Wessing 2022) Particularly, considering the interoperability feature of metaverse, this becomes even more complex (World Economic Forum 2023).

4. Conclusion

This paper is an attempt to understand the impediments, opportunities and scope of patents in metaverse. The analysis of this paper has not been restricted to patent law of any particular jurisdiction. Metaverse as a technology has immersion and dissolving the boundaries at its core. Restricting the analysis to patent law of any single jurisdiction would be devoid of any broad analysis from multiple angles for any metaverse related patent. For instance, the notion of inventorship differs in a nuanced way for different jurisdictions. For a comprehensive understanding, it was required that it be considered from perspectives of patent laws of multiple countries. Analysing each concept with regards to the respective patent laws of the three prominent jurisdictions reflected in the paper is much beyond the scope of this article. The focal point of analysis has therefore been core concepts of patents and not any single jurisdiction. The conception of 'Jurisdictional Interoperability' as reflected in the WEF report on 'Interoperability in Metaverse' should drive the future discourse of patent law and metaverse. The report mentions that how there needs to be a collective understanding of multiple metaverse experience across myriad regulations and locations should be coherently considered so that the ultimate use of metaverse remains lawful (World Economic Forum 2023). Patent is a territorial concept and therefore laws of individual countries will remain vital. However, patents in metaverse have different set of challenges due to the features analysed in this paper. It was rightly pointed out in one of the recent judgments by the Indian court that there is a pressing need to take into account 'the march of technology in the digital space ... so that patent law is not outpaced and patenting itself does not become irrelevant in the years to come' (Opentv Inc vs The Controller Of Patents And Designs 2023). Any reform in patent system of different jurisdictions with regards to patentability criteria, subject matter eligibility, ownership and patent enforcement, done to attune with the new technology like that of metaverse shall therefore be a welcome step.

Disclosure statement

No potential conflict of interest was reported by the author(s).

ORCID

Prajakta Kale http://orcid.org/0000-0001-9770-4570

References

"2106 Patent Subject Matter Eligibility [R-10.2019]". n.d. USPTO. Accessed August 5, 2023. https://www.uspto.gov/web/offices/pac/mpep/s2106.html.

"2186 Relationship to the Doctrine of Equivalents [R07.2022]". n.d. USPTO. Accessed August 5, 2023. https://www.uspto.gov/web/offices/pac/mpep/s2186.html.

Abbot, Ryan. 2019. "Everything is Obvious." *UCLA Law Review* 66 (2).

Abbott, Ryan. 2019. "The Artificial Inventor Project." WIPO Magazine. December 2019. https://www.wipo.int/wipo_magazine/en/2019/06/article_0002.html.

AGFA NV & Anr v The Assistant Controller of Patents and Designs & Anr [2023] Delhi HC. 2023.

Alice Corp v CLS Bank International. 2014. 573 US 208.

Bainbridge, David. 2014. *Information Technology and Intellectual Property Law*. 6th ed. London: Bloomsbury Professional.

Basham, Victoria. 2021. "South Africa Issues World's First Patent Listing AI as Inventor." Global Legal Post. Accessed July 28, 2021. https://www.globallegalpost.com/news/south-africa-issues-worlds-first-patent-listing-ai-as-inventor-161068982.

Bentley, Lionel, Brad Sherman, Dev Gangjee, and Phillip Johnson. 2022. *Intellectual Property Law*. 6th ed. Oxford: OUP.

Berger, Adam. 2023. "What Is Metaverse?: Arts, Entertainment and Sports in Metaverse." Meta, Coursera. 2023.

Bidar, Musadiq. 2022. "Companies Race to Build 'Digital Twins' in the Metaverse." Money Watch. March 17, 2022. https://www.cbsnews.com/news/metaverse-amazon-bmw-lockheed-martin-adobe-digital-twin/.

Boreham, Jack. 2022. "An In-Depth Guide on Metaverse Avatars & How to Create One." The Metaverse Insider. July 2022. https://metaverseinsider.tech/2022/07/16/metaverse-avatars/.

"Break down Walls to Build a More Connected Virtual World.". n.d. Ready Player Me. Accessed June 21, 2023. https://readyplayer.me/about.

Cantley, Beckett, and Geoffrey Dietrich. 2015. "The Metaverse: A Virtual World with Real World Legal Consequences." *Rutgers Computer and Technology Law Journal* 49 (1): 1–25.

Chan, Kevin. 2023. "Metaverse: What Are the Economic Benefits?" World Economic Forum. Accessed June 22, 2023. https://www.weforum.org/agenda/2023/06/what-will-be-the-economic-benefits-of-the-metaverse/.

Cook, Trevor. 2018. *A User's Guide to Patents*. 5th ed. Hayward Heath: Bloomsbury Professional.

Decosta, Frank. 2017. "Intellectual Property Protection for Artificial Intelligence." Finnegan. 2017. https://www.finnegan.com/en/insights/articles/intellectual-property-protection-for-artificial-intelligence.html.

"Demystifying the Virtual Reality Landscape.". n.d. Intel. Accessed June 17, 2023. https://www.intel.in/content/www/in/en/tech-tips-and-tricks/virtual-reality-vs-augmented-reality.html.

Diaz, Adriana. 2022. "Disturbing Reports of Sexual Assaults in the Metaverse: 'It's a Free Show'." New York Post. May 2022. https://nypost.com/2022/05/27/women-are-being-sexually-assaulted-in-the-metaverse/.

Dmitry, Baraishuk. 2023. "What Is Artificial Intelligence? AI vs Traditional Software." Belitsoft. 2023. https://belitsoft.com/ai-development/artificial-intelligence-vs-conventional-software#:~:text=While%20conventional%20software%20is%20programmed,we%20have%20to%20write%20code.

Ethicon, Inc. v. United States Surgical Corp. 1998. 135 F.3d 1456.

European Innovation Council and SMEs Executive Agency. 2022. "Intellectual Property in the Metaverse. Episode III: Patents." 2022. https://intellectual-property-helpdesk.ec.europa.eu/news-events/news/intellectual-property-metaverse-episode-iii-patents-2022-05-30_en.

"European Patent Convention.". n.d.-a. Accessed August 5, 2023. https://new.epo.org/en/legal/epc/2020/a52.html#:~:text=(1)%20European%20patents%20shall%20be,are%20susceptible%20of%20industrial%20application.

European Patent Convention. n.d.-b. Accessed August 5, 2023. https://new.epo.org/en/legal/guidelines-epc/2023/g_ii_4_1.htm.

"Everyday Examples of Mixed Reality.". 2019. https://academyxi.com/everyday-examples-of-mixed-reality/.

Fonarov, Oleg. 2022. "What Is The Role Of NFTs In The Metaverse?" Forbes Technology Council. Accessed March 11, 2022. https://www.forbes.com/sites/forbestechcouncil/2022/03/11/what-is-the-role-of-nfts-in-the-metaverse/?sh=5195d756bb87.

G 0001/19 (Pedestrian simulation). 2021.

Gartner. n.d. "Digital Twin." Accessed June 22, 2023. https://www.gartner.com/en/information-technology/glossary/digital-twin.

Gerratana, Frank, and Amritaa Ganguly. 2023. "Intellectual Property for the Metaverse." 2023. https://www.mintz.com/insights-center/viewpoints/2231/2023-05-24-intellectual-property-metaverse.

Glee, Alex. 2022. "Metaverse Patents for Innovation Insights." 2022. https://www.slideshare.net/alexglee/metaverse-patents-for-innovation-insights.

Gokhale, Sameer. 2022. "AI as a Tool for the 'PHOSITA.'" Lexology. January 2022. https://www.lexology.com/library/detail.aspx?g=fd5ef6f0-5982-4d24-b4d2-0838453e2560.

Graylin, Alvin. 2022. "AWE Asia 2022 Main Stage: Metaverse Metamorphosis." 2022. https://www.google.com/search?q=alvin+graylin+htc+ai+metaverse&rlz=1C1CHBF_enIN992IN992&oq=alvin+graylin+htc+ai+metaverse&aqs=chrome.69i57.14568j0j7&sourceid=chrome&ie=UTF-8#fpstate=ive&vld=cid:722d3944,vid:C8RK6kemLwE.

"Haptic Technology.". n.d. Wikipedia. Accessed June 18, 2023. https://en.wikipedia.org/wiki/Haptic_technology.

Hayes, Adams. 2023. "Augmented Reality (AR) Defined, With Examples and Uses." Investopedia. 2023. https://www.investopedia.com/terms/a/augmented-reality.asp#:~:text=Augmented%20reality%20uses%20the%20existing,on%20their%20phone%20or%20tablet.

In re Petrus A.C.M. 2007. *NUIJTEN*.

"Intellectual Property for the Metaverse.". 2023. The National Law Review. 2023. https://www.natlawreview.com/article/intellectual-property-metaverse.

Jablonski, Sylvia. 2021. "Are NFTs The New Crypto? A Guide to Understanding Non-Fungible Tokens." Forbes Business Council. Accessed June 9, 2021. https://www.forbes.com/sites/forbesbusinesscouncil/2021/06/09/are-nfts-the-new-crypto-a-guide-to-understanding-non-fungible-tokens/?sh=594377763d95.

Jaswant, Shilpa, and Prajakta Kale. 2021. "Smart Contracts and Blockchain: Legal Issues and Implications for Indian Contract Law." *International Review of Law, Computer and Technology* 36 (3), https://www.tandfonline.com/toc/cirl20/36/3?nav=tocList.

jones day. 2023. "Generative AI-Assisted Patent Inventorship Questions Remain." June 2023. https://www.jonesday.com/en/insights/2023/06/generative-aiassisted-patent-inventorship-questions-remain.

Katopis, Chris. 2022. "Blockchain IP: DAOs Are Innovative—But Will They Be Inventors?" IPwatchdog. Accessed August 10, 2022. https://ipwatchdog.com/2022/08/10/blockchain-ip-daos-innovative-will-inventors/id=150806/.

Kompella, Kashyap. 2020. "How Machine Learning Differs from Traditional Software?" The Hindu Business Line. Accessed November 25, 2020. https://bloncampus.thehindubusinessline.com/columns/future-tense/how-machine-learning-differs-from-traditional-software/article33178445.ece.

Lee, Alex. 2022. "AI for Metaverse x Web 3 Overview." 2022. https://www.slideshare.net/alexglee/ai-for-metaverse-x-web3-overview.

Levine, Marne. 2023. "What Is Metaverse?: This Is the Metaverse." Meta, Coursera. 2023. https://www.coursera.org/learn/what-is-the-metaverse/lecture/7dRj9/this-is-the-metaverse.

Li, Elisa. 2022. "China: Design Patents and the Metaverse." National Law Review, Accessed August 22, 2022. https://www.natlawreview.com/article/china-design-patents-and-metaverse.

Lv, Zhihan. 2023. "Generative Artificial Intelligence in the Metaverse Era." *Cognitive Robotics* 3: 208–217. https://doi.org/10.1016/j.cogr.2023.06.001.

Mandhani, Apoorva. 2023. "Intellectual Property in the Age of AI — Why Delhi HC Wants Govt to Relook Patents Act." The Print. Accessed May 16, 2023.

Marr, Bernard. 2022. "The Important Difference Between Web3 And The Metaverse." Forbes. Accessed February 22, 2022. https://www.forbes.com/sites/bernardmarr/2022/02/22/the-important-difference-between-web3-and-the-metaverse/?sh=77882adf5af3.

Mathys&Squire. 2021. "G1/19: EPO Enlarged Board of Appeal Hands down Decision on Patentability of Simulations and Computer-Implemented Inventions." Accessed March 11, 2021. https://www.mathys-squire.com/insights-and-events/news/g1-19-epo-enlarged-board-of-appeal-hands-down-decision-on-patentability-of-simulations-and-computer-implemented-inventions/.

Matveev, Anton, and Elizaveta Martyanova. 2022. "Patentability of Computer Program Algorithms in the G20 States." *BRICS Law Journal* 9 (3): 144–173. https://doi.org/10.21684/2412-2343-2022-9-3-144-173.

Maura, O'Malley. 2023. "UK Supreme Court Grapples with Whether AI Can Be a Patent Inventor as DABUS Case Is Heard." Global Legal Post. Accessed March 7, 2023. https://www.globallegalpost.com/news/uk-supreme-court-grapples-with-whether-ai-can-be-a-patent-inventor-as-dabus-case-is-heard-1273622924.

minesoft. n.d. "Patenting Innovations in the Metaverse." Accessed February 10, 2024. https://minesoft.com/patenting-innovations-in-the-metaverse/.

Opentv Inc vs The Controller Of Patents And Designs. 2023.

Ouyong, Zin, Zhen Sun, and Xu Xinzhen. 2022. "Patent System in the Digital era - Opportunities and new Challenges." *Journal of Digital Economy* 1 (3): 166–179. https://doi.org/10.1016/j.jdec.2022.12.003.

"Overview: The TRIPS Agreement.". n.d. World Trade Organization. Accessed June 22, 2023. https://www.wto.org/english/tratop_e/trips_e/intel2_e.htm#:~:text=The%20TRIPS%20Agreement%20requires%20Member,novelty%2C%20inventiveness%20and%20industrial%20applicability.

The Patents Act. 1970. India: https://www.ipindia.gov.in/writereaddata/Portal/IPOAct/1_113_1_The_Patents_Act_1970_-_Updated_till_23_June_2017.pdf.

The Patents Act. 1977. UK. https://www.gov.uk/guidance/the-patent-act-1977/section-2-novelty.

Patents Act. 1977. UK. https://www.legislation.gov.uk/ukpga/1977/37/section/7#:~:text=%283%29%20In%20this%20Act%20%E2%80%9Cinventor%E2%80%9D%20in%20relation%20to,invention%20and%20%E2%80%9Cjoint%20inventor%E2%80%9D%20shall%20be%20construed%20accordingly.

Perez, Sarah. 2020. "Amazon Rolls out a New AR Shopping Feature for Viewing Multiple Items at Once." Techcrunch. 2020. https://techcrunch.com/2020/08/25/amazon-rolls-out-a-new-ar-shopping-feature-for-viewing-multiple-items-at-once/.

Pila, Justine. 2020. "Adapting the Ordre Public and Morality Exclusion of European Patent Law to Accommodate Emerging Technologies." *Nature Biotechnology* 38 (5): 555–557. https://doi.org/10.1038/s41587-020-0504-5.

Ponde, Nikhilesh. 2023a. "What Is Metaverse?: Avatars in the Metaverse." Meta, Coursera. 2023. https://www.coursera.org/learn/what-is-the-metaverse/lecture/kCu17/avatars-in-the-metaverse.

Ponde, Nikhilesh. 2023b. "What Is Metaverse? :Interoperability in the Metaverse." Meta, Coursera. 2023. https://www.coursera.org/learn/what-is-the-metaverse/lecture/7g6lp/interoperability-in-the-metaverse.

Prudy, Mark. 2022. "AI and Machine Learning: How Metaverse Could Change Work." Harvard Business Review. April 2022. https://hbr.org/2022/04/how-the-metaverse-could-change-work.

Pumfrey, Nicholas, Martin J. Adelman, Shamnad Basheer, Raj Dave, Peter Meier-Beck, Yukio Nagasawa, Maximilian Rospatt, and Martin Sulsky. 2009. "The doctrine of equivalents in various patent regimes-does anybody have it right?" *Yale Journal of Law & Technology* 11: 261–308. https://openyls.law.yale.edu/bitstream/handle/20.500.13051/7764/11_11YaleJL_Tech261_2008_2009_.pdf?sequence=2#:~:text=The%20doctrine%20of%20equivalents%20is,the%20bounds%20of%20the%20patent.

Recktorchek, Jan. 2022. "Patenting the Metaverse – Possibilities for Companies in Another World." TaylorWessing. 2022. https://www.taylorwessing.com/en/insights-and-events/insights/2022/05/patenting-the-metaverse.

R K Dewan & Co. 2020. "Commercial Benefits of Patenting." Lexology. Accessed June 3, 2020. https://www.lexology.com/library/detail.aspx?g=ed127557-e0cc-4026-974c-9a11ba9f5166.

Salazar, Rodolfo. 2023. "The Metaverse And AI: A Powerful Combination For Business Growth And Innovation." Forbes Agency Council. 2023. https://www.forbes.com/sites/forbesagencycouncil/2023/04/14/the-metaverse-and-ai-a-powerful-combination-for-business-growth-and-innovation/?sh=238095dd69a1.

Sample, Ian. 2020. "What Are Deepfakes – and How Can You Spot Them?" The Guardian. Accessed January 13, 2020. https://www.theguardian.com/technology/2020/jan/13/what-are-deepfakes-and-how-can-you-spot-them.

Schneider, Jacob. 2022a. "The Metaverse: Patent Infringement in Virtual Worlds." Holland & Knight/IP Decode Blog. 2022. https://www.hklaw.com/en/insights/publications/2022/08/metaverse-patent-infringement-in-virtual-worlds.

Schneider, Jacob. 2022b. "The Metaverse: Decentralized Autonomous Organizations (DAOs)." Holland & Knight IP/ Decode Blog. Accessed November 22, 2022. https://www.hklaw.com/en/insights/publications/2022/11/the-metaverse-decentralized-autonomous-organizations-daos.

Shaikh, Shabib, Alok Khode, and Nishad Deshpande. 2018. "Prior Art Searches in Software Patents-Issues Faced." *Journal of Intellectual Property Rights* 23 (November): 243–249.

Sinhal, Devansh. 2022. "What Are the Differences and Similarities between Web 1.0, Web 2.0, and Web 3.0?" Coinswitch. 2022. https://coinswitch.co/switch/crypto/comparing-web-1-web-2-and-web-3/.

"Software Patent Registration.". 2023. Indiafilings. 2023. https://www.indiafilings.com/learn/software-patent-registration/.

Spring, Louisa. 2023. "What Is the Metaverse?" Meta, Coursera. 2023. https://www.coursera.org/learn/what-is-the-metaverse/lecture/B2QEX/xr-in-the-metaverse.

Suthersanan, Uma, Graham Dutfield, and Kit Boey Chow, eds. 2007. *Innovation Without Patents: Harnessing the Creative Spirit in a Diverse World*. UK: Edward Elgar

Talon, Kettj. 2022. "L'Oréal Expands in the Metaverse." Nssgclub. 2022. https://www.nssgclub.com/en/beauty/29059/oreal-professionel-metaverse-trademark.

Tao, Fei, He Zhang, Ang Liu, and A. Y. C. Nee. 2019. "Digital Twin in Industry: State-of-the-Art." *IEEE Transactions on Industrial Informatics* 15 (4): 2405–2415. https://doi.org/10.1109/TII.2018.2873186.

TedKBL. 2021. "What Is Direct vs Indirect Infringement of Patents." Berkley Law and Technology Group LLP. 2021. https://bltg-ip.com/what-is-direct-vs-indirect-infringement-of-patents/.

Terra, John. 2023. "What Is Web 1.0, Web 2.0, and Web 3.0? Definitions, Differences & Similarities." Simpliliearn. 2023. https://www.simplilearn.com/what-is-web-1-0-web-2-0-and-web-3-0-with-their-difference-article#:~:text=Web%201.0%20is%20the%20%22read,towards%20decentralized%2C%20nearly%20anonymous%20platforms.

Teska, Kirk. 2008. "Invention [Software Patents 101]." *Spectrum, IEEE*.

Thaler v. Comptroller General of Patents Trade Marks and Designs. 2021.

Thaler v. Vidal. 2022. 2021–2347.

Title 35- Patents. n.d. US: https://uscode.house.gov/view.xhtml?req=granuleid:USC-prelim-title35-section100&num=0&edition=prelim.

"Virtual Reality.". n.d. Wikipedia. Accessed June 17, 2023. https://en.wikipedia.org/wiki/Virtual_reality#20th_century.

"VR v. AR v. MR: What You Need to Know.". n.d. Intel. Accessed June 18, 2023. https://www.intel.in/content/www/in/en/tech-tips-and-tricks/virtual-reality-vs-augmented-reality.html.

Wendt, Jeffrey. 2020. "Review of 'Digital Twin' Patents in Industry." Linkedin. Accessed April 30, 2020. https://www.linkedin.com/pulse/review-digital-twin-patents-industry-jeffrey-l-wendt/.

Wessing, Taylor. 2022. "Patenting the Metaverse - Possibilities for Companies in Another World." Lexology. 2022. https://www.lexology.com/library/detail.aspx?g=eab55573-aa82-4148-87e6-c43b39712da3.

"What Is AI?". 2023. McKinsey & Company. 2023. https://www.mckinsey.com/featured-insights/mckinsey-explainers/what-is-ai.

"What Is an Avatar, and How to Create a Metaverse Avatar?". n.d. PlugXR. Accessed June 21, 2023. https://www.plugxr.com/augmented-reality/how-to-create-metaverse-avatar/.

"What Is Metaverse? : A Community Focused Economy.". 2023. Meta, Coursera. 2023. https://www.coursera.org/learn/what-is-the-metaverse/supplement/MpCQu/a-community-focused-metavers e-economy.

"What Is Metaverse?: What Decentralization Means in the Metaverse.". 2023. Meta, Coursera. 2023. https://www.coursera.org/learn/what-is-the-metaverse/supplement/quklD/what-decentralization-means-in-the-metaverse.

"What Is the Metaverse?". 2022. Mckinsey & Company. 2022. https://www.mckinsey.com/featured-insights/mckinsey-explainers/what-is-the-metaverse.

White, Christopher, and Hamid Piroozi. 2019. "Drafting Patent Applications Covering Artificial Intelligence Systems." American Bar Association. 2019. https://www.americanbar.org/groups/intellectual_property_law/publications/landslide/2018-19/january-february/drafting-patent-app lications-covering-artificial-intelligence-systems/.

World Economic Forum. 2023. "Interoperability in the Metaverse." https://www3.weforum.org/docs/WEF_Interoperability_in_the_Metaverse.pdf.

World Economic Forum in association with Accenture. 2023. Interoperability in the Metaverse.".

World Intellectual Property Organization. 2023. "IP Is Key for Incentivizing Metaverse Investments and Innovations, WIPO DG Says." Accessed March 31, 2023. https://www.wipo.int/about-ip/en/frontier_technologies/news/2023/news_0001.html?trk=public_post_comment-text.

Xie, Wen. 2022. "How to Patent Artificial Intelligence and Machine Learning Models." Forbes Business Council. Accessed August 29, 2022.

Contours of data protection in India: the consent dilemma

Aafreen Mitchelle Collaco

ABSTRACT
Amid the rapid advancement of digital technology in India, there is a growing concern regarding data protection and digital privacy. The recent DPDP Act 2023 also reflects the significant emphasis on a robust privacy practice. This paper examines the effectiveness of consent, a crucial principle and a subject of many debates in data privacy regimes. Despite being a cornerstone of privacy regimes globally, the consent-based approach has significant limitations. For instance, its binary character allows for a yes or no response and its inability to guarantee data subjects to make an informed choice. The study is set against the prominent data breaches and the Indian Government's effort to strengthen data protection measures. The study also examines the theoretical and legal aspects of consent by analysing the fundamental ideas that form the basis of the DPDP Act, 2023, protecting the consent framework. It questions whether the current form of the Act aligns with the landmark Privacy Judgement. It concludes by exploring alternative and more adaptable mechanisms for implementing informational privacy that might effectively address the specific issues in the Indian context while taking inspiration from other jurisdictions like the EU.

1. Introduction

India's approach towards its privacy regime has undergone a transition over the years since the Privacy Judgement. Despite the change, some of the core principles remain intact. For instance, to govern informational privacy, the essential principle is consent. Consent is often included in data protection regimes as a mechanism for regulating sensitive and personal data use. Frequently, when we discuss various realms, the one question that comes up is what constitutes free and informed consent.

The paper aims not to determine the correct approach towards consent; instead, it is to lay down alternatives towards the approach of consent in the current data protection regime. The uncertainty and ambiguity towards the notion of consent can be witnessed in the Supreme Court's ruling on the Right to Privacy (Justice K.S. Puttaswamy (Retd.) & Anr. v. Union of India 2017). Even though the Supreme Court determined the Right to Privacy as a fundamental right under the *Aadhaar* Judgement and struck down some elements of the *Aadhaar* scheme, it did find an undeniable argument for putting reasonable limits on privacy on the grounds of public interest.

Similarly, the Report of the Committee of Experts (Justice K.S. Puttaswamy (Retd.) & Anr. v. Union of India. 2017) recommends that the consent framework be made in the form and substance. Certain obligations must be imposed on data fiduciaries to protect data principals' rights to ensure fair and reasonable data processing. Hence, the new Digital Personal Data Protection (DPDP) Act 2023 (GoI, Digital Personal Data Protection Act 2023) goes above and beyond the global standard of 'fair and reasonable' compared to the previous iterations.

The primary means of achieving data protection and informational privacy is through a legal and policy regulatory framework. The introduction of a legislative framework, like the EU GDPR, has prompted governments worldwide to adapt their administrative practices to protect data collection, processing, and dissemination. All privacy regulations worldwide are built upon the principle of notice and consent, but how they implement it varies. The actual efficiency of the consent principle is still up for debate. Consent is now regarded as one of the most efficient strategies for safeguarding data privacy and plays a crucial role in data collection. Although it may be a good tool for securing data privacy, the notice and consent approach must make a better trade-off between privacy and competing concerns. The right of data subjects to make an informed and free decision is not upheld. The consent-based approach justifies data usage and processing in any format. The binary nature of the opting-out mechanism is one of its main criticisms. The user may only opt out in this case after opting in. As a result, more is needed to mitigate the problem of informed consent non-compliance.

In the current digital era, issues related to data privacy are on the rise in India. Additionally, with initiatives like 'Digital India', the Government of India seems to be working closely on introducing digitisation in the mainstream. There are diverse statutes and rules such as (IT Act and regulations, IP, contracts, and crimes offer to impose civil and criminal liability) in India, which address privacy concerns; however, a robust regulatory framework around data protection and data privacy is just initiated. Now that the DPDP Act 2023 is implemented in its current form, it might help balance an individual's rights vis-à-vis the State.

The paper is structured as follows: first, it offers to lay down a backdrop on the rising concerns of Data Protection in India by analysing the Privacy Judgement and what followed later in the realm of privacy and consent jurisprudence. The ideas behind the intersection of data protection and privacy often overlap. While they might be related to data protection, data protection is primarily concerned with regulating data processing, while data privacy concerns broader rights-based issues. Even in terms of the approaches, in the EU, the data protection regime is conflicted between the balance of a welfarist approach vis-à-vis an individualist approach or consumer approach (Brownsword 2006). The paper aims to promote substantive standards for protecting digital privacy and advancing collective welfare.

Secondly, the discussion moves on to the evolution of the DPDP Act 2023 by examining its historical developments. This section offers an examination of the challenges and approaches toward the building up of the new data protection regime. The paper then moves on to a detailed analysis of the consent framework under the DPDP Act 2023. The DPDP Act 2023 contemplates substantive limits imposed on data processing even when consent is obtained. Though necessary, these limits are introduced through a concept of 'legitimate use' of data. Such an approach may be authoritarian as it may, in some circumstances, override consent. However, it offers the potential to advance border goals, such as creating a robust digital environment. The paper finally suggests that the direction proposed under the DPDP Act 2023 may be beneficial, whether the intent is to support a welfarist or consumer approach. This is done by comparing the EU perspectives to the Indian regime and understanding whether the EU model is suited to the Indian context or not.

2. Rising concerns of data protection in India and the notion of consent

a. Privacy and consent – from the lens of the Indian judiciary

The fundamental concept of privacy is recognising individuals' rights to choose what they want to share and what they don't. One of the first cases in India where the idea of consent was discussed was in *R. Rajagopal v. State of Tamil Nadu* (R. Rajagopal v. State of Tamil Nadu 1994). Here, the courts held that any publication which seeks certain kinds of personal information was contingent on prior consent (R. Rajagopal v. State of Tamil Nadu 1994). Nevertheless, the Court also pointed out specific exceptions to the rule in the case of public documents and records. Similarly, in *Suchita Srivastava v. Chandigarh Administration* (Suchita Srivastava v. Chandigarh Administration 2009), the court considered consent an integral part of privacy while recognising a woman's reproductive choice. The courts delved into the significance of self-determination and what it means when the notion of privacy was discussed under Article 21 (Right to Life and Liberty) of the Constitution. The concept of the right to liberty may be understood in various ways, allowing for essential interventions to safeguard rights and obligations towards others.

When the Supreme Court ruled out the essence of privacy in *Puttaswamy*, the narrative shifted. Justice Puttaswamy, a former High Court judge in Karnataka, filed a writ suit in 2012 challenging the legality of the Aadhaar programme because it lacked legislative support. *The Aadhaar (Targeted Delivery of Financial and Other Subsidies, Benefits, and Services)* Act, 2016 (*'Aadhaar Act'*) was passed by the government in 2016. The Aadhaar programme was launched by the Indian government, under which each citizen of India received a unique 12-digit identity number based on their biometric and demographic information. The Unique Identification Authority of India (*'UIDAI'*) claims to have provided more than 120 crore Indian citizens with Aadhaar numbers as of this writing (UIDAI n.d.). UIDAI oversees Aadhaar's enrolment and authentication, including 'the security of identity information and authentication records of individuals' (UIDAI n.d.). Numerous challenges have been filed since 2015, contesting different elements of the Aadhaar project. Due to the uncertainty surrounding the status of the right to privacy, a constitutional bench was established to address two key issues: first, whether the ratio decidendi in *M.P. Sharma* and *Kharak Singh* concluded that there is no fundamental right to privacy, and second, whether the subsequent cases jurisprudentially uphold the right to privacy? (Justice K.S. Puttaswamy (Retd.) & Anr. v. Union of India. 2017).

On 24th August 2017, the Nine-Judge constitution bench unanimously held the right to privacy as a Fundamental Right under Article 21 of the Indian Constitution (*Puttaswamy*

I) (Justice K.S. Puttaswamy (Retd.) & Anr. v. Union of India. 2017). The 547-page landmark decision overruled the verdicts in the *M.P. Sharma* (M.P. Sharma and Ors. V. Satish Chandra, District Magistrate, Delhi and Ors. 1950) and *Kharak Singh* (Kharak Singh v. State of U.P. 1963), which clearly stated the right to privacy, not as a right protected under the Indian Constitution.

Justice DY Chandrachud heavily relied on the jurisprudence of privacy and recognised choice and autonomy as an inherent aspect of the right to privacy (Justice K.S. Puttaswamy (Retd.) & Anr. v. Union of India. 2017, 248, 297). Justice Chandrachud emphasises that 'Apart from safeguarding privacy, data protection regimes seek to protect the autonomy of the individual. This is evident from the emphasis in the European data protection regime on the centrality of consent'. (Justice K.S. Puttaswamy (Retd.) & Anr. v. Union of India. 2017).

Previously, in *M.P. Sharma* and *Kharak Singh*, an eight-bench and six-bench court held that the Indian Constitution does not protect the right to privacy. The Supreme Court overturned the *M.P. Sharma* and *Kharak Singh* instances in *Puttaswamy I*, upholding the right to privacy as a fundamental freedom. According to Article 21 of the Indian Constitution, the right to privacy is acknowledged as inseparable from the right to life and the right to personal liberty. It also opened the doors for various privacy aspects, including informational privacy.

> Informational privacy is a facet of the right to privacy. The dangers to privacy in an age of information can originate not only from the State but from non-state actors as well. We commend the Union Government on the need to examine and put into place a robust regime for data protection. The creation of such a regime requires a careful and sensitive balance between individual interests and legitimate concerns of the State. (Justice K.S. Puttaswamy (Retd.) & Anr. v. Union of India. 2017, 268)

The notion of the right to privacy has been extensively discussed in the *Puttsawamy I* judgement and linked to liberty and human dignity in several ways. Emphasis can be placed on privacy rising from a right to liberty or privacy as a feature of human dignity. Different interpretations of the right to liberty may allow intervention required to safeguard long-term liberties and reciprocal obligations to others. Human dignity itself may be used as a justification for freedom or restriction.

Returning to the question of the constitutional validity of Aadhaar, however, it touched upon aspects of consent. Consent finds its way in parts of *Puttaswamy I* when the Court deals with 'informational self-determination'. The judgement also emphasises the Group of Experts on Privacy Report (GoI, Sri Krishna Report 2017), which laid out all the necessary privacy principles. Likewise, the principle of consent is mentioned in various places, such as in data collection, purpose limitations, and the ability to access and correct data (Justice K.S. Puttaswamy (Retd.) & Anr. v. Union of India. 2017, 177).

In *K.S. Puttaswamy v. Union of India (Puttaswamy II)* (Justice K.S. Puttaswamy v. Union of India 2019), which mainly dealt with questioning the constitutional validity of the Aadhaar, however, did touch upon aspects of consent. While tackling the issue of Aadhaar's constitutionality, Justice Sikri emphasised consent and the importance of individual dignity. In the majority opinion, Justice Sikri discussed two facets of the dignity of an individual and how the same should be protected. He states that: -

> It is the balancing of two facets of dignity of the same individual. Whereas, on the one hand, right of personal autonomy is a part of dignity (and right to privacy), another part of dignity of the same individual is to lead a dignified life as well (which is again a facet of Article 21 of the Constitution). Therefore, in a scenario where the State is coming out with welfare schemes, which strive at giving dignified life in harmony with human dignity and in the process some aspect of autonomy is sacrificed, the balancing of the two becomes an important task which is to be achieved by the Courts. (Justice K.S. Puttaswamy v. Union of India 2019, 537–538)

It is crucial to delve into the details of the above paragraph because Justice Skiri departed from the earlier judgement (*Puttaswmay I*), making the idea of consent autonomous. Justice Sikri devised a community approach, where the right of personal autonomy becomes part of dignity, which is further considered 'public good'. In his dissent, Justice Chandrachud points out that even in the pretext of a welfare state, the right to live a dignified life while accessing a welfare scheme (in the current case, *'Aadhaar'*) seems to be more of a sacrifice than an alternative for an individual to choose (Justice K.S. Puttaswamy (Retd.) & Anr. v. Union of India. 2017, 254). Justice Chandrachud again goes back to the individual-based approach. Taking Aadhaar as an example, even though it has been made voluntary, there is no option to opt out of it (Justice K.S. Puttaswamy (Retd.) & Anr. v. Union of India. 2017, 66). Thereby making consent a one-time choice. In the dissent, Justice Chandrachud again observed that the possibility of opting out must always be vested in the individual (Justice K.S. Puttaswamy (Retd.) & Anr. v. Union of India. 2017, 152). He emphasises that consent, transparency and control over information are essential elements in privacy, making the 'individual' a central component of the privacy jurisprudence.

Therefore, the Court found that certain aspects of the *Aadhaar* plan did not comply with the ruling's stipulation that the right to privacy may only be violated by just, fair, and reasonable laws. According to the judgement, the *Aadhaar* programme generally served a significant social or public purpose, and the Act's validity could be mainly sustained. Also, Based on the proportionality principle, using biometric data to obtain government services was constitutional. The Court also determined that some aspects of the *Aadhaar* programme had to be either repealed or modified since they conflicted with the constitutionally guaranteed right to privacy. We can conclude that the legislature did not seem to adopt the Court's welfarist approach. However, a more general approach is noticed further with the introduction of the upcoming bills on data protection, where one can see the role of the data controller being more proactive in safeguarding the consent to ensure individual interest.

b. The report of the Committee of Experts and consent

After the decision in *Puttaswmay*, the Government of India constituted a Committee of Experts to draft a legal framework around data protection and privacy; Justice Shri B N Srikrishna, committer, released a White Paper on Data Protection Framework for India on 27th November 2017 (GoI, Sri Krishna Report 2017). The objective of the Committee was to safeguard the right to privacy of individuals and balance the interest and collective interest of the State. The Committee observed and recommended that the State formulate a robust data protection framework that protects the citizens from the dangers of informational privacy from State and non-state actors and serves as a common good (GoI, Sri Krishna Report 2017, 5). As an observation, the primary goal of the approach was to ensure that personal data is safeguarded not only from breaches but also to empower citizens to protect their privacy rights in the digital space.

The Committee acknowledged the importance of consent by allowing the data subjects to exercise autonomy (GoI, Sri Krishna Report 2017, 24). It laid a foundation by stating,

> The notice and choice framework to secure an individual's consent is the bulwark on which data processing practices in the digital economy are founded. It is based on the philosophically significant Act of an individual providing consent for certain actions pertaining to her data. (GoI, A Free and Fair Digital Economy, Protecting Privacy, Empowering Indians 2018a)

The Committee also stated that sometimes users cannot provide meaningful Consent (GoI, A Free and Fair Digital Economy, Protecting Privacy, Empowering Indians 2018a). This is the case, especially in an online environment where users may not have complete information about how their data is stored or processed.

Similarly, it is argued that consent must be regulated in case consent is not given in an informed manner. Moreover, the Committee disregarded the normative significance of consent, which would be unsuitable due to existing practical functions. Although these consent issues seem genuine, the uncertainty of being completely abolished remains uncertain. Similarly, the uncertainty of attaining explicit consent in every circumstance may invite the problem of consent fatigue.

Furthermore, it stated,

> A preponderance of evidence points to the fact that the operation of notice and consent on the internet today is broken. Consent forms are complex and often boilerplate … Any enumeration of a consent framework must be based on this salient realisation the internet today, consent does not work. (GoI, A Free and Fair Digital Economy, Protecting Privacy, Empowering Indians 2018a)

Nevertheless, the Committee believed a better consent framework would help build a better privacy policy. The Committee does draw certain advantages of providing consent – first, it respects the user's autonomy. Second, it also provides clarity to the data collector to whom the consent is given to disclaim liability (GoI, A Free and Fair Digital Economy, Protecting Privacy, Empowering Indians 2018a, 34). The requirements of consent are further classified as free, fair, informed, specific, explicit and capable of being withdrawn (GoI, A Free and Fair Digital Economy, Protecting Privacy, Empowering Indians 2018a, 37).

The Committee argued vehemently in favour of a different legal structure to guarantee fairness in data processing, which would check the inescapable disparities in bargaining power between data fiduciaries and data principals. Moreover, the Committee stated that fair and reasonable conditions concerning consent should be made explicitly. Hence, preliminary deliberations on the implementation of consent and deemed consent under the data protection regime were placed prior to the DPDP Act 2023. Further, The Committee indicated that consent could be implied in some circumstances depending on particular situations. The Committee also emphasised that the 'fair and reasonable' criterion should go beyond mere procedural duty and include substantial significance. These requirements should be based on the principle of avoiding the use of data for purposes that may not align with the data principal's best interest or go beyond their reasonable expectation (GoI, A Free and Fair Digital Economy, Protecting Privacy, Empowering Indians 2018a, 37). As suggested by the Committee, these requirements serve as an additional measure to protect information privacy and go beyond the criteria of obtaining consent, which we realise is missing in the current regime.

c. The making of the DPDP Act 2023

On 27th July 2018, the Draft Personal Data Protection Bill 2018 (GoI, The Personal Data Protection Bill 2018b) was put out by the J. Sri Krishna Committee. On 11th December 2019, a new version of the Personal Data Protection (PDP) Bill 2019 was introduced (GoI, The Personal Dara Protection Bill 2019). Later, the Joint Committee of Parliament (JPC) received a review copy of this draft from both chambers of Parliament. The Data Protection (DP) Bill 2021 (GoI, The Joint Parliamentary Committee on Personal Data Protection Bill 2021) was finally shared by the JPC after two long years, only for it to be withdrawn on 3rd August 2022, following years of discussion. Later, in November 2022, the new Bill, Digital Personal Data Protection (DPDP) Bill 2022 (GoI, Digital Personal Data Protection Bill 2022), was released for public comments. Finally, the DPDP Act 2023 (GoI, Digital Personal Data Protection Act 2023) became the law on data protection in India.

While drafting the PDP Bill 2019 and presenting it to the Indian Parliament, the EU's General Data Protection Regulation (EU GDPR) (Council Regulation (EU) 2016/679 General Data Protection Regulation 2016) was initially kept in mind. The Bill was created to safeguard both the cross-border flow of data and citizens' data. The Bill outlined several duties and rights for enterprises and people. It established the Data Protection Authority (DPA) (GoI, The Joint Parliamentary Committee on Personal Data Protection Bill 2021, Clause 41), whose responsibility was to preserve people's privacy interests. The Asia-Pacific Economic Cooperation (APEC) Privacy Framework (APEC Privacy Framework 2005) also served as a basis for the Bill. The Bill's goal was to provide a legal framework that would support the expansion of the digital economy while safeguarding the privacy of its users.

The DPDP Act 2023 fundamentally moves away from the suggested regulatory and institutional construction framework. The PDP Bill 2019 did indicate the establishment of an autonomous regulatory body. Data Protection Authority (DPA) was introduced with the EU perspective kept in mind. However, the Indian DPA was designed to have a broader regulatory authority than DPAs under the EU GDPR. The DPA would be responsible for formulating specific codes or rules around the collection and storage of data.

Moreover, the DPDP Act 2023 emphasises establishing a Data Protection Board of India (DPBI) (GoI, Digital Personal Data Protection Act 2023, Section 18), which will facilitate overseeing the prevention of data breaches and direct any urgent remedial or mitigation measures. The DPBI is reasonably different from the DPA as the DPBI lacks the authority to establish regulations and the capacity to carry out investigations.

The PDP Bill's 2019 approach aligns with the Committee's suggestion. As suggested by the Committee, the responsibility to provide evidence lies with the person who controls the data (i.e. Data Fiduciary). However, any legal consequence which leads to the lawful withdrawal of consent must be endured by the Data Principal. It is essential to discuss the historical insight as it helps us navigate which elements of the original draft have been retained. Three observations can be noted from the previous iterations of the legislation. The 2018 and some aspects of the 2019 draft focused a lot on the notion of data protection, for instance, mandating the protection of even non-personal data, which only caused more confusion than clarity on the objective of the law. Instead, the DPDP Act 2023 is a welcome move focusing on data privacy, especially in the digital realm. Secondly, the shift can also be felt in reducing overall compliances, making the new Act more accessible and industry-friendly. Lastly, the DPDP Act 2023 has been pivotal in eliminating the role of the regulatory body and has limited the role of DPBI to data breach remediation and business compliance.

The above discussion indicates that the Indian Government and the Parliament have shifted their approach towards data protection law and its importance in the Indian economy. Many factors include the Supreme Court's declaration of privacy as a fundamental right or the numerous debates on EU GDPR. Similarly, the fundamental growth of the Digital Indian economy has played a vital role in eliminating major compliance roadblocks, which the previous iteration of the Act stated.

2. The evolution of consent jurisprudence pre DPDP Act 2023

Before one examines the current standing of consent under the DPDP Act, 2023, it is imperative to appreciate the journey since the introduction of the PDP Bill, 2019 and the DPB 2021. One needs to understand the distinct nature of the concept of data fidelity under the Indian data protection regime. The rationale behind introducing the idea of the Data Fiduciary instead of a Data Controller is deliberate. The Committee was inspired by the work of Jack Balkin, who had developed a theory of informational fiduciaries in his paper (Balkin 2015). He observed that designating a specific group of organisations to gather and use personal data as fiduciaries in the context of the data they possess about a person is one method to improve data protection. While it may not be possible for the government or any entity to control every aspect of how private businesses utilise, he points out that there are some privacy concerns that governments can safeguard about the interchange and use of specific categories of information.

Further, Balkin suggests that organisations hold themselves out to the public in their private information, which should be held to such assertions (Balkin 2015). Therefore, keeping Balkin's theory in mind, the Committee recommended that Data Fiduciaries uphold the trust of the Data Principal. Hence, the notion of Consent by Data Fiduciaries becomes even more imperative.

Consent is one of the most crucial components of the data protection regime (GoI, The Personal Dara Protection Bill 2019, Clause 11). Heavily drawn by the EU General Data Protection Regulation, the PDP Bill 2019 stated that personal data could be processed based on free and informed consent, additionally, specific consent that even allows withdrawal regime (GoI, The Personal Dara Protection Bill 2019, Clause 11). If the data were processed without consent, such cases would attract a penalties regime (GoI, The Personal Dara Protection Bill 2019, Clause 11, 57). The Bill created a separate category for sensitive personal data and sought explicit consent for processing sensitive personal data (GoI, The Personal Dara Protection Bill 2019, Clause 7).

Further, notice concerning the rights and obligations of the users and the data fiduciary also needed to be shared (GoI, The Personal Dara Protection Bill 2019, Clause 7). In the case of trans-border sharing of sensitive personal data, the same could be made only after the user consented. The Bill also protected the user from transferring critical personal data outside the country, except on specific grounds (GoI, The Personal Dara Protection Bill 2019, Clause 41).

The concept of Notice and Consent was further read with the principle of purpose limitation, which stated that the Data Fiduciary would be required to store the data only for the *necessary period and purpose of data collection* (GoI, The Personal Dara Protection Bill 2019, Clause 5,6,8,9 and 10). Consequently, as the user had the right to withdraw, they also had the right to be forgotten, where the user could request the Data Fiduciary to restrict or prevent the disclosures of personal data (GoI, The Personal Dara Protection Bill 2019, Clause 20). The PDP Bill 2019 followed the harm-based model to seek protection for the users but failed to define the word 'harm'. It stated explicit consent from the users who need to be *informed and free*. Thus, the focus is more on disclosures than the right to privacy.

Later, in 2021, the Bill's scope was expanded to cover non-personal data. The earlier iterations of the draft bill did not include this. The Committee's report stated that they had decided against including non-personal data to be controlled by the same rules as personal data. This action was exceptional and unprecedented compared to global regulatory frameworks like the EU GDPR. Only personal data is covered by the GDPR, but non-personal data is subject to different legislation that oversees its free transfer throughout the EU.

Under the DP Bill 2021, it was imperative to obtain consent from the Data Principals freely while collecting and processing the data (GoI, The Joint Parliamentary Committee on Personal Data Protection Bill 2021, Clause 11). It was also important to explicitly state why the data was collected and processed (GoI, The Joint Parliamentary Committee on Personal Data Protection Bill 2021, Clause 11). Hence, the purpose for which the data was being processed and collected had to be defined clearly (GoI, The Joint Parliamentary Committee on Personal Data Protection Bill 2021, Clause 11). The Bill featured a few standard sections, but in its current form, it permitted data processing without consent while ignoring the justifications for the extensive exclusions. Concerns about abusing the 'public order' (GoI, The Joint Parliamentary Committee on Personal Data Protection Bill 2021, Clause 12) exemption provision were raised. Any exceptions granted by a government body needed to pass the test of proportionality and necessity criteria (European Data Protection Supervisor n.d.). Such broad exemptions would result in bulk surveillance without a regulated legal process.

The PDP Bill 2019 also introduced a new idea known as 'Consent Managers'. This is absent from the EU GDPR. The framework for consent management was influenced by recent efforts in India to create a digital public infrastructure that would simplify sharing data through responsible intermediaries (GoI, The Personal Dara Protection Bill 2019, Clause 23). Like a Data Fiduciary, a consent manager provides an accessible, transparent, and interoperable platform for a data principle to provide, withdraw, evaluate, and manage their Consent (GoI, The Personal Dara Protection Bill 2019, Clause 23(3)). The Committee, in their report, had suggested a similar architecture in the form of consent dashboards to relieve the perils of consent fatigue (GoI, Sri Krishna Report 2017, 80).

Under the PDP Bill 2019, Data Principals could use consent managers to exercise their rights to confirmation, access, correction and portability of data (GoI, The Personal Dara Protection Bill 2019, Clause 23(4)). Moreover, the consent managers were to register under the Data Protection Authority (DPA) to govern their technical and operational regulations (GoI, The Personal Dara Protection Bill 2019, Clause 23(5)). Under the PDP Bill 2019, a consent manager was likely to work as a data fiduciary and a third-party agency on behalf of the data principals.

3. The consent framework under the Digital Personal Data Protection Act, 2023

The Digital Personal Data Protection Act, 2023 (GoI, Digital Personal Data Protection Act 2023) is the fifth iteration of India's Data Protection regime. The DPDP Act 2023 eliminates all references to non-personal data and solely pertains to digitised personal data. It does away with the classifications of datasets like sensitive personal data and critical personal data. It also forgoes other compliances, such as data localisation requirements for non-personal data (GoI, Digital Personal Data Protection Act 2023, Section 3) and data portability. The DPDP Act, 2023 applies to digital personal data collected online from Data Principal and offline, which is subsequently digitised.

According to the DPDP Act 2023, Data Fiduciaries must seek the Data Principal's consent before processing personal data (GoI, Digital Personal Data Protection Act 2023, Section 4). They must give detailed notice of the data sets they intend to collect and their intended uses (GoI, Digital Personal Data Protection Act 2023, Section 6). The message should be written in clear and plain language (GoI, Digital Personal Data Protection Act 2023, Section 6(1)). The Data Fiduciary must offer the data principal the choice of accessing the request for consent in either English or any other language listed in the Eighth Schedule to the Indian Constitution (GoI, Digital Personal Data Protection Act 2023, Section 5(3)). This move was made keeping in mind the intention of the Bill to make it inclusive, accessible and straightforward, especially for the rural population (Sur and Choudhury 2022). However, such a move could be challenging for online platforms solely supporting the English language. Hence, it is worthwhile that platforms should ideally offer consent in the languages that they support.

The DPDP Act 2023 indicates consent to be free, specific, informed and unambiguous (GoI, Digital Personal Data Protection Act 2023, Section 6(1)). Consent may also be withdrawn at any point in time (GoI, Digital Personal Data Protection Act 2023, Section 6(4)). Additionally, once the consent is withdrawn, the Data Fiduciaries must cause the Data Fiduciary to stop processing the Data Principal's personal data. Unless otherwise permitted under the DPDP Act, 2023, or it is necessary to process the Data Principal's data without their consent (GoI, Digital Personal Data Protection Act 2023, Section 8 (7)). Hence, the consent provided by the data principal must have explicit affirmative action and signify the purpose. Additionally, once the data principal withdraws their consent, such withdrawal should not affect the legality of data collected and processed based on the consent before its withdrawal.

The Act also recognises the role of 'consent managers'. This has been retained from the PDP Bill 2019. Moreover, the DPDP Act 2023 has defined consent managers as Data Fiduciaries, which empower Data Principals to 'give, manage, review and withdraw her consent through an accessible, transparent and interoperable platform' (GoI, Digital Personal Data Protection Act 2023, Section 6(7)). Here, the Data Principals have the option to share consent as well as withdraw it through the consent manager. To fulfil the withdrawal process, the consent manager must offer the Data Principal a precise method or process to 'give, manage, review or withdraw' their consent. When a Data Principal's Consent is revoked, Data Fiduciaries need to ensure, within a reasonable time, that the Data Principal's data is no longer processed.

a. 'Deemed Consent' vs. 'Certain Legitimate Uses' – is it different?

The DPDP Bill 2022 introduced the concept of 'Deemed Consent' (GoI, Digital Personal Data Protection Bill 2022, Clause 8). Here, the Data Principal was deemed to have given consent, i.e., where consent was not expressly needed. This might have been inspired by the Singaporean PDPA 2012, but now has been replaced with the terminology 'Certain Legitimate Uses' (SG 2012, Section 15).

Deemed consent included situations where the data principals voluntarily provide their data or are reasonably expected to and for the performance of any function under any law (GoI, Digital Personal Data Protection Bill 2022, Clause 8(1),8(2)). For instance, the purpose could be to avail of services such as obtaining licenses, permits or certificates. This clause is no different from the current section on 'Certain Legitimate Uses' (GoI, Digital Personal Data Protection Act 2023, Section 7). That is hardly a change in its approach but a mere change in nomenclature. Even though the Act proclaims 'legitimate uses' to be in favour of public interest (GoI, Digital Personal Data Protection Act 2023, Section 7 (g)) and in consonance with the concept of alternate grounds of processing under the EU GDPR, the way DPDP Act 2023 has worded this clause opens doors to broad and vague interpretation. In the earlier iterations of the Act, stakeholders had requested more clarity of terms like 'fraud' and 'networking and informational security', which was added to the list of grounds under which entails 'public interest' (GoI, Digital Personal Data Protection Bill 2022, Clause 8). Correspondingly, grounds such as 'recovery of debt' (GoI, Digital Personal Data Protection Bill 2022, Clause 8(g)) and 'credit scores' (GoI, Digital Personal Data Protection Bill 2022, Clause 8 (d)) were put under the broad ambit of 'public interest'. Although the current provisions of the Act may still be used as a lawful basis for processing, the need for a 'reasonable expectation' of processing is no longer necessary.

Moreover, the examples under Section 7 of the DPDP Act 2023 suggest that the Data Principal may withdraw consent; however, it is not apparent how the process would be carried out when information is shared on a one-off basis. Similarly, the provisions that enable data processing by the State have been made subject to the relevant legislation or policy enacted by the cantal government. Considering the concerns voiced throughout the JPC and consultation process on certain exceptions, this may be a favourable move and contribute to cross-border data transfers in the long run (GoI, Digital Personal Data Protection Act 2023, Section 7(b)). Interestingly, there is also a requirement for processing data previously consented to for availing any subsidy or benefit available in government records (GoI, Digital Personal Data Protection Act 2023, Section 2(f)). This again highlights a bit of a contradiction in re-using or re-purposing existing stored data in government records. Especially considering the ongoing Aadhaar data leak fiascos, the state needs to ensure the correct mechanism for storing and processing such sensitive data. One can also notice a dilution of user protection compared to the earlier iterations of the Bill with the introduction of 'certain legitimate uses'.

b. Children's and persons with disability's consent under the DPDP Act 2023.

The Act defines the term 'child' as someone below eighteen years of age (GoI, Digital Personal Data Protection Act 2023, Section 2(f)). Data Fiduciaries must obtain verifiable parental/guardian consent before processing children's and persons with disabilities' data (GoI, Digital Personal Data Protection Act 2023, Section 9(1)). The Data Fiduciaries are prohibited from tracking or sharing targeting advertisements to children. In the previous iterations, the proceeding of children's data was deemed a Significant Data Fiduciary (SDF) (GoI, Digital Personal Data Protection Bill 2022, Clause 11). However, the same is no longer the case. The DPDP Act 2023 notably grants the Central Government the authority to exclude specific categories of data fiduciaries and processing activities from the need to acquire parental agreement and the prohibition on behavioural monitoring. Furthermore, it also allows the Central Government to relieve data fiduciaries from some requirements while processing children's data in specified circumstances.

The consent framework in the Act has some changes compared to previous bill iterations. For instance, an itemised notice format is no longer needed. Additionally, a notice must be provided to the data principal before the consent request stating the purpose of processing, explicitly mentioning the rights to withdraw consent, and a proper grievance redressal.

4. EU's perspective on consent and its influence on DPDP Act 2023.

The EU law on data protection ensures that consent is at the heart of safeguarding data protection. However, the issue of informational self-determination is still undetermined. The role of consent under EU laws is much more complex as the data protection law separates data protection from data privacy (Omotubora and Basu 2020). Hence opening a pandora of questions which is beyond the scope of this paper. In this section, I attempt to unpack the relevance of the EU's approach and India's attempt to mirror the role of consent.

The EU GDPR replaced the European Data Protection Directive in 2016 (Directive 95/46/EC 1995). On top of updating European data protection legislation, it was designed to increase uniformity throughout Europe by becoming a regulation (rather than a directive) and entering into force on 25th May 2018. The growing number of data protection legislation reflects the importance of data protection and countries' desire to meet EU standards (Omotubora and Basu 2020). The EU GDPR has influenced EU markets and has been a foundation for new regimes.

The EU GDPR defines personal data broadly enough to cover information about an identified or identifiable person (Council Regulation (EU) 2016/679 General Data Protection Regulation 2016, Article 4). A set of data protection principles, including 'lawfulness, fairness, and transparency', 'purpose limitation', 'data minimisation', 'storage limitation', 'integrity and confidentiality', and 'accountability', must be followed by those who must process personal data in accordance with data protection laws. Article 6 of the EU GDPR helps to evaluate whether processing is permitted. Through Article 9 of the EU GDPR, specific categories of data are eligible for enhanced safeguards under data protection legislation. Unique category data cannot be processed unless one of many exceptions applies. According to Article 9(2)(a), 'the data subject has given explicit consent to the processing' is the first possible exemption.

One of the guiding concepts for preserving individual privacy under EU GDPR is consent. Before collecting, processing, or storing a person's personal data, an organisation should obtain that person's express and explicit consent (Council Regulation (EU) 2016/679 General Data Protection Regulation 2016, Article 6). The consent has to be freely given, specific, informed, and clear (Council Regulation (EU) 2016/679 General Data Protection Regulation 2016, Article 4(11)). Individuals also have the freedom to change their minds at any moment. Organisations that fail to get legitimate consent or improperly manage consent withdrawal may suffer serious repercussions, including fines and legal action. Businesses may develop explicit consent rules and processes, offer readily available data processing information, and routinely review and update their privacy policies to maintain compliance. EU GDPR gives people more authority to regulate their personal data and assert their privacy rights.

EU GDPR has also raised the threshold of valid consent, especially in cases related to a children's consent (Council Regulation (EU) 2016/679 General Data Protection Regulation 2016, Article 8) or the right to erasure (Council Regulation (EU) 2016/679 General Data Protection Regulation 2016, Article 17). However, when the controller is a public entity, or there may be a blatant power imbalance between the parties, the EU GDPR discourages reliance on consent (Council Regulation (EU) 2016/679 General Data Protection Regulation 2016, Recital 43).

EU GDPR models have been adopted all around the world. The EU GDPR emphasises the principle of consent because privacy and security of personal data have always been at the forefront of the European Union (Charter of Fundamental Rights of the European Union (2012/C 326/02) 2012). Recital 6 of the EU GDPR also clarifies that the 'processing personal data should be designed to serve mankind' (Council Regulation (EU) 2016/679 General Data Protection Regulation 2016, Recital 6).

Consent, as required under the EU GDPR, seems more stringent than the existing DPDP Act 2023. Comparing the DPDP Act 2023 to the existing laws in India, the notion of consent meets the criteria set forth in the Indian Contract Act 1872, where it is understood to be an act that must not result from any undue influence, fraud or misrepresentation (GoI, The Indian Contract Act, 1872 n.d., Section 14). If one tends to raise the threshold as discussed under EU GDPR, it might not be seen from the lens of a welfarist approach. Instead, an increase in the threshold might value the individualist approach, as discussed in the aforementioned sections. Still, in the long run, it might seem to hamper the growth of business and opportunities in the digital space.

Moving on to the grounds of processing personal data for lawful purposes, the Act governs the processing to be made for the data for which the Data Principle has given her consent or for certain legitimate use. (GoI, Digital Personal Data Protection Act 2023, Section 4(1)(a) and (b)). Lawful purpose means 'any purpose which is not expressly forbidden by law' (GoI, Digital Personal Data Protection Act 2023, Section 4(b).). The uncanny similarity of this provision mirrors Article 8 of the Charter of Fundamental

Rights of the European Union, which entails that personal data must be processed in a fair manner for specified purposes and on the basis of obtaining the consent of the person concerned or any other 'legitimate basis laid down by law' (Charter of Fundamental Rights of the European Union (2012/C 326/02) 2012, Article 8).

Similarly, the EU GDPR ensures the processing of data in a fair and transparent manner (Council Regulation (EU) 2016/679 General Data Protection Regulation 2016, Article 5 (1)(a)). Prima facie, the DPDP Act 2023 might concern itself with fair data processing, but the notion of 'fair processing' does not occur in the Act explicitly. Hence, in the Indian context, any lawful purpose for processing data might just ensure procedural safeguards to fairness than substantive ones. Thus, the fair processing of data may not always in favour of an individual's interests.

5. Future of consent and the rise of informational privacy in India: a way forward

There have been several concerns regarding the approach of consent and its implementation. For instance, the notion of deemed consent might seem an adequate approach prima facie as it helps to curtail the issue of consent fatigue. Yet, there are many challenges and problems of infringement of privacy rights. While there might be several issues in the concept of consent, it is essential to study and analyse the notion once the DPDP Act 2023 is in full force. This section will address a few alternative and necessary safeguards India can device from other jurisdictions.

Several scholars have also suggested replacing the principle of consent with accountability, which is considered counterproductive (Matthan 2017a; 2017b). In his paper, Solove questions if the data collection process can be meaningfully consented to (Solove 2013, 1880). Similarly, some studies state that individuals often don't understand what they consent to while agreeing to privacy policies online (Bhandari et al. 2017). According to Schwartz, the principle of notice and consent is not based on free choice because of a lack of market options and information (Schwartz 2000, 815). According to Matthan, the accountability principle makes the data controller or fiduciary more responsible for collecting and using the data (Matthan 2017a; 2017b, 4). The burden of risk now shifts to the data controller (Matthan 2017a; 2017b). This is not to be compared with the harm-based approach, where causing harm and financial penalties act as the deterrent for the data controller; instead, this is a rights-based approach, where the individual would have the right to safeguard their interest. This could be achieved through an opting-out model or the right to fair treatment (Matthan 2017a; 2017b). In his article, Bhatia observes that consent should not be a one-time waiver of an individual's right to control personal information. Instead, it must extend to a specific use of the information, even after one has consented to use the data (Bhatia n.d.).

Now, an opt-out model might work, but to ensure that the clause on 'certain legitimate uses' under the DPDP Act 2023 respects information self-determination, there is a need to provide better alternatives, such as a 'soft opt-in and out' practised in jurisdictions in the UK, Canada and Singapore (Gupta and Naithani 2023). India could implement a similar safeguard to the soft opt-in concept, enabling data principals to opt-out if consent is assumed.

In some recent examples, it will be clear how this soft opt-out might be relevant. In 2019, the Union Home Secretary of India issued an order that authorised security and intelligence agencies (Economic Times 2018) to intercept, monitor, and decrypt information generated, transmitted, received, or stored in any computer resource. The same has been done under the exception laid down in Section 69(1) of the Information Technology (IT) Act 2000 r/w rule 4 of the Information Technology (Procedure and Safeguards for Interception, Monitoring and Decryption of Information) Rules, 2009. Likewise, the Union Government of India has passed The DNA Technology (Use and Application) Regulation Bill, 2018 (PRS Legislative Research n.d.). The Bill highlights the use of DNA technology as evidence in criminal and civil matters. Other features of the Bill include establishing the DNA Regulatory Board and the National and Regional DNA Data Banks, which would be further used for scientific research and study. For every DNA sample collection, the consent of the individuals is required; however, certain exceptions have been enlisted in the Bill. For instance, the consent of individuals in case of DNA profiling in civil matters is not required.

Similarly, storing DNA profiles relating to civil matters without the individual's consent may violate the citizen's right to privacy. The Bill is also susceptible to specific human rights violations leading to communal and racial profiling. Therefore, whether this Bill would stand judicial scrutiny is another question. Nevertheless, the fact that one's fundamental right to privacy is being violated in terms of consent cannot be ignored. Citing the aforementioned examples, one can conclude the importance of a soft opt-out. Otherwise, this could give rise to untoward situations where individuals might not have the right and control over their personal and sensitive data.

Another criticism of opting out is its binary nature (F. H. Cate 2012). Here, the user can opt out only after opting in. Hence, it does not help mitigate the issue of non-compliance with informed consent. In their paper, Tene and Poonetsky discuss that consent and data minimisation principles should be loosened to ensure more substantial access (Tene and Polonetsky 2013). To enable better choices for individuals, they suggest that the user should have more knowledge about how their information will be used; only then would they be capable of making informed choices (Tene and Polonetsky 2013). Hence, it is imperative to determine the purpose and scope of collecting data. Even though the DPDP Act 2023 lists instances where such data can be collected, the exemptions are too broad, making the implementation arbitrary.

Additionally, the principle of consent has the inherent contradiction of taking certain rights away on the pretext of protecting privacy (Allen 1999). Allen presents a different view of privacy, and she differentiates decisional privacy from other forms of privacy, such as proprietary, physical or informational (Allen 1999). Decisional privacy is a mechanism to allow decisions on free will, whereas the others are related to personal disclosure (Allen 1999). Notice and consent seem to be an effective tool, but there is a poor trade-off between privacy and competing concerns, and it fails to ensure an informed and free choice. The consent-based approach pretty much reflects the legitimation of the use and processing of data in any form. According to Burman, the Notice and Consent framework may be counterproductive and give rise to moral hazard as users might rely more on regulation than self-awareness (Burman 2020).

One of the most challenging criteria for informed consent is the exact need to be easy and accessible for the user, and many times, this has been difficult to achieve

(Sinha and Mason 2016). In her paper, Gindin believes that due to the lengthy and complicated language of the notice, most people find it challenging to share their consent in an informed manner (Gindin 2009). Similarly, the notice should be adequate if available in the local language, especially in India. For instance, the Netherlands' Supervisory Authority fined TikTok (a popular social media app) 750,000 Euros for not offering privacy statements in Dutch. The regulators clearly stated that TikTok failed to define the scope of collecting, using, and processing personal data clearly in the local language (Euronews 2021). Such an example reinstates that compliance with the notice and consent principle is becoming imperative but challenging to implement in this rapidly growing technological world and the Big Data era. The DPDP Act 2023 does facilitate the introduction of consent in local languages (GoI, Digital Personal Data Protection Act 2023, Section 5(3)). India, too, is moving towards an accessible digital space where language is not a barrier, but the understating of privacy rights might be. In fact, consent in the context of standard form contracts or online transactions is insufficient or even accurately indicative of the preferences of the people who give it. By establishing conditions for consent that are free, informed, precise, unambiguous, and capable of withdrawal, such as those contained in the EU GDPR and the DPDP Act 2023, statutory processes may try to protect people against what is known as 'forced' consent.

The DPDP Act 2023 raises the threshold for valid consent and allows for assumed consent in limited circumstances. However, at the same time, it places certain obligations on the Data Fiduciary to ensure data processing is commenced in a 'fair and reasonable' manner. This is a deliberate move by the legislatures to ensure there is no unequal bargaining power between Data Principals and Data Fiduciaries. This threshold may seem higher than EU GDPR, even though the DPDP Act 2023 and the previous iterations of the Bill appear to be inspired by EU GDPR.

While reflecting on the current Act, it is evident that it covers the procedural aspect of consent and caters to substantive protections due to the requirement of consent being fair and reasonable. The Act calls for the data fiduciary to consider the interests of the data subject and, at the very least, make sure those interests aren't compromised in a way that's out of proportion to the objectives to be accomplished. Subsequently, it is imperative that data fiduciaries consider societal norms and values while collecting and processing data.

7. Conclusion

India has a vast population. Rendering a consent-based approach in every aspect might be implausible. The Digital Personal Data Protection Act 2023 takes action to guarantee that permission to process personal data in India is meaningful and informed. However, it continues by imposing obligations on corporations to refrain from abusing the inescapable disparities in relative bargaining situations. The Act also aims to acknowledge more widely the circumstances required for trust in a contemporary information economy. Although the Sri Krishna Committee Report stressed that a privacy and data protection framework must serve 'the common good', it acknowledged the significance of consent as a safeguard in its comments on the previous iterations of the Bill.

One can observe the notion and what it means for a data fiduciary to act honestly concerning a data subject is given more significant substance by the job of a data fiduciary as it is now defined by the DPDP Act 2023 than has previously been the case with data protection authorities in Europe. It goes beyond the notion that businesses must be honest and avoid dishonest or deceitful tactics. It imposes a duty on the institutions to behave in a 'fair and reasonable' manner.

In the *Puttswamy* judgement, it was evident that the Supreme Court implied data protection and informational privacy as an essential part of the Right to Privacy. Given that EU GDPR separates the right to privacy from the right to data protection, it is reasonable to suppose that this extraction will have regulating effects that might lead to the acceptance of varying expectations. The form and substance of a right to fair processing and the link to the purpose of individual's permission as a safeguard are all affected differently by various interpretations of the right to privacy and its connection to data protection. A weak understanding and implementation of consent, which is not supported by other forms of substantive and procedural protection, does not provide either autonomy or privacy. This is not meant to downplay the importance of consent. Contrarily, if a substantive test of fairness is effectively applied, there is less of a need to operate with a high bar for valid permission, which would deter the use of consent as a legal justification for the processing. Consent has its limitations in protecting people's reasonable expectations of privacy, and substantive safeguards may be seen as enhancing both people's autonomy by giving them the freedom to live their lives fully without having to worry about making countless decisions that will affect how they will live in the future, as well as advancing more collectivist goals.

Disclosure statement

No potential conflict of interest was reported by the author(s).

References

Allen, Anita L. 1999. "Coercing Privacy." *William & Mary Law Review* 40: 723.

APEC. 2005. *APEC Privacy Framework*. https://www.apec.org/publications/2005/12/apec-privacy-framework.

Balkin, Jack M. 2015. "Information Fiduciaries and the First Amendment." *U.C. Davis Law Review* 1183.

Bhandari, Vrinda, Amba Kak, Smriti Parsheera, and Faiza Rahman. 2017. *Social Science Open Access Repository*. Accessed May 30, 2023. https://nbn-resolving.org/urn:nbn:de:0168-ssoar-54766-2.

Bhatia, Gautam. n.d. *The Supreme Court's Right to Privacy Judgment IV: Privacy, Informational Self-Determination, and the Idea of Consent, Idea of Consent, Indian Constitutional Law and Philosophy*. Accessed May 30, 2023. https://indconlawphil.wordpress.com/2017/08/30/the-supreme-courts-right-to-privacy-judgment-iv-privacy-informational-self-determination-and-the-idea-of-consent/.

Brownsword, Roger. 2006. *Contract Law: Themes for the Twenty-First Century*. OUP.

Burman, Anirudh. 2020. *Carnegie India*. March 09. https://carnegieindia.org/2020/03/09/will-india-s-proposed-data-protection-law-protect-privacy-and-promote-growth-pub-81217last.

Cate, Fred H. 2012. *Technology|Academics|Policy Notice and Consent in a World of Big Data*. November 26. Accessed May 30, 2023. https://www.techpolicy.com/NoticeConsent-inWorldBigData.aspx.

Charter of Fundamental Rights of the European Union (2012/C 326/02). 2012. https://eur-lex.europa.eu/legal-content/EN/TXT/HTML/?uri=CELEX%3A12012P%2FTXT.

Council Regulation (EU) 2016/679 General Data Protection Regulation. 2016. April 27. https://gdpr.eu/tag/gdpr/.

Economic Times. 2018. *The Economic Times*. December 21. https://economictimes.indiatimes.com/news/politics-and-nation/10-central-agencies-can-now-snoop-on-any-computer-they-want/articleshow/67188875.cms?from=mdr.

Euronews. 2021. *Dutch Data Protection Authority fines TikTok € 750,000 over privacy flaw*. July 22. https://www.euronews.com/next/2021/07/22/dutch-data-protection-authority-fines-tiktok-750-000-over-privacy-flaw.

Gindin, Susan E. 2009. "Nobody Reads Your Privacy Policy or Online Contract? Lessons Learned and Questions Raised by the FTC's Action Against Sears." *Northwest Journal of Technology and Intellectual Property* 8: 1.

GoI. 2017. "White Paper of the Committee of Experts on a Data Protection Framework for India." Accessed May 30, 2023." http://planningcommission.nic.in/reports/genrep/rep_privacy.pdf.

GoI. 2018a. "A Free and Fair Digital Economy, Protecting Privacy, Empowering Indians." Accessed January 2024. https://www.meity.gov.in/writereaddata/files/Data_Protection_Committee_Report.pdf.

GoI. 2018b. *The Personal Data Protection Bill*. https://www.meity.gov.in/writereaddata/files/Personal_Data_Protection_Bill,2018.pdf.

GoI. 2019. *The Personal Dara Protection Bill*. http://164.100.47.4/BillsTexts/LSBillTexts/Asintroduced/373_2019_LS_Eng.pdf.

GoI. 2021. *The Joint Parliamentary Committee on Personal Data Protection Bil*. https://drive.google.com/file/d/1emcAB8HjE2oCC_Dl6zR5YPnPQ5iwwwCT/view?ref=static.internetfreedom.in.

GoI. 2022. *Digital Personal Data Protection Bill*. https://www.meity.gov.in/writereaddata/files/The%20Digital%20Personal%20Data%20Potection%20Bill%2C%202022_0.pdf.

GoI. 2023. *Digital Personal Data Protection Act*.

GoI. n.d. *The Indian Contract Act, 1872*. https://lddashboard.legislative.gov.in/actsofparliamentfromtheyear/indian-contract-act-1872.

Gupta, Indranath, and Parth Naithani. 2023. "What is Left of Consent When it is Deemed Consent: A Data Protection Experiment in India." *Journal of Data Protection & Privacy* 6 (1): 71–83.

Justice K.S. Puttaswamy (Retd.) & Anr. v. Union of India. 2017. 10 SCC 1 (The Supreme Court of India, September 28).

Justice K.S. Puttaswamy v. Union of India. 2019. 1 SCC 1 (The Supreme Court of India).

Kharak Singh v. State of U.P. 1963. AIR 1963 SC 1295 (The Supreme Court).

Matthan, Rahul. 2017a. *Takshashila Institution, Beyond Consent - A New Paradigm for Data Protection*. July. https://static1.squarespace.com/static/618a55c4cb03246776b68559/t/62a6beb7e9a41c52669d188b/1655094971332/TDD-Beyond-Consent-Data-Protection-RM-2017-03.pdf.

Matthan, Rahul. 2017b. *Takshashila Institution, Beyond Consent - A New Paradigm for Data Protection*. July. Accessed May 30, 2023. https://static1.squarespace.com/static/618a55c4cb03246776b68559/t/62a6beb7e9a41c52669d188b/1655094971332/TDD-Beyond-Consent-Data-Protection-RM-2017-03.pdf.

M.P. Sharma and Ors. V. Satish Chandra, District Magistrate, Delhi and Ors. 1950. SCR 1077 (The Supreme Court of India).

Omotubora, Adekemi, and Subhajit Basu. 2020. "Next Generation Privacy." *Information & Communication Technology Law*, 151–173.

PRS Legislative Research. n.d. *The DNA Technology (Use and Application) Regulation Bill 2019*. https://www.prsindia.org/sites/default/files/bill_files/DNA%20Technology%20Bill%2C%202018%20as%20passed%20by%20LS.pdflast.

R. Rajagopal v. State of Tamil Nadu. 1994. 6 SCC 632 (The Supreme Court of India).

Schwartz, Paul M. 2000. "Internet Privacy and the State." *Connecticut Law Review*.

SG. 2012. *Personal Data Protection Act*. https://sso.agc.gov.sg/Act/PDPA2012.

Sinha, Amber, and Scott Mason. 2016. *A Critique of Consent in Information Privacy*. January 11. https://cis-india.org/internet-governance/blog/a-critique-of-consent-in-information-privacy.

Solove, Daniel. 2013. "Privacy Self Management and the Consent Dilemma." *Harvard Law Review* 126: 1894–1900.

Suchita Srivastava v. Chandigarh Administration. 2009. 9 SCC 1 (The Supreme Court of India).

Sur, Aihik, and Deepsekhar Choudhury. 2022. *Money Control*. August 03. https://www.moneycontrol.com/news/business/complicated-data-protection-bill-would-have-hurt-startups-rajeev-chandrasekhar-8947571.html.

Tene, Omer, and Jules Polonetsky. 2013. "Big Data for All: Privacy and User Control in the Age of Analytics." *Northwest Journal of Technology and Intellectual Property* 11: 239.

UIDAI. n.d. *Unique Identification Authority of India*. Accessed January 20, 2024. https://uidai.gov.in/aadhaar_dashboard/.

Standardised cookie banner: a solution to the cookie consent problem

Paarth Naithani

ABSTRACT
Cookies are an essential part of today's internet. In the EU, the ePrivacy Directive (read with the EU GDPR) requires prior informed consent for using cookies. Usually, websites use cookie banners to meet the informed consent requirement. However, due to a lack of harmonisation of cookie law across the EU, varying cookie guidelines by data protection authorities of different member states, and varying implementation of cookie consent requirements by websites, users face differing cookie banners on different websites. Having to face differing cookie banners requires additional cognitive effort and time to read, understand, evaluate, and select options on each banner. Moreover, the way consent is sought remains deceptive. Websites use dark patterns, vague language, positive framing, and nudging to elicit user consent. This paper proposes standardised cookie banners to solve the various problems with cookie consent banners. The paper suggests that the standardised banner must have standardised timing of display, position on the website, text and language, presentation, consent options, and way of consenting.

Introduction

Internet cookies are small pieces of information stored on user devices, allowing websites to recognise the users' devices (ICO UK 2020). While cookies can be used for necessary purposes (such as remembering what product is placed in an online shopping cart), cookies can also be used for privacy-invasive purposes such as tracking user behaviour across websites (ICO UK 2020). Cookies are categorised as session cookies (automatically deleted on closing the browser) or persistent cookies (remain stored until they reach their expiration date), first-party cookies (cookies set by the data controller operating the visited website) or third-party cookies (cookies stored by data controllers that do not operate the visited website) (Article 29 Working Party 2012).

Cookies are of various kinds, such as user input cookies that keep track of users' input on the website, authentication cookies that identify the user once the user has logged in, multimedia player session cookies that store the technical data to play back video or audio content, user interface customisation cookies such as language preference cookies or result display preference cookies, social plug-in content sharing cookies that allow social media networks to identify their members, third-party advertising cookies, first-party analytics cookies, and user centric security cookies (Article 29 Working Party 2012). Cookies can also be multipurpose cookies that are used for several purposes (Article 29 Working Party 2012).

The use of cookies can be disadvantageous to users for various reasons. Cookies can be used to link online behaviour to personally identifiable information (Kierkegaard 2005). Companies can sell this data, leading to possible re-uses of the data and individuals' loss of control over personal data (Kierkegaard 2005). Third parties can collect clickstream data via third-party cookies and engage in online profiling through data mining (Debusseré 2005). Users could receive advertisements they do not wish to receive and may be nudged into disadvantageous consumer decisions (Wein 2022). There may be negative consequences such as adverse insurance decisions, material losses such as higher prices, and immaterial losses such as anxiety (Wein 2022).

The EU ePrivacy Directive and the EU General Data Protection Regulation (GDPR) regulate cookies. Article 5(3) of the ePrivacy Directive requires prior consent for 'storing of information, or the gaining of access to information already stored, in the terminal equipment'. This provision applies to cookies as cookies involve storing and gaining access to information from user devices (Article 29 Working Party 2010). Prior consent is required for cookies (such as tracking cookies) that are not covered by Article 5(3) exceptions (Article 29 Working Party 2012). The requirement of consent under the ePrivacy Directive corresponds to the requirement of consent under the EU GDPR (EDPB 2020). The requirement of consent under the proposed ePrivacy Regulation, which is proposed to replace the ePrivacy Directive, also corresponds to the requirement of consent under the GDPR (Article 9, proposed ePrivacy Regulation).

The EU member states have established different levels of protection given the minimum harmonisation requirement of the ePrivacy Directive (Cofone 2017). Besides, different member states' Data Protection Authorities (DPAs) have proposed differing cookie guidelines. For instance, there are divergences in the cookie guidelines of the UK ICO, the French CNIL, the German DPA and the Spanish DPA (Voisin et al. 2020). The guidelines vary on whether scrolling a website constitutes consent for cookies, what cookie options must be provided, whether granular consent options should be part of the first or second layer of the cookie banner, and whether cookie walls are allowed (and under what conditions) (Voisin et al. 2020).

Cookie law has been called a regulatory failure because of low levels of compliance (Leenes 2015). It has been found that applicable laws are violated by 89% of consent banners as they do not comply with the legal requirement for cookie banner text (Hofslot et al. 2022; Santos et al. 2021). A large-scale study suggests that the very basic compliance in displaying a cookie banner was missing in a substantial proportion of websites in Greece and the UK (Kampanos and Shahandashti 2021). Many websites did not provide direct opt-out, nudged users, and made it more difficult to reject cookies than to consent to cookies (Kampanos and Shahandashti 2021). Other problems include websites bypassing consent to track users through third-party cookies (Gotze et al. 2022). A study indicates that 9%–90% of government websites of G20 countries are found to track users in a widespread manner without their consent (Gotze et al. 2022).

The problem also lies with consent management platforms used by websites to obtain user consent. A study suggested that consent management platforms implemented cookie banners that did not comply with EU data protection law (Matte, Bielova, and Santos 2020). Another study suggested that default templates for cookie consent notices offered by consent management platforms contain dark patterns (Stöver et al. 2022).

To address the problems with cookie banners, this paper proposes standardised cookie banners as a solution. The paper is structured as follows – first, the paper describes the existing problems with cookie banners and argues how standardised cookie banners can help address the problems. Second, the paper discusses how cookie banners can be standardised. Finally, the paper discusses how standardised cookie banners can be implemented.

The problems with cookie banners

Cookie banners vary across websites, from confirmation-only notices to binary choice notices and category-based notices (Utz et al. 2019). The banners that provide granular consent options vary in whether the options are present on the first layer of the cookie banners or subsequent layers, and whether the options are pre-selected. Banners also differ in their position on the webpage, the text and language used, and the presentation of information. The differences in cookie banners impact whether and how users interact with the banners. A study suggests that interaction with cookie banners is substantially impacted by even seemingly small implementation decisions (Utz et al. 2019).

The problem with differing cookie banners on different websites is that it takes users additional time and cognitive effort to read, understand, evaluate, and choose the preferred option on each website. For users who do not want to allow cookies, they must know how to reject cookies on different banners. The process is annoying when there is no 'reject cookies' button or when it is not easy to reject cookies requiring navigating to subsequent layers of cookie banners (Fassl, Gröber, and Krombholz 2021) or unchecking ticked checkboxes. This can lead to consent fatigue when 'users simply agree to the data privacy disclosure when asked for their consent, without reading the disclosure or thinking about what it means' (Wein 2022, 307). For users who are unaware of cookies, are not adept at navigating cookie banners, or are unwilling to take the effort to reject cookies, the maze of differing cookie banners would make them click the prominently displayed 'accept cookies' button so that the cookie banner disappears.

Other problems compound the problem of navigating differing cookie banners on different websites. One of such problems is that websites often manipulate users into consenting to cookies through various dark patterns (Brignull et al. 2023). The EDPB has defined dark patterns as 'interfaces and user experiences … that lead users into making unintended, unwilling and potentially harmful decisions regarding the processing of their personal data' (EDPB 2022, 2). Dark patterns involve using behavioural economics to make it quicker, more convenient and appealing to consent (Seuchter et al. 2020). Websites also exploit cognitive and behavioural biases to cause errors in judgment and behaviours using design elements such as visibility and attractiveness of choice (Dougherty 2020).

The presentation of choice to consumers can be manipulative because of the use of defaults (predefined settings that need active steps to change), sensory manipulation (visual and aural features steering users), sludge (excessive unjustified friction to do what one wishes) and dark nudges (removed friction to make ill-considered decisions) (CMA 2022). The choice information can be manipulative because of the use of framing (how decision-related information is presented), complex language (presenting obscure choices or sentence structure, making information difficult to understand), and information overload (giving too much information so that the most relevant information is difficult to find) (CMA 2022).

Dark patterns on cookie consent banners include pre-selection of options that users do not often change, misdirection to select a privacy-unfriendly option (such as by diverting attention), forcing the user to make a consent choice using tracking walls ('take cookies or leave the website' choice) or obstructing or hiding information to make it difficult to refuse or withdraw consent (Martini and Drews 2022). The difficulty in finding opt-out settings makes users habitually choose the 'accept all cookies' option (Böhme and Köpsell 2010; Fernandez et al. 2021).

Besides, websites use technical jargon and ambiguous language on cookie banners (Santos et al. 2021). Positive framing is used to nudge users to share consent by providing a partial view that neglects negative aspects of consenting, such as targeted ads (Santos et al. 2021). Negative framing is used to pressurise users and nudge them by exploiting loss aversion (Acquisti et al. 2017; Santos et al. 2021). It leads to developing wrong mental models of what happens when one does not consent (Bongard-Blanchy et al. 2021; Santos et al. 2021).

Notably, user choices are significantly affected by dark patterns used by websites. A study suggests that designers of cookie banners can design manipulative banners to 'effectively boost relative consent rates by 85% and thereby collect data on additional 17% of their total website users' (Bauer, Bergstrøm, and Foss-Madsen 2021, 5).

The outlined problematic website practices violate EU data protection law. Dark patterns on websites are against the principle of transparency (Article 12 GDPR) and conditions of consent (Article 4(11) and 7 GDPR) (EDPB 2022). Dark patterns are manipulative and unfair to the user, and challenge fair processing which requires that data is not obtained using deception or without the data subjects' knowledge (Leiser et al. 2022). Dark patterns challenge the ethos of data protection by design and default under Article 25 GDPR (Leiser et al. 2022). Dark patterns also violate the easily accessible and intelligible information requirement under Article 12(1) GDPR (EDPB 2022).

Various other data protection requirements are violated. For instance, pre-selected checkboxes are against the requirement of consent through an unambiguous indication and clear affirmative action (Martini and Drews 2022). Using pre-ticked boxes results in invalid consent as per the CJEU Planet49 judgement (Bundesverband v Planet49 2019), and violates Article 25(2) GDPR. Further, hiding the 'reject cookies' button leads to invalid consent. It must be as easy to refuse cookies as it is to accept them (CNIL 2022). Using positive and negative framing on cookie banners is against free and informed consent. Using technical and ambiguous language on cookie banners is against the requirement of clear and plain language (Article 12(1) GDPR).

Standardised cookie banner: a solution to the problems

A solution to the above-mentioned problems is a standardised cookie consent banner. Standardised banners can help users effortlessly navigate banners, help websites comply with cookie law requirements, and help supervisory authorities monitor compliance with cookie law. For users, it would save them the additional time and cognitive effort it takes to navigate differing cookie consent banners on different websites by having to evaluate different options on each website. Using standardised banners across websites would save users time as they would be accustomed to the banner. The standardised banner can be designed to be non-manipulative and non-complicated, thereby helping users make meaningful choices across websites.

Standardised cookie banners can also help improve websites' compliance with cookie law requirements. Many websites do not have a cookie banner that complies with basic data protection requirements. Websites could adopt the standardised banner to comply with data protection requirements. It would save websites the task of interpreting data protection requirements to design cookie banners.

Standardised cookie banners can help supervisory authorities monitor compliance. When cookie banners are not standardised across websites, authorities need to make a case-by-case assessment of whether each banner is compliant with data protection requirements. However, it is difficult to manually detect dark patterns in cookie banners, given that the volume of cookie banners makes it beyond human capacity to detect, report and penalise (Soe, Santos, and Slavkovik 2022). Manual detection of violations is not scalable and is also time-consuming (Santos, Bielova, and Matte 2019). On the other hand, cookie consent banners with a standardised design can help automate the detection of cookie consent violations (Santos, Bielova, and Matte 2019).

Standardised cookie banner: essential considerations

The standardised cookie banner must be designed to comply with data protection requirements including transparency, fairness, accountability, consent and data protection by default. Standardised banners must be designed to be free of dark patterns. The standardised cookie banner must present the user with a neutral choice that does not nudge the user to accept or reject cookies.

The following sub-sections propose how cookie banners can be standardised by standardising display timing, position, text and language, presentation, cookie consent options, and way of consenting on the banner.

Display timing of the standardised cookie banner

The ePrivacy Directive requires prior informed consent for using non-necessary cookies (Article 29 Working Party 2013). Thus, the standardised cookie banner must be displayed before non-necessary cookies are stored on the user's device. The non-necessary cookies must not be stored until the user accepts cookies on the standardised cookie banner.

Article 5(3) of the ePrivacy Directive 2002/58/EC amended by Directive 2009/136/EC provides two exemptions to the consent requirement, which are strict necessity to provide an explicitly requested service and 'technical storage or access for the sole purpose of carrying out the transmission of a communication over an electronic communications network' (communication exemption). It is important to note that the first exemption is only for 'strictly necessary' cookies and not for cookies that are merely important or reasonably necessary (ICO UK 2019). An example of cookies that are not strictly necessary is first-party analytics cookies. Consent is required for such cookies as per a European Data Protection Supervisor decision (EDPS 2022). The communication exemption requires communication to be 'impossible' without the cookie (ICO UK 2019). The test is 'if cookies are disabled, the service will not work' (Article 29 Working Party 2012, 3). Cookies that merely assist the communication are not covered (ICO UK 2019).

While the cookie banner must be displayed immediately on the user entering the website (Article 29 Working Party 2013), there is a need to standardise the time of display of the cookie banner. This is because some websites constantly display the cookie banner until the user makes a consent choice. On other websites, the cookie consent banner disappears when the user does not interact with the banner and continues to use the website.

In this respect, it is essential to consider that merely scrolling through a website must not be construed as acceptance of cookies. As silence and inactivity do not constitute consent (Recital 32 GDPR), consent must not be inferred when the user scrolls the website without interacting with the cookie banner. The cookie banner must not disappear unless the user has expressed an active choice (Article 29 Working Party 2013) by clicking a button on the cookie banner. It would help ensure that unambiguous consent is sought (Article 29 Working Party 2013). Action such as clicking the 'more information' option on the cookie banner must not be taken as an indication of consent (Article 29 Working Party 2013).

Position of the standardised cookie banner

The standardised cookie banner must appear at a fixed position on each website. The interaction rates with the cookie banner depend on the chosen position (Utz et al. 2019). Another important consideration is non-hindrance of the users' view of the website. Thus, a standardised cookie consent banner must not be positioned in a way that blocks the users' view of the website. The banner must not force the user to make a choice and not allow access to the website until the user has made a choice (Santos, Bielova, and Matte 2019). Recital 32 of the GDPR must be respected, which requires consent requests not to be 'unnecessarily disruptive to the use of the service for which it is provided' (Santos et al. 2021).

The standardised banner must not be a tracking wall (hereinafter cookie wall) that blocks access to the website until the user selects the 'accept cookies' option. Recital 25 of the ePrivacy Directive states that 'access to specific website content may still be made conditional on the well-informed acceptance of a cookie or similar device, if it is used for a legitimate purpose.' It is important to note that the term 'specific website content' implies that general access to the website should not be made conditional on the acceptance of non-essential cookies (ICO UK 2019). Also, the term 'legitimate purpose' excludes analytics services or online advertising (ICO UK 2019).

The EDPB has recognised that cookie walls are against freely given consent as there is no genuine choice (EDPB 2020). Freely given consent implies that the provision of a service should not be made conditional on personal data processing not necessary for that purpose (Article 7(4) GDPR). Therefore, access to a website cannot be made conditional on the user's consent to cookies (EDPB 2020). The EDPB has stressed the need for an explicit provision in the ePrivacy Regulation prohibiting cookie walls (EDPB 2021).

The Eurobarometer on ePrivacy suggests that 64% of respondents feel that 'it is unacceptable to have their online activities monitored in exchange for unrestricted access to a certain website' (European Commission 2016, 5). Cookie walls leave the users with no real choice and constrain them to consent (European Commission 2017). A laboratory test by the Joint Research Centre (European Commission) has shown that most users consent when the option is take-it-or-leave-it (European Commission 2017). However, lesser users consent when there is an option to use the website without accepting cookies (European Commission 2017).

Websites also use cookie paywalls where users can either accept tracking or pay money to access the website (Morel et al. 2022). Presently, there are divergences in opinions about the legality of cookie paywalls. While the previous stance of the Austrian DPA was that cookie paywalls are, in principle, valid (Morel et al. 2022), the Austrian DPA has recently ruled against cookie paywalls in a complaint by NOYB – European Center for Digital Rights (IAPP 2023). On the other hand, the French CNIL has proposed a case-by-case analysis of cookie paywalls considering evaluation criteria such as the presence of real and fair alternative ways to access content, reasonable price of the paywall, paywall being limited to fair remuneration for the offered service, and paywall not imposing acceptance of all trackers on a website (IAPP 2022; Morel et al. 2022). Divergences in guidelines around cookie paywalls make it difficult to automate the auditing of cookie paywalls by DPAs (Morel et al. 2022). While a detailed discussion around cookie paywalls is beyond the scope of this paper, cookie paywalls potentially violate freely given consent as the user cannot refuse consent without the adverse consequence of having to pay a sum of money (Morel et al. 2022). Thus, the standardised cookie banner must not be a cookie paywall.

Text and language of the standardised cookie banner

The standardised cookie banner must use standardised language to convey standardised information. The style, formatting, punctuation and writing can be standardised (European Commission n.d.). The standardised banner must fulfil the requirement of informed consent. For consent to be informed, information must be provided about the data controller's identity, the purpose of processing, the type of data, and the right to withdraw consent (EDPB 2020). Thus, the standardised banner must provide information about the use of cookies, the categories of cookies by purpose, the data controllers' identity, and ways of withdrawing consent to cookies. The link to additional information must be provided on the cookie banner (DPC Ireland 2020a).

The language used to provide the information must be intelligible (Article 12 GDPR). Clear and plain language must be used (Recital 42, GDPR), which requires that 'information should be provided in as simple a manner as possible, avoiding complex sentence and language structures' (Article 29 Working Party 2018, 8). Concrete and definitive information must be provided, leaving no room for varied interpretations (Article 29 Working Party 2018).

Misleading statements that confuse the user, positively or negatively frame the information, and conceal relevant details must be avoided (Santos et al. 2021). Ambiguous and vague language must not be used, leaving the data subject unsure of data processing and how to exercise control over personal data (EDPB 2022). Textual strategies influencing user choice must be avoided, including motivational language, blame and uncertainty (Hofslot et al. 2022). The users must not be confirm-shamed to make them feel shame or guilt to influence their choice (Habib et al. 2022). The users must not be emotionally steered by giving them a highly positive or negative outlook, making them feel good, safe or scared (EDPB 2022).

Presentation of the standardised cookie banner

Standardised cookie banners must be presented in a standardised visual style that is not manipulative. Data subjects must not be left in the dark by making information unclear and unintelligible (EDPB 2022). For instance, visual signifiers must not be mixed up to appear contradictory to actual settings (EDPB 2022). Marked checkboxes must be used to avoid confusion about their functionality (DPC Ireland 2020b). Sliders may confuse individuals when they are unmarked and even when they are colour coded because the colours may not be accessible or self-explanatory to people who do not see the same colour in the same way (DPC Ireland 2020b).

The information must not be hidden in plain sight by using visual style to nudge users towards privacy-invasive options and away from privacy-advantageous options (EDPB 2022). Banners must not use font sizes or colours that make content less visible so that it is overlooked or made difficult to read (e.g. a light colour on a white background) (EDPB 2022). This would violate the intelligible and easily accessible requirement under Article 12, GDPR (EDPB 2022). The contrast between the text and the button background should not make the text unreadable (EDPB 2023). Besides, it is crucial to consider accessibility issues such as colour blindness (DPC Ireland 2020b).

The colours and contrasts of buttons and the background should not lead to highlighting one button, such as the 'accept cookies' button. (EDPB 2023) The various options on cookie banners must be equally prominent (DPC Ireland 2020b). For instance, the accept and reject cookies buttons and granular options must be presented in the same visual style, including colour, font, and font size. It would help create a balanced choice between accepting and rejecting cookies (Toth, Bielova, and Roca 2022).

Standardising cookie consent options

The cookie consent options must be standardised. The banner must provide the option to accept all cookies, reject all cookies, and accept cookies by categories of purpose. All the options must be provided on the first layer of the cookie banner.

On the banner, the 'reject cookies' button must be provided alongside the 'accept cookies' button because freely given consent requires that it must be as easy to reject cookies as it is to accept cookies (CNIL 2022). It must not take longer than necessary to reject cookies by having to complete more steps to activate a data protection control than to choose a data invasive option (EDPB 2022).

Granular options to accept selected categories of cookies by purpose must be provided. The GDPR requires that consent must be granular and specific, i.e. separate consent is required for each purpose of processing, and there must be separate opt-in for each purpose (EDPB 2020). Merely providing an 'accept all' cookies option would result in invalid consent as the user must be able to provide granular consent (Article 29 Working Party 2017). A study suggests the disadvantage of bundling consent for cookies by only providing an 'accept all' cookies button alongside the 'reject all' cookie button (Utz et al. 2019). Users tend to accept cookies rather than reject cookies when presented with a binary choice (Utz et al. 2019).

The granular options must be provided on the first layer of the cookie banner. A study has suggested that 93% of internet users stop at the first layer of cookie banners and do not visit the second layer to customise their cookie settings (Nouwens et al. 2020). When granular options are provided on the first layer, it decreases the possibility of accepting all cookies. (Habib et al. 2022; Nouwens et al. 2020) Another study suggests that not having an opt-out on the first layer increases consent rates by 22–23 percentage points, and providing granular options on the first layer reduces consent rates by 8–20 percentage points. (Nouwens et al. 2020).

Further, cookie consent options must not be pre-ticked as per Recital 32 of GDPR and the Planet49 judgement of the CJEU. This would help avoid deceptive snugness which involves enabling privacy-invasive settings by default that users are unlikely to change (EDPB 2022).

The labels for purposes of using cookies can also be standardised. Standardising the labels for purposes of processing can make the consent meaningful and help clarify the processing purposes for the affected parties (Grafenstein 2018). It is essential to standardise the labels because, when differing terms are used on different websites to describe the same purpose, it raises doubts about whether users can associate the different terms with the same idea (Santos et al. 2021). For instance, the purpose of advertising is mentioned differently on banners across websites using terms such as 'marketing (content), targeted/tailored ads, ad(s) delivery/personalization/measurement, and promotional offers' (Santos et al. 2021, 3). Standardising the labels would avoid different interpretations for different people (Santos et al. 2021). The labels must convey purposes without using 'legalistic, technical or specialist language or terminology' (Article 29 Working Party 2018, 10).

Besides, cookies must not be wrongly categorised to seek exemption from the consent requirement. Importantly, cookies can be exempt from consent by relying on the exemptions, when the cookies are not used for additional purposes (Article 29 Working Party 2012). When the same cookie is used for various purposes, the exemption only applies if all the purposes individually benefit from the exemption (Article 29 Working Party 2012). Thus, cookies used for both necessary and non-necessary purposes must not be categorised as necessary cookies under the exemption.

The proposed ePrivacy Regulation provides the grounds on which cookies can be used (Article 8). Compared to the ePrivacy directive, an additional ground introduced by the proposed ePrivacy Regulation is the necessity for web audience measuring carried out by the provider of requested information society service (Article 8). The EDPB has stressed the need for the ground of audience measurement not to be broadly interpreted as it could lead to a lower level of protection for user devices (EDPB 2021). The EDPB has suggested that the web audience measurement ground must not lead to singling out or profiling individuals or the collection of navigation information across websites (EDPB 2021).

Other than standardised options to consent to cookies, there must be information about how consent can be withdrawn. As per Article 7(3) GDPR, consent must be allowed to be withdrawn as easily as it is given. Websites can use links placed at a visible and standardised place on the website that allow withdrawal of consent (EDPB 2023).

Standardising the way of consenting

The Article 29 Working Party has stated that consent for cookies must be given through active behaviour (Article 29 Working Party 2013). The action should be 'based on a traceable user-client request towards the website' (Article 29 Working Party Working 2013, 4). Unambiguous consent requires that it must be obvious that the individual has consented (EDPB 2020). The user choice must be an active indication of wishes, leaving no doubt about the users' intention (Article 29 Working Document 2013).

The EDPB has stated that 'merely proceeding with a service cannot be regarded as an active indication of choice' (EDPB 2020, 18). One cannot infer consent from 'merely continuing the ordinary use of a website' (EDPB 2020, 19).

Making the click of the 'accept button' the standardised action to consent across websites would help curtail website practices of assuming consent from user silence or inactivity. A study indicates that users tend to believe that their data is not collected unless they make a decision (Utz et al. 2019). Any user action other than clicking the 'accept cookies' button must not be assumed as consent.

Other considerations for standardising cookie banners

Other factors should be considered while designing the standardised cookie banner. It is essential to consider that varied audiences of differing knowledge and attitudes towards cookies and privacy would use the standardised cookie banner. Thus, a standardised cookie banner must be designed by studying what would meaningfully work for different people. A large-scale study can be carried out to understand user knowledge, attitude and behaviour towards cookies to design the cookie banner (Bavel and Rodríguez-Priego 2016).

It is important to consider balancing the users' interests with the interests of those parties collecting information through cookies (including websites and advertisers). For instance, it would not be in the interest of websites to show cookie consent banners that dissuade people from being tracked (Mondschein 2016). At the same time, it would not be in the user's interest to see cookie consent banners that persuade them to accept all cookies.

The standardised cookie banner can be designed considering factors such as the usability and likeability of the banner. Users do not uniformly like all UI designs of different cookie banners (Singh et al. 2022). Liking is impacted by decision-making time, transparency, and ease of use (Singh et al. 2022). Besides, usability aspects can be considered, including user needs, sentiment, ability and effort (Habib et al. 2022). Usability and likeability are important to avoid annoyance and sub-optimal choices affecting free consent and user privacy (Singh et al. 2022).

The standardised cookie banner must be designed to allow the automated detection of violations. While this paper has suggested how standardised cookie banners must look and read, there are ways of standardising how cookie banners operate to store consent. It has been suggested that, to automatically detect violations, there is a need for standardising the structuring and storage of consent (Santos, Bielova, and Matte 2019). Developing a standardised cookie banner that enables automated violation detection would promote transparency and accountability.

Another factor to consider is automating user consent decisions across websites. While it is debatable whether consent decisions must be automated, standardised cookie banners can facilitate automated consent decisions. Automated tools can help read standardised cookie banners on different websites and make consent choices on behalf of the user. Automated tools that accept only necessary cookies can be developed (Fassl, Gröber, and Krombholz 2021; Yue, Xie, and Wang 2010).

Implementing standardised cookie banners

Standards are specifications for best practices that provide efficient solutions (Kamara and Kosta 2016). In the past, standards have been developed addressing the communication between websites and potential visitors (W3C 2018). There have been attempts to standardise privacy policies to enable the use of automated analysis tools, potentially helping regulators, individuals and websites (Binns 2014). There have been suggestions to present cookie policies in a standardised manner to help reduce deception in cookie policies (Seuchter et al. 2020). There have been attempts at standardising consent, for instance, ISO/IEC 29184:2020 titled 'Information technology — Online privacy notices and consent'. The Directive 2011/83/EU (EU Consumer Rights Directive) is an example where standardised text is prescribed that can be used in standard contractual forms (Annexure 1).

The GDPR has envisaged the process of standardisation. Article 12 of the GDPR provides that information required when data are collected from the data subject can be provided alongside standardised icons. Article 12 of the GDPR empowers the EU Commission to adopt delegated acts determining the information to be presented by icons and the procedures for providing standardised icons. The power of the Commission to adopt delegated acts under the GDPR is mentioned in Recital 166. Recital 166 of the GDPR states that the Commission has the power to adopt acts as per Article 290 of the TFEU to fulfil the GDPR objectives and protect the fundamental right to personal data protection. Article 92 of the GDPR requires that the European Parliament and the Council should be informed when the Commission adopts a delegated act. Article 92 further states that the delegated act would enter into force only when there is no objection. These delegated acts can help create a more consistent application of the law across the EU and help supplement the GDPR while fulfilling the objectives of the GDPR (Tosoni 2020).

Standardisation by adopting delegated acts must be done with appropriate consultations at the expert level (Recital 166). Article 29 Working Party has recognised that efforts to create standardised icons must follow an evidence-based approach with extensive research involving industry and the wider public (Article 29 Working Party 2018). The consultations must also include the EDPB (Tosoni 2020). Thus, experts can be engaged to study how cookie consent banners can be standardised, so they work well for different users. There is a need to study the intelligibility and the effectiveness of user interfaces through 'mechanisms such as user panels, readability testing, formal and informal interactions and dialogue with industry groups, consumer advocacy groups and regulatory bodies' (Article 29 Working Party 2018, 7).

The process of standardisation has also been envisaged under the proposed ePrivacy Regulation. Article 8 of the proposed ePrivacy Regulation provides that standardised icons can be used alongside the information that needs to be provided. Article 8 further states that the Commission can adopt delegated acts laying down the procedures for providing and determining the information presented by standardised icons. While the process for standardisation has been envisaged for icons, the proposed ePrivacy Regulation could be revised to include standardisation of cookie banners.

Another way to standardise cookie banners is for the EU Commission to request EU Standardisation Organisations to develop a standardised cookie consent banner like the Commission has requested EU Standardisation Organisations in the past to develop privacy-related standards (Kamara 2017). Such a request can be a Commission Implementing Decision (Kamara 2017). The process would establish a standard which would also be an agreed way of meeting the legal requirements (Kamara 2017). Standards can be imposed as regulatory obligations to ensure compliance with data protection regulation (Kosta and Stuurman 2015).

Another way to implement standardised cookie banners is for the EDPB to develop guidelines to propose the template for standardised cookie banners. The EDPB can propose harmonised EU-level guidelines on how cookie disclosures must be transparent and readable, considering consumer behaviour research (Luzak 2014). The process of creating harmonised guidelines for a standardised cookie banner would be facilitated with the implementation of the ePrivacy Regulation.

The passage of the ePrivacy Regulation would result in a harmonised cookie consent requirement across the EU member states. The proposed ePrivacy Regulation provides consent as a ground for using cookies (Article 8). The definition of consent has previously been harmonised by the GDPR. The enactment of the ePrivacy Regulation would lead to better harmonisation than the existing minimum harmonisation required by ePrivacy Directive. While directives seek to harmonise national legislation by requiring minimum standards and objectives, there could be varying data protection standards as member states enact their own law based on the directives (Deloitte 2017). On the other hand, Regulations directly apply in the member states without needing to be transposed into national law, and Regulations supersede incompatible national law provisions (European Parliament n.d.).

Thus, with the enactment of the ePrivacy Regulation which would be read with the GDPR, there would be a harmonised cookie consent requirement in the EU. This could facilitate the creation of a standardised cookie banner for the EU based on the harmonised cookie consent requirement.

The main challenge is to bring together different stakeholders to work on creating a standardised cookie banner that would address the concerns with cookie consent. As discussed in this section, the EDPB can suggest guidelines for a standardised cookie banner, or the EU Commission can adopt delegated acts or a Commission Implementing Decision for standardisation of cookie banners. However, the likelihood of seeing standardised banners depends on how different stakeholders receive and act upon the idea of standardised cookie banner proposed in this paper.

Conclusion

This paper proposes a standardised cookie consent banner to solve various problems associated with cookie consent. Presently, cookie consent requirement is not harmonised across the EU, and websites use differing cookie consent banners. This makes users face the cognitive effort of navigating differing text and language, presentation, and consent options on different websites' cookie banners. Besides, there are other problems with cookie consent banners, such as dark patterns that manipulate users into making privacy-invasive decisions. A standardised cookie banner across websites can help address these concerns. It can make it easy for users to navigate the banner across websites, easy for websites to comply by adopting the standardised banner, and easy for supervisory authorities to monitor compliance by automated detection of violations.

This paper proposes that the standardised banner must have standardised timing of display, position on the website, text and language, presentation, consent options, and ways of consenting. The standardised banner must be displayed on entering the website and the banner must be displayed until the user has clicked an option on the banner. Consent must not be inferred from any other action such as scrolling a website, and non-necessary cookies must not be stored until the user has accepted cookies. The standardised banner must be displayed so that it doesn't hinder the users' view of the website. The banner must not be a blocking banner that forces the user to choose to proceed on the website, and it must not be a tracking wall that forces the user to accept cookies to proceed on the website. The banner must be displayed at a fixed position on each website. Standardised information must be provided on the banner about the use of cookies, categories of cookies by purpose, data controllers' identity and ways of withdrawing consent. The information must be provided in standardised and definitive language that is neutral and not misleading or manipulative. The visual style (colour, font, font size, etc.) of the banner must be standardised. On the standardised banner, there must be 'Accept All' option, 'Reject All' option, and the option to accept cookies by categories of purposes. All the options must be on the first layer of the cookie banner and presented as a balanced choice. The options must not be pre-ticked. The labels of the categories of purposes must be standardised, and cookies must not be wrongly categorised. The way of consenting must be standardised. Only clicking the 'accept cookies' button must be construed as consent, and no other user action must be assumed as consent.

The factors to consider while developing the standardised banner include how varied audiences with different knowledge and attitudes would interact with the banner, evaluating the usability and likability of the banner, allowing automated detection of violations, and allowing automated consent decisions across websites.

Banners can be standardised by – (1) relying on provisions on standardisation in the GDPR and proposed ePrivacy Regulation that allow the EU Commission to adopt delegated acts, or (2) the EU Commission requesting Standardisation Organisations to develop the standardised banner, or (3) the EDPB developing guidelines that propose the template for the standardised banner. With the passage of the ePrivacy Regulation, the cookie consent requirement could be harmonised across the EU, facilitating the standardisation process.

A standardised cookie consent banner across websites would address the concerns with cookie consent, make decision-making on cookie banners convenient for website users, and simplify cookie law compliance and regulation.

Disclosure statement

No potential conflict of interest was reported by the author(s).

References

Research Publications

Acquisti, Alessandro, et al. 2017. "Nudges for Privacy and Security: Understanding and Assisting Users' Choices Online." *ACM Computing Surveys (CSUR)* 50 (3): 1–41. https://doi.org/10.1145/3054926.

Bauer, Jan M., Regitze Bergstrøm, and Rune Foss-Madsen. 2021. "Are you Sure, You Want a Cookie?– The Effects of Choice Architecture on Users' Decisions About Sharing Private Online Data." *Computers in Human Behavior* 120: 106729. https://doi.org/10.1016/j.chb.2021.106729.

Binns, Reuben. 2014. "Standardised Privacy Policies: A Post-mortem and Promising Developments." In *W3C Privacy Workshop: Privacy and User-Centric Controls.* https://www.w3.org/2014/privacyws/pp/Binns.pdf.

Böhme, Rainer, and Stefan Köpsell. 2010. "Trained to Accept? A Field Experiment on Consent Dialogs." *In Proceedings of the SIGCHI Conference on Human Factors in Computing Systems,* 2403–2406. https://doi.org/10.1145/1753326.1753689.

Bongard-Blanchy, Kerstin, Arianna Rossi, Salvador Rivas, Sophie Doublet, Vincent Koenig, and Gabriele Lenzini. 2021. "I am Definitely Manipulated, Even When I am Aware of It. It's Ridiculous!" - Dark Patterns from the End-User Perspective." In *Designing Interactive Systems Conference*: 763–776. https://doi.org/10.1145/3461778.3462086.

Cofone, Ignacio N. 2017. "The way the Cookie Crumbles: Online Tracking Meets Behavioural Economics." *International Journal of Law and Information Technology* 25 (1): 38–62.

Debusseré, Frederic. 2005. "The EU e-Privacy Directive: A Monstrous Attempt to Starve the Cookie Monster?" *International Journal of Law and Information Technology* 13 (1): 70–97.

Dougherty, Christie. 2020. "Every Breath You Take, Every Move You Make, Facebook's Watching You: A Behavioral Economic Analysis of the US California Consumer Privacy Act and EU EPrivacy Regulation." *NEULR* 12: 629.

Fassl, Matthias, Lea Theresa Gröber, and Katharina Krombholz. 2021. "Stop the Consent Theater." *In Extended Abstracts of the 2021 CHI Conference on Human Factors in Computing Systems*, 1–7. https://doi.org/10.1145/3411763.3451230.

Fernandez, Carlos B., Dimitris Chatzopoulos, Dimitrios Papadopoulos, and Pan Hui. 2021. "This Website Uses Nudging: Mturk Workers' Behaviour on Cookie Consent Notices." *Proceedings of the ACM on Human-Computer Interaction* 5 (CSCW2): 1–22. https://doi.org/10.1145/3476087.

Gotze, Matthias, Srdjan Matic, Costas Iordanou, Georgios Smaragdakis, and Nikolaos Laoutaris. 2022. "Measuring Web Cookies in Governmental Websites." *In 14th ACM Web Science Conference 2022,* 44–54. https://doi.org/10.1145/3501247.3531545.

Grafenstein, M. 2018. "Regulation as a Facilitator of Startup Innovation: The Purpose Limitation Principle and Data Privacy." In *Entrepreneurial Innovation and Leadership*, edited by N. Richter, P. Jackson, and T. Schildhauer. Cham: Palgrave Pivot. https://doi.org/10.1007/978-3-319-71737-1_4.

Habib, Hana, Megan Li, Ellie Young, and Lorrie Cranor. 2022. ""Okay, Whatever": An Evaluation of Cookie Consent Interfaces." In *Proceedings of the 2022 CHI Conference on Human Factors in Computing Systems*: 1–27. https://doi.org/10.1145/3491102.3501985.

Hofslot, Marieke Van, Almila Akdag Salah, Albert Gatt, and Cristiana Santos. 2022. "Automatic Classification of Legal Violations in Cookie Banner Texts." In *Proceedings of the Natural Legal Language Processing Workshop* 2022: 287–295. https://doi.org/10.18653/v1/2022.nllp-1.27.

Kamara, Irene. 2017. "Co-regulation in EU Personal Data Protection: The Case of Technical Standards and the Privacy by Design Standardisation Mandate." *European Journal of Law and Technology* 8 (1): 1–24. https://www.ejlt.org/index.php/ejlt/article/view/545.

Kamara, Irene, and Eleni Kosta. 2016. "Do Not Track Initiatives: Regaining the Lost User Control." *International Data Privacy Law* 6 (4): 276–290. https://doi.org/10.1093/idpl/ipw019.

Kampanos, Georgios, and Siamak F. Shahandashti. 2021. "Accept All: The Landscape of Cookie Banners in Greece and the UK." In *ICT Systems Security and Privacy Protection: 36th IFIP TC 11 International Conference, SEC 2021, Oslo, Norway, June 22–24,* 2021: 213–227. Springer International Publishing.

Kierkegaard, Sylvia Mercado. 2005. "How the Cookies (Almost) Crumbled: Privacy & Lobbyism." *Computer Law & Security Review* 21 (4): 310–322. https://doi.org/10.1016/j.clsr.2005.06.002.

Kosta, Eleni, and Kees Stuurman. 2015. "Technical Standards and the Draft General Data Protection Regulation." In *The Law, Economics and Politics of International Standardization (Forthcoming).* Cambridge University Press. https://doi.org/10.2139/ssrn.2642331.

Leenes, Ronald. 2015. "The Cookiewars: From Regulatory Failure to User Empowerment?" *The Privacy & Identity Lab: 4 Years Later The Privacy & Identity Lab* 2015: 31–49. https://pure.uvt.nl/ws/portalfiles/portal/9020466/Ronald_Leenes_The_cookiewars.pdf.

Leiser, M. R., Eleni Kosta, Ronald Leenes, and Irene Kamara. 2022. "Dark Patterns: The Case for Regulatory Pluralism Between the European Unions Consumer and Data Protection Regimes." In *Research Handbook on EU Data Protection Law*, 240–269. Edward Elgar Publishing Ltd. https://doi.org/10.4337/9781800371682.00019.

Luzak, Joasia A. 2014. "Privacy Notice for Dummies? Towards European Guidelines on How to Give "Clear and Comprehensive Information" on the Cookies' use in Order to Protect the Internet Users' Right to Online Privacy." *Journal of Consumer Policy* 37: 547–559. https://doi.org/10.1007/s10603-014-9263-3.

Martini, Prof, and Christian Drews. 2022. "Making Choice Meaningful–Tackling Dark Patterns in Cookie and Consent Banners through European Data Privacy Law." Available at SSRN 4257979. https://doi.org/10.2139/ssrn.4257979.

Matte, Célestin, Nataliia Bielova, and Cristiana Santos. 2020. "Do Cookie Banners Respect My Choice?: Measuring Legal Compliance of Banners from IAB Europe's Transparency and Consent Framework." *In 2020 IEEE Symposium on Security and Privacy (SP)*, 791–809. https://doi.org/10.1109/SP40000.2020.00076.

Mondschein, Christopher F. 2016. "Some Iconoclastic Thoughts on the Effectiveness of Simplified Notices and Icons for Informing Individuals as Proposed in Article 12 (1) and (7) GDPR." *European Data Protection Law Review* 2: 507. https://doi.org/10.21552/EDPL/2016/4/9.

Morel, Victor, Cristiana Santos, Yvonne Lintao, and Soheil Human. 2022. "Your Consent Is Worth 75 Euros A Year-Measurement and Lawfulness of Cookie Paywalls." *In Proceedings of the 21st Workshop on Privacy in the Electronic Society*, 213–218. https://doi.org/10.1145/3559613.3563205.

Nouwens, Midas, Ilaria Liccardi, Michael Veale, David Karger, and Lalana Kagal. 2020. "Dark Patterns After the GDPR: Scraping Consent Pop-Ups and Demonstrating their Influence." *In Proceedings of the 2020 CHI Conference on Human Factors in Computing Systems*, 1–13. https://doi.org/10.1145/3313831.3376321.

Santos, Cristiana, Nataliia Bielova, and Célestin Matte. 2019. "Are Cookie Banners Indeed Compliant with the Law? Deciphering EU Legal Requirements on Consent and Technical Means to Verify Compliance of Cookie Banners." *arXiv preprint arXiv:1912.07144*. https://doi.org/10.48550/arXiv.1912.07144.

Santos, Cristiana, Arianna Rossi, Lorena Sanchez Chamorro, Kerstin Bongard-Blanchy, and Ruba Abu-Salma. 2021. "Cookie Banners, What's the Purpose? Analyzing Cookie Banner Text Through a Legal Lens." *In Proceedings of the 20th Workshop on Workshop on Privacy in the Electronic Society*, 187–194. https://doi.org/10.1145/3463676.3485611.

Seuchter, Gerhard, Sabine Prossnegg, Veronika Beimrohr, and Dawn Branley-Bell. 2020. "The Crux of Cookies Consent: A Legal and Technical Analysis of Shortcomings of Cookie Policies in the Age of the GDPR." *Jusletter IT*, https://doi.org/10.38023/5f700184-d8ee-4bdb-b906-7cde70fbf0a2.

Singh, Ashutosh Kumar, Nisarg Upadhyaya, Arka Seth, Xuehui Hu, Nishanth Sastry, and Mainack Mondal. 2022. "What Cookie Consent Notices Do Users Prefer: A Study In The Wild." In *Proceedings of the 2022 European Symposium on Usable Security*: 28–39. https://doi.org/10.1145/3549015.3555675.

Soe, Than Htut, Cristiana Teixeira Santos, and Marija Slavkovik. 2022. "Automated Detection of Dark Patterns in Cookie Banners: How to do It Poorly and Why It is Hard to do It Any Other Way." *arXiv preprint arXiv:2204.11836*.

Stöver, Alina, Nina Gerber, Christin Cornel, Mona Henz, Karola Marky, Verena Zimmermann, and Joachim Vogt. 2022. "Website Operators are not the Enemy Either-Analyzing Options for Creating Cookie Consent Notices Without Dark Patterns." *Mensch und Computer 2022-Workshopband*.

Tosoni, Luca. 2020. "Article 92 Exercise of the Delegation." In *The EU General Data Protection Regulation (GDPR): A Commentary*, edited by Christopher Kuner, Lee A Bygrave, Christopher Docksey, and Laura Drechsler, 1268–1277. Oxford University Press. https://doi.org/10.1093/oso/9780198826491.003.0140.

Toth, Michael, Nataliia Bielova, and Vincent Roca. 2022. "On Dark Patterns and Manipulation of Website Publishers by CMPs." In *PETS 2022-22nd Privacy Enhancing Technologies Symposium*: 478-497. https://inria.hal.science/hal-03577024.

Utz, Christine, Martin Degeling, Sascha Fahl, Florian Schaub, and Thorsten Holz. 2019. "(Un) informed Consent: Studying GDPR Consent Notices in the Field." *In Proceedings of the 2019 acm sigsac Conference on Computer and Communications Security*, 973–990. https://doi.org/10.1145/3319535.3354212.

Wein, Thomas. 2022. "Data Protection, Cookie Consent, and Prices." *Economies* 10 (12): 307. https://doi.org/10.3390/economies10120307.

Yue, Chuan, Mengjun Xie, and Haining Wang. 2010. "An Automatic HTTP Cookie Management System." *Computer Networks* 54 (13): 2182–2198.

Guidelines and official documents

Article 29 Working Party. 2010. "Opinion 2/2010 on Online Behavioural Advertising." https://ec.europa.eu/justice/article-29/documentation/opinion-recommendation/files/2010/wp171_en.pdf.

Article 29 Working Party. 2012. "Opinion 04/2012 on Cookie Consent Exemption." https://ec.europa.eu/justice/article-29/documentation/opinion-recommendation/files/2012/wp194_en.pdf.

Article 29 Working Party. 2013. "Working Document 02/2013 providing guidance on obtaining consent for cookies." https://ec.europa.eu/justice/article-29/documentation/opinion-recommendation/files/2013/wp208_en.pdf.

Article 29 Working Party. 2017. "Opinion 01/2017 on the Proposed Regulation for the ePrivacy Regulation (2002/58/EC)." https://ec.europa.eu/newsroom/article29/items/610140/en.

Article 29 Working Party. 2018. "Guidelines on Transparency under Regulation 2016/679." https://ec.europa.eu/newsroom/article29/items/622227/en.

Bavel, R. van, and Nuria Rodríguez-Priego. 2016. "Testing the Effect of Cookie Banners on Behaviour." EUR 28287 EN, Joint Research Centre (European Commission). https://doi.org/10.2791/22197.

Bundesverband der Verbraucherzentralen und Verbraucherverbände - Verbraucherzentrale Bundesverband e.V. v Planet49 GmbH [2019] CJEU ECLI:EU:C:2019:801.

Competition and Markets Authority. 2022. "Online Choice Architecture How Digital Design can Harm Competition and Consumers Discussion Paper." https://assets.publishing.service.gov.uk/media/624c27c68fa8f527710aaf58/Online_choice_architecture_discussion_paper.pdf.

Directive 2002/58/EC of the European Parliament and of the Council of 12 July 2002 concerning the processing of personal data and the protection of privacy in the electronic communications sector (Directive on privacy and electronic communications) OJ L 201, 31.7.2002, p. 37–47; Directive 2009/136/EC of the European Parliament and of the Council of 25 November 2009 amending Directive 2002/22/EC on universal service and users' rights relating to electronic communications networks and services, Directive 2002/58/EC concerning the processing of personal data and the protection of privacy in the electronic communications sector and Regulation (EC)

No 2006/2004 on cooperation between national authorities responsible for the enforcement of consumer protection laws OJ L 337, 18.12.2009, p. 11–36.

Directive 2011/83/EU of the European Parliament and of the Council of 25 October 2011 on consumer rights, amending Council Directive 93/13/EEC and Directive 1999/44/EC of the European Parliament and of the Council and repealing Council Directive 85/577/EEC and Directive 97/7/EC of the European Parliament and of the Council Text with EEA relevance OJ L 304, 22.11.2011, p. 64–88.

Deloitte. 2017. "The Proposed ePrivacy Regulation: The Commission's and the Parliament's Draft s at a Crossroads?" https://digital-strategy.ec.europa.eu/en/library/evaluation-and-review-directive-200258-privacy-and-electronic-communication-sector.

European Commission. 2016. "Eurobarometer on ePrivacy." https://digital-strategy.ec.europa.eu/en/library/eurobarometer-eprivacy.

European Commission. 2017. "Ex-post REFIT Evaluation of the ePrivacy Directive 2002/58/EC." https://digital-strategy.ec.europa.eu/en/library/proposal-regulation-privacy-and-electronic-communications.

European Data Protection Board. 2020. "Guidelines 05/2020 on Consent under Regulation 2016/679." https://edpb.europa.eu/our-work-tools/our-documents/guidelines/guidelines-052020-consent-under-regulation-2016679_en.

European Data Protection Board. 2021. "Statement 03/2021 on the ePrivacy Regulation. Adopted on 9 March 2021." https://edpb.europa.eu/system/files/2021-03/edpb_statement_032021_eprivacy_regulation_en_0.pdf.

European Data Protection Board. 2022. "Guidelines 3/2022 on Dark Patterns in Social Media Platform Interfaces: How to Recognise and Avoid Them." https://edpb.europa.eu/our-work-tools/documents/public-consultations/2022/guidelines-32022-dark-patterns-social-media_en.

European Data Protection Board. 2023. "Report of the Work Undertaken by the Cookie Banner Taskforce." https://edpb.europa.eu/system/files/2023-01/edpb_20230118_report_cookie_banner_taskforce_en.pdf.

European Data Protection Supervisor. 2022. "Decision of the European Data Protection Supervisor in complaint case 2020-1013 submitted by Members of the Parliament against the European Parliament." https://noyb.eu/sites/default/files/2022-01/Case%202020-1013%20-%20EDPS%20Decision_bk.pdf.

ICO, UK. 2019. "Guidance on the Use of Cookies and Similar Technologies." https://ico.org.uk/for-organisations/guide-to-pecr/guidance-on-the-use-of-cookies-and-similar-technologies/.

DPC Ireland. 2020a. "Guidance Note: Cookies and Other Tracking Technologies." https://www.dataprotection.ie/sites/default/files/uploads/2020-04/Guidance%20note%20on%20cookies%20and%20other%20tracking%20technologies.pdf.

DPC Ireland. 2020b. "Report by the Data Protection Commission on the use of cookies and other tracking technologies." https://www.dataprotection.ie/sites/default/files/uploads/2020-04/Report%20by%20the%20DPC%20on%20the%20use%20of%20cookies%20and%20other%20tracking%20technologies.pdf.

Web Pages

Brignull, Harry, Mark Leiser, Cristiana Santos, and Kosha Doshi. 2023. "Deceptive Patterns" https://www.deceptive.design.

CNIL. 2022. "Cookies: FACEBOOK IRELAND LIMITED fined 60 million euros." https://www.cnil.fr/en/cookies-facebook-ireland-limited-fined-60-million-euros.

European Comission. n.d. "01. Web Writing Overview." https://wikis.ec.europa.eu/display/WEBGUIDE/01.+Web+writing+overview.

European Parliament. n.d. "Sources and Scope of European Union Law." https://www.europarl.europa.eu/factsheets/en/sheet/6/sources-and-scope-of-european-union-law.

IAPP. 2022. "CNIL Publishes Cookie Wall Evaluation Scheme." https://iapp.org/news/a/cnil-publishes-cookie-wall-evaluation-scheme/.

IAPP. 2023. "Austria DPA Rules against Newspaper Cookie Paywalls in NOYB Complaint." https://iapp.org/news/a/austria-dpa-rules-against-newspaper-cookie-paywalls-in-noyb-complaint/.

Information Commissioners' Office (ICO), UK. 2020. "What are Cookies and Similar Technologies?". https://ico.org.uk/for-organisations/guide-to-pecr/guidance-on-the-use-of-cookies-and-similar-technologies/what-are-cookies-and-similar-technologies/.

Voisin, Gabriel, Ruth Boardman, Simon Assion, Clara Clark Nevola, Lupe Sampedro, and Ester Vidal. 2020. "ICO, CNIL, German and Spanish DPA Revised Cookies Guidelines: Convergence and Divergence." IAPP. https://iapp.org/resources/article/ico-and-cnil-revised-cookie-guidelines-convergence-and-divergence/.

W3C. 2018. "Platform for Privacy Preferences (P3P) Project." https://www.w3.org/P3P/.

When it's cute but also dark: critical analysis of *FarmVille 3's* game design in the digital economy

Caroline Stockman, Anthony O'Connell and Emma Nottingham

ABSTRACT

'Cute design' or 'cuteness' is a known design and development trend in the digital economy, with a proven advertising and marketing appeal to both children and adults. However, we postulate that it may also be an effective dark pattern. The following analysis uses the popular online game *FarmVille 3* to illustrate the potential dark side of cuteness in digital game design. Through an explorative game analysis, the cute aesthetic can be identified as pervasive and multi-factored. At the same time, the history and economic steer behind the game shows a clear interest in user data ownership and control. Here, we flag cute design as a risk to human autonomy, and therefore a significant regulatory concern. This original conceptualisation of 'cute but dark' design is significant in its potential to manipulate the consumer autonomy of both children and adults. Current regulatory frameworks should empower the end user against the manipulate steer of cute but dark design, considering cultural nuances of what might be deemed cute user interfaces, and the vulnerabilities of certain consumer groups. Regulatory development should constitute a more streamlined approach to dark patterns, that enables a thriving digital economy while maintaining rigorous consumer protection.

Introduction

In this paper, we raise 'cute design' of popular information technologies as a potential red flag in regard to data ownership and control. End-user autonomy is potentially undermined through interaction with digital platforms which utilise cute design. Cute design can steer end-user behaviour and is particularly alluring to children. We postulate that cute design of end-user interfaces could be a dark pattern tactic, following the extensive OECD (2022) report on dark commercial patterns, and consider that 'cute but dark' design should be added to the current discourse (including the OECD report). Further, we argue that regulatory frameworks would benefit from a more streamlined approach to dark patterns, that empowers end users against the manipulative steer of cute but dark design, showing sensitivity to individual and cultural perceptions of what makes digital design appear cute, as well the vulnerabilities of certain consumer groups such as children.

This analysis is situated in a digital context where big tech companies, including online game providers, have been penalised for exploiting end-user data, including children's data (Brown 2023). Negligent privacy and data handling measures have been specifically noted for the mobile app market that targets children (or their parents) as end users (Jibb et al. 2022). This paper comes at a time when dark patterns are being considered globally, by leading organisations including the Organisation for Economic Co-operation and Development (OECD), Competition and Markets Authority (CMA), and the Federal Trade Commission (FTC), and when national and international organisations, such as the 5Rights Foundation (2023) and Defend Digital Me (2021), are advocating for the increased protection of children's data rights.

This paper contextualises dark pattern literature and provides an overview of cute design principles and impact. It focuses on the cute aesthetic of the end-user interface, alongside the underlying data protection management. For this, it draws on concrete examples of *FarmVille 3*'s end-user interface and data protection policies, as the game has been previously critiqued as an example of the big data economy, with related ethical concerns about transparency and end-user autonomy (Willson and Leaver 2015). This paper adds to that discussion by critiquing how cute design can be operationalised in the data economy as a dark pattern in itself, or to mask an underlying dark pattern in data protection practices. Although we acknowledge heightened risks for end users of all ages, we are particularly concerned with the rights and wellbeing of children who are (legally or otherwise) exposed to cute but dark design. With reference to related legal frameworks and policies such as the UK General Data Protection Regulation and the Age Appropriate Design Code published by the UK's Information Commissioner's Office (ICO), we discuss how the regulatory framework in the UK does not conclusively address cute design for any end user, and highlight where it should specifically address children's rights and protection. We emphasise where the cute aesthetic could be addressed, where it can enable successful digital business and appealing gameplay, or where it should be more clearly considered as a powerful tool for end-user manipulation in the digital economy.

The issues raised in this paper and the scope of the analysis is not limited to *FarmVille 3* specifically. It is used as an illustration for a critically overlooked risk: when cute design becomes a risk to a person's autonomy. It crucially highlights the significance to the regulatory frameworks of data protection and ethical software development.

Dark design

What is a dark pattern?

Dark patterns aim to 'steer, deceive, coerce, or manipulate consumers into making choices, including regarding purchases, their personal data or attention time, which may not be in their best interests' (OECD 2022, 9). The term's originator, Brignull (2010), now favours 'deceptive design' or 'deceptive patterns' to capture this purposeful design tactic. The concept has also been described as 'manipulative design features' (Radesky et al. 2022), 'persuasive design' (5Rights Foundation 2023) or 'evil by design' (Nodder 2013) and has some overlap with 'choice architecture' (Thaler and Sunstein 2013). In general, these terms capture design tactics that prioritise commercial interests over the end user. Interface design choices can lead to end users disclosing substantial amounts of data, which can then be sold to third party on-sellers or data brokers, and making choices that they might not have otherwise made had they been fully informed or provided with alternatives (Mathur et al. 2019, 2). The distortion of consumer behaviour has been identified by the Competition and Markets Authority (2022) as a key type of harm associated with choice architecture. Mathur, Mayer, and Kshirsagar (2021, 14) identify the cognitive burden of dark patterns, as they intentionally colonise a person's attention, energy, and time. Dark patterns can undermine end user's ability to freely decide their interactions with a technology, since platforms are frequently designed to constrain autonomy and choice, despite often giving consumers an illusion of some control or optionality (Hartzog 2018). In the gaming context Zagal, Bjork, and Lewis (2013, 7) coined the term 'Dark Game Design Patterns' which they describe as 'a pattern used intentionally by a game creator to cause negative experiences for players which are against their best interests and likely to happen without their consent'. They suggest that the interests of game developers and game players are sometimes at odds.

Children have specifically been identified as being too young to understand pervasive design tactics (Radesky et al. 2022; 5Rights Foundation 2023, 18). Marketing techniques habitually take advantage of the increased vulnerability of children as online consumers (Jibb et al. 2022; Kennedy, Jones, and Janine 2019). Cute design is key example of a marketing technique which appeals to both adult and child consumers. Although cute design is not explicitly mentioned in dark patterns literature, it could be considered an example of 'emotional steering', which refers to techniques that provoke emotional responses in the end user, perhaps making them feel 'good, safe or rewarded' or 'scared, guilty or punished' (European Data Protection Board 2023). Eliciting emotional responses, either positive or negative, might lead to end users making decisions that go against their data protection interests. The next section critically analyses cute design for this emotional steer on decision-making, thereby outlining its cute but dark potential.

Cute design

What is cute design?

'Cute design' or 'cuteness' is a known design and development trend pertaining to various consumer technologies. While it can relate to both software and hardware, we particularly consider the end-user interface, being a software interface that is made for the customer, player, or end user, and is distinct from the developer interface (in what follows, these terms will be used interchangeably). Cuteness in the end-user interface may be expressed in sound, functionality, or visuals, such as avatars, icons, and colours. Mara and Appel (2015) for example empirically verified that identical robots are considered cuter when displaying a 'head tilt' rather than an upright head posture. A technology's whole aesthetic may be deemed cute or a singular feature can be identified as cute.

Cute can be defined as 'being attractive in an adorable or endearing way' (Hellén and Sääksjärvi 2013). It can pervade any feature, whether functional or aesthetic, such as avatars, characters, colours, sounds and animations. Dale (2017) describe this as 'the Aww factor', a verbal expression of finding something cute. But while seemingly simple, cuteness does have its complexities. There is no definitive list of characteristics that make something cute. There are, however, some leitmotifs that can be found in marketing, design, and human behaviour studies.

The 'Baby Schema' or 'Kindchenschema' described by Lorenz (1971) is one of those common themes. It can materialise as an avatar or other character visualisation that has an unusually large head in proportion to its body, large eyes, small nose, high forehead, short extremities, and an oddly elastic or clumsy consistency when moving (Lorenz 1971, 154–162). In a small empirical study with young female participants, Glocker et al. (2009) verify that 'high baby schema' pictures of infants are indeed considered cuter than those with 'low baby schema', which feature a narrower face, smaller eyes and a big nose. Either way, they found the baby schema activates a brain region associated with reward processing and biological motivation.

Expressions of emotion can also be deployed in the cute aesthetic. In a study using pictures of infants, Hildebrandt (1983) found that smiling infants were considered cuter than those expressing neutral or negative emotions. Even when the characters are not human but only a smiling 'blob of soft, doughy matter' (Ngai 2012, 64), much like the Bugbies of popular children's TV CBeebies, they can still be perceived as cute.

Language can also be 'cutified' (Ngai 2012, 87), much like 'baby talk' is often expressed by higher intonation, simpler lexicon, and weak syntax. Animated characters in the end-user interface will often speak in high voices, or simple sounds. However, cute design can also be enhanced by incapacitation. For example, characters that cannot speak or do not have a mouth. This, again, is unlikely to be accidental. (See part b in 2.2 Cute Design Consumer Impact). Emotional expression remains important but can be achieved by other semiotics. For example, Cauldwell and Lacey (2020) discuss colour, light and other graphics that communicate cute moods and sentiments such as a 'heart light', a circular light in the centre of the chest (2020, 959). In one of the few empirical studies considering auditory cues of cuteness, Shin and Mattila (2021) find that baby laughs are considered more cute than adult laughs. This corresponds with other studies on auditory cuteness, that found sounds from toys or in music boxes scored high in cuteness if they were high frequency, low energy, much like 'the vocal tract of infants' (Huron 2015). This corresponds to an aspect in the design of Lv et al.'s (2022) empirical study which notes a girl's voice as significantly cuter than a woman's voice.

Cute design consumer impact

It needs us

Cuteness can be associated with vulnerability, dependency, and neediness. This perception of cuteness can be theorised as a spark for the human want to care for what is cute and quickly form a positive affective bond. Glocker et al. (2009) found that this spark readily happens when viewing cute infants, regardless of biological ties.

Cauldwell and Lacey (2020) highlight the Darwinian associations of Lorenz's (1971) 'Baby Schema'. They emphasise 'an evolutionary function of cuteness' as 'the "bias" towards cute significantly enhances the chances of offspring survival' (Cauldwell and Lacey 2020, 957). They refer to Turkle (2010, 8), who states that the cute aesthetic of home robots aims to 'push our Darwinian buttons'. Auditory cues can also to spark a care-taking response, associating cute sounds with being 'fragile, delicate, innocent and vulnerable' (Huron 2015). This aligns with findings that 'babyfacedness' negatively impacts perceptions of competence (Poutvaara, Jordahl, and Berggren 2009), and that people engaging with 'very cute' animals are motivated to be more careful than they are with 'slightly cute' ones (Sherman, Haidt, and Coan 2009). The assumption is that we are psychologically driven to remain close to what is cute and that something cute needs us, potentially overriding autonomous decisions to disengage.

We can trust it

Power differentials have been considered key to cute aesthetic (Ngai 2012, 91). What appears as vulnerable and in need of care is difficult to simultaneously perceive as a threat. The interpretation that something is vulnerable often comes with an association of powerlessness, which can prompt the need to care. However, this illusion of powerlessness can be a dangerous form of deception, to persuade the end user to trust a manipulative tactic. Cute design often maximises this impression of powerlessness by stimulating pity (Harris 2000). A cute avatar, for example, might be weakened, stunted, or limited in some way. Again, this can stimulate the end user's moral code to care and instils trust. Harris (2000, 5) identifies this as a certain sadism of cute design. Intentional design can therefore offer the end user a reassuring digital experience by stimuli of perceived weakness but in actuality be rendering the end users themselves disempowered.

We should play with it

Lorenz' (1971) framework theorises that cute design sparks an innate caring for what is cute. In contrast, Sherman and Haidt (2011) emphasise a socialisation response to cuteness. They suggest that cuteness is not just about instilling a care-taking response but is connected to motivations for social interaction and can elicit affiliative behaviours towards a cute entity, such as touching, holding, petting, playing or talking. An end user might bond with a cute image or a cute gadget by giving it a name. This process, known as anthropomorphisation (attributing humanlike properties to non-human agents or objects), reinforces the emotional connection (Sherman and Haidt 2011).

Through an empirical study, Shin and Mattila (2021) found that cuteness can be deployed in marketing to encourage consumer engagement. Even when cuteness was only conveyed through auditory stimuli, it was effective in steering human behaviour. Lv et al. (2022) found similar results for both visual and auditory stimuli. However, they also note an important difference, that because cute can be considered incompetent, it is preferred for applications that do not require a knowledge-based functionality. The main interpretive appeal is on emotional grounds, making cute design ideally suited for light-hearted, fun gameplay. This builds on childhood theories that idealise the utopia of human childhood and related play. They suggest that when adults perceive something as cute, it triggers an engagement that is marked by a social interaction that they recognise as child-like.

It defines us

Cuteness is theorised as a core spark for the human psyche and socialisation behaviour. This also brings about a defining quality to mark our social status and connections. For example, 'baby talk', as discussed above, is a way of expressing a cuteness response. Whether it's about socialisation (Sherman and Haidt 2011) or biological care response

(Lorenz 1971), the 'baby talk' communication marks the hierarchical relation between a stronger party and something or someone weaker. In interface design, the end user is often made to feel like the stronger party.

Cuteness can also be used as a code for communication. For example, the rounded shapes, colours, and uses of common emoji sets in digital language correspond to cute design. According to a 2015 report, '78 percent of women are frequent users of emoji (using them several times per week), while only 60 percent of men use emoji as frequently. With age also playing a factor, younger audiences showed greater usage of emojis' (Shaul 2015). Language defines social groups, and emojis in particular allow a form of child-like communication in fun pictorial language. This plays into the socialisation response again, on a biopsychological level, as 'social connection can lower anxiety and depression, help us regulate our emotions, lead to higher self-esteem and empathy, and actually improve our immune systems. By neglecting our need to connect, we put our health at risk' (House, Landis, and Umberson 1988). It implies that humans are biologically driven to respond to socialisation stimuli, and a shared language will reaffirm closeness and familiarity from the outset.

Limitations of cute design

End-user context

Perceptions on what is deemed cute can vary culturally. Dale (2017) for example discuss semantic differences between the English 'cute' and the Japanese '*kawaii*'. The latter could be considered cute from a UK perspective but may also have a subtle cultural divergence. A study by Kumagai (2022) shows factors associated with *kawaii* can include baby-like features, femininity and roundness. The study also makes detailed observations about phonetic and phonological patterns, for example, that nasal sounds are considered *kawaii*, or other sounds that can be made with pouting lips.

Aside from cultural context, other factors can play a role. For example, Glocker et al. (2009) note that some studies conclude that women are usually more responsive to the 'Baby Schema' than men, but that there are still inconclusive findings in this regard. In addition, there may be individual variation. For example, not all end users will consider a dog avatar as cute. Cauldwell and Lacey (2020, 957) therefore point out that it may be preferable to deploy imaginary characters and avatars rather than mimic existing animals, as these could be associated with pre-existing experiences and emotions that are negative.

Software and hardware

While we pose cute design as significant, it is important to note that, as a consumer engagement tactic, it operates simultaneously to other design features. This poses a clear limitation to the effectiveness of cute design as a dark pattern on its own. Cute design is most likely found in operation with other design tactics that seek to manipulate the end user.

One such feature constitutes stimuli of personal narrativising (Cauldwell and Lacey 2020, 960). For example, prompting the end user to personalise an avatar, giving it a name and visual optionality. Through gameplay, the character may evolve, creating the perception of responsiveness and growth. The more personalised this narrative functionality is, the more an end user will bond with the technology. The emotional investment of 'the story' builds a foundation for the initial spark of the cute design feature.

Other gameplay tactics build on the foundation of behaviourist reward theory, also used in consumer enticement to gamble, which can become addictive. For example, Albarrán-Torres (2016) critically discusses cuteness as a tactic to mask the problematic consumption of gamble-play media as it can make gambling look and feel harmless. The use of rewards has been said to provide the end user with a dopamine hit and children have been identified as particularly vulnerable to this persuasive design tactic, which encourages the end user to seek immediate gratification (5Rights Foundation 2023, 19–22).

Technological determinism

The end user is not deterministically influenced by a technology. Stockman (2019) discusses how technological determinism implies that technology will have a linear and unavoidable effect on people, while (socio)constructivist views on technology will forefront human autonomy, flexibility, and unpredictability. While predictable effects of cute design have been empirically verified, it is important to maintain that the nature of the human mind is still a considerable force against the manipulative steer of dark patterns. Even frameworks such as Lorenz' (1971) 'Baby Schema' are essentially reductive to human autonomy. For that reason, such theories are also socially and politically dangerous (Dale 2017). It is this human element which should be empowered and protected by the regulatory frameworks, in view of cultural nuances and specific vulnerabilities of certain consumer groups.

Game analysis

Mobile gaming and FarmVille

The global games market, including mobile and other platforms, generated more than $184 billion in 2022 (Newzoo 2022). Mobile gaming makes up the majority of revenue. Compared to traditional gaming media, mobile games do not often demand a high initial purchase cost, but instead rely on micro-transactions or data brokering as a business model. Jibb et al. (2022) point out that this creates serious and oft-overlooked risks to children and their parents, as children's data are among the worst in terms of the number of associated third-party trackers. They also conclude that in-app purchase options pervade the end-user experience and include manipulative delivery methods. A recent example of consumer manipulation of this kind occurred when Epic Games was fined £201 m due to dark patterns that allegedly tricked players into 'making unintended game purchases' (Brown 2023). The FTC claimed that Epic Games used design tricks to get players 'of all ages' to unintentionally make in-game purchases using real money, with 'counterintuitive, inconsistent, and confusing button configuration' that led to unwanted purchases (Brown 2023). At the time of writing, the FTC website stated that users *Fortnite* (a popular online game owned by Epic Games), who were charged for unwanted purchases, can apply for a refund until January 2024 (FTC 2023).

Drawing on *FarmVille* as a concrete example of the cute aesthetic, we critique cute design as potential mask for dark pattern tactics. We do not theorise that cute design will always mean that there is a dark pattern at play. However, where cute design is used in order to manipulate the user and disguise a dark pattern(s), we advocate that these should be referred to using the notion of 'cute but dark' design or patterns. The findings of this analysis are not limited to *FarmVille*, as cute but dark patterns are likely to be found in an array of online games as well as other applications and software. Nevertheless, *FarmVille* is a useful case study by which cute design can be analysed in the context of dark patterns. This serves as a foundation for scholars, end users (children or adults), software developers, policymakers and legislators to carefully consider cute but dark design in their respective significance.

FarmVille is an agriculture simulation game developed by the company Zynga in 2009. Gameplay involves various aspects of farmland management, such as ploughing land, planting, growing and harvesting crops, as well as raising livestock. The first *FarmVille* game was a Flash game available via the social networking website Facebook. The game series remains free-to-play. After launching on Facebook in 2009, *FarmVille* became the most popular game on the site and held that position for over two years. In 2011, Zynga accounted for 12% of Facebook's total profits (Willson and Leaver 2015, 150). Daily active users peaked at 40 m in 2022 (Statista 2023). On 27 September 2020, Zynga announced that it would discontinue the Facebook game on 31 December 2020, as Facebook no longer supported Flash Player games. Following this, *FarmVille 2* and *FarmVille 3* were offered on mobile devices. The focus of this paper, *FarmVille 3* was released in November 2021 and can be played on Android, iOS, Adobe Flash and HTML5 platforms.

Cuteness and data protection

In what follows, we juxtapose the cute aesthetic with the relevant data protection mechanisms, and how the former may interfere with end-user autonomy over the latter. We specifically consider Zynga's Terms of Service (Last Amended: 16th of June 2022), hereafter referred to as 'the Terms', and Community Rules (Last Amended: 21st of May 2018) as well as Take-Two Interactive Software Privacy Policy, hereafter referred to as 'the Privacy Policy' (Last Amended: 26th of April 2023). The analysis is structured in five components that mimic the end-user engagement after download: (1) the app icon, (2) the loading screens, (3) the opening trailers, (4) the recurring pop-ups on start, (5) the game world.

1. The app icon

An app's icon is an important prompt for brand recognition, marketing appeal, and consumer interaction. It is the first point of engagement after download. Current design philosophy indicates that the icon should be reflective of the experience that the end user should expect when interacting with a product: 'increasing downloads, advertising your app's look/style and communicating your app's function' (Workerbee 2017). *FarmVille 3*'s icon at the time of writing shows a woman dressed in casual clothing with a piglet in her arms, having lifted it to her chest, and pressing her nose to its face. The surrounding space has been left empty, suggesting that there is no other information that is required by the end user to understand the expected experience. Though the gameplay is presented as a farm simulation game, the app's icon is more indicative of a 'human-animal' socialisation experience. Cute design is utilised in the promise of connection, through the character designs and emotive poses expressed. Dale (2017) suggests that behind people's willingness to engage with cuteness is a 'drive to enjoy it'... which lurks behind any desire to nurture or engage a cute object'. This nurturing is captured in the small image of the app's icon. The representation of the human to the animal mimics the pose of a mother and child embracing, with their close physical proximity and both facial expressions indicating a strong emotional and happy bond. The end user is more likely to identify with the human character presented, yet during gameplay this character becomes disembodied (apart from cut-scenes). Animals appear as 'NPCs' (non-playable characters) and therefore act more like objects than end-user-steered avatars. It is not possible to pick up animals, and the implied bonding is not a goal within the gameplay. In many ways, the app's icon is not a representation of the gameplay. It only serves to spark engagement when opening the app.

The app's icon further shows both human and animal with eyes closed, suggesting trust and comfort. Neither appears to fear any harm, intrinsic to the cute aesthetic. The piglet has its head titled slightly to the side, suggesting a submission to the parental figure of the mother. In the disembodied state of the gameplay, the end user is cast in the implied role of nurturer. The disarming nature of this pattern merges with a numerical counter during gameplay, therefore offering a nurture success in some regard.

In addition to the design elements of the characters, the choice of colours plays a large part in what message the app icon conveys, and how the user perceives the other visual features displayed. Initially, the colours can be seen to support the cuteness of the characters, soft and muted yellows, pinks, and reds blend together to create a warmth which supports the imagery and draws the user in to the intimacy of the portrayed connection. Desaturated bright colours are considered to be friendly and support the cute design (Anthony 2010). Yet the physiological effects of the colour red make it powerful for encouraging impulse buys, and among large retailers, 59% incorporate red into their branding (Webber 2018). A sense of urgency is incorporated into app icon design more generally, by showing notifications in a red bubble on the top right corner, and a number indicating how many notifications are waiting for the player in the game.

Even before gameplay, *FarmVille 3* utilises the concept of warm, caring, and safe social relationships. The game app's icon is designed for a powerful approach motivation, positive affective bonding and a highly reassuring consumption experience. The end-user decision to download and then open the app goes hand in hand with a data protection decision. As a Zynga product, *FarmVille 3* players must agree to Zynga's Terms of Service. These can be found on the product company website (zynga.com). End users are only formally prompted to agree to these when making an account and it is possible to download *FarmVille 3,* and play it indefinitely, without making an account. In addition, other accounts may be needed, or in some cases are needed, in order to access the game. For example, an Apple account will be needed to download the game via the Apple Store onto a personal iPhone. Zynga's Terms of Service also implies additional compliance to the Community Rules and Take-Two Interactive's Privacy Policy, which is Zynga's parent company. The Privacy Policy considers common topics of data protection regulation such as the collecting and sharing of personal data, data security, and children's privacy. Playing *FarmVille 3* as a thirteen-year-old child therefore places the onus on the child as the end user to read and understand Zynga's Terms of Service, the Community Rules, Take-Two's Privacy Policy. In addition, they will need to have read and understand the Terms of Service of the platform from which the download has occurred (such as Apple or Google), any social networks that interact with the game, any platforms or products that process payments if/when they are made (i.e. PayPal), and any other third-party advertising or marketing interests that run across all of the previously stated platforms and products.

2. The loading screens

An initial assumption appears to be made in the data protection policies that playing the game will simply mean the player has agreed to the Terms: 'When you use our Services, you agree to be bound by these terms and conditions. If you don't agree to all the terms and conditions, you must not use our Services.' This also includes any changes that are made at any point, which 'may' (or by implication, may not) be flagged by additional notice such as email. Formal acknowledgement of end-user agreement to the Terms, Community Rules, or Privacy Policy is prompted when loading the app (after download) as a tick-box screen. The decision is presented as all-or-nothing: other than 'Accept', the only other option is to close the app.

As previously stated, making an account is not required. Yet the Privacy Policy details that personal data can be collected after downloading company software 'even if you do not register for the Services', including:

- name, email address, phone number, photo, mailing address / zip code, payment or purchase information, age, gender, password, platform ID, software products played, survey data, geolocation, and user device information
- gameplay information (platform ID or gaming service ID, game achievements, game scores and performance, IP address, MAC address or other device IDs, other platform / device information, and other information and statistics)
- user name, friends list, and other 'account information necessary to provide the Services or a purchased in-game item' when accessing through third-party platform accounts such as Facebook

This data may be collected by explicit consent or automatically, through tracking technologies, or third-party exchange agreements. It operates across devices and platforms, powerfully linking personal data as individual consumer profiles, and nuanced market insights. The onus is on the end user to follow links to these company policies, to read and understand them, before clicking 'Accept' and thereby resisting the call to play the game as encouraged by the cute design. In their article on Zynga's data mining practices, Willson and Leaver (2015) raise the question:

> What might the responsibilities and also the capacities be of those who offer services to people as a commercial endeavour seemingly for free, but with the trade-off of the release

> of personal and network information without a clear understanding of what will happen to this (personal) information? (p.154)

Targeted advertising is noted as one of the data use intentions in the Privacy Policy. The Policy overtly states that 'In the last 12 months, Take-Two has sold and/or shared unique identifiers, IP address, as well as Internet/Electronic Activity and Profile Inferences with third-party advertising providers to enable us to provide personalized advertising to you and others like you.' Opting out of such commercial use of personal data is accurately noted as a right. Under Article 21 of the UK GDPR, it is posed as a right to object. The Privacy Policy suggests that to opt out, the end user can do so by clicking on the link in the site footer, and separately linked on the Privacy Policy's page upon expanding the collapsed text. This brings the end user to a new page (Last Amended: 29th March 2023), explaining the right to object in legalese, six new suggested links for more help and information, and a dominantly placed suggestion to adjust browser privacy controls. For example, 'an "opt-out" cookie will be stored in your browser indicating that you do not want to receive targeted advertisements'. Somewhat problematic to the legal framework is that an opt-in stance seems to be implied. Further complicating the proposed solution is that the Privacy Policy also stated that 'Our system may not respond to Do Not Track requests or headers from some or all browsers.' It is unclear which browsers would be unsuccessful, or why the system would be unresponsive to these.

The data protection decision-making versus the game's engagement stimuli pose an interesting real-world versus fictional world duality. Further design features of the app mimic this. Initially, a black loading screen appears with a delayed publisher logo appearing. No audio or visual stimuli occurs for approximately four to five seconds, prior to the corporate branding. The software then switches to the main loading screen. This delay creates a boundary between the real-world digital economy and the game's world. It mirrors the initial cinematic trailer (discussed in the next step below) between the mundane and the idyllic worlds. In total, the prompt to launch the app and the second loading screen takes approximately eight seconds. This is the currently held attention span for digital technologies, according to Microsoft; 'people now generally lose concentration after eight seconds' (McSpadden 2015). As such, at the transition into the title loading screen, the user will break from their focus on the screen, and as such the repetition of scrolling messages at the bottom of the screen will be the last conscious engagement. These messages often contain suggestions to make purchases to both improve and personalise gameplay experience.

The second loading screen shows the game logo, characters, and a collection of farm animals. Following the break between reality and game offered in the first loading screen, the second loading screen invites the end user into the game world and reminds them of the different social experiences open to those that enter the game environment. The design of the loading screen shows many different animals and humans together in harmony, with a sense of life, energy, and unity present in the depiction. The animals are engaged in different forms of happy social interaction, and the user's gaze is led up to the empty space between a woman and a horse. Both seemingly welcoming the user: the woman waving a greeting, and the horse having brought a gift of flowers. The empty space could offer the end user to place themselves within the picture, so as to complete the pyramid structure of the characters' arrangement on the hay bales. Altogether, the picture presents a happy, safe community.

The game utilises many aspects of Lorenz's (1971) 'Baby Schema' in its design aesthetics, such as a; 'large head, … large eyes, chubby cheeks, … and plump body shape'. These features combine in a way that can be perceived as cute and elicits caretaking behaviour from the end user. This extends to animals, such as the water buffalo, which might not be considered cute in real-world manifestations. However, with shaggy hair covering the buffalo's eyes, exaggerated plump body shape, and the nuzzling behaviour, a sense of vulnerability and dependency is created. This can spark a human want to care for what is cute, and quickly form a positive affective bond. Additionally, design features exaggerate poses and animal behaviours which can signal an open, playful, and supportive community to the end user. For example, the cat sat upon the farm hand's lap shows positive effects of interaction, with a smiling facial expression and head tilt. Further, the dog is shown engaged in a tug of war with a goat while a second goat chews on the same scarf. Although this scene may imply aggressive behaviour, it is stylised to be fun and harmless, in accordance with cute design principles.

The game environment features many aesthetic choices to mimic the cuteness shown within the character design. There is a distinct absence of hard edges, hard shadows, and all environmental assets contain soft and round elements, including items which one would normally expect to be straight, such as the fence beams which have enough breaks in their continuity to remove the straightness of their normal design. There is little sign of civilisation, with two (also cute) farm buildings strewn out in the background. These design choices spread into the extra-environmental assets of the game's logo, which contains the product title. Font can be 'cutified' when the width exceeds the height; 'letters of lower height-to-width ratio are perceived as cuter and thus more preferable than thinner ones' (Xie et al. 2023). Accordingly, the *FarmVille 3* logo has even been carefully designed so that the end user may see some form of cuteness, and develop a positive affective bond with the product.

The initial stimulus of the app's icon is powerfully reinforced through the loading screens, alongside a real-world versus fictional world disassociation. The fictional world appears to be highly cute, implying safety and trustworthiness. The data protection decision is all-or-nothing, and places great responsibility on the end user to disengage with the alluring gameplay stimuli.

3. The opening trailers

A one-time introductory video auto-plays upon the end user selecting a new game. This opening cinematic serves two purposes: first, it creates a call to action, thus providing purpose, and a reason for the events of the game. The second, to call into question whether the protagonist (the end user) is happy with their current situation. It prompts to consider the alternative of the idealistic game world. The narrative starts by defining the social relationship to the farm's owner, Marie. She is a childhood friend, and as such is a part of an existing social group with the end user. This reinforces trust and defines the end user's position. Marie is therefore part of the close friend status. Massot (2019) identified the importance of childhood friends, stating that they

> were witnesses of our first steps, in every way. Together with our neighbors and classmates, we learned to add and subtract, to write in cursive, to play games and sports, and so forth.

> Maybe we learned to play musical instruments together. Above all, we had fun together, and shared countless experiences during that stage of our lives.

The friend status of Marie prompts the player to remember the emotions they felt during their real-world childhood friendships. In doing so, *FarmVille 3* is able to hide the call to action behind an established sense of community and trust with a familiar frame of reference for the end user. The message is clear: save the farm and help your friend. It fits the cute aesthetic. This cut-scene is the only instance of the player having a physical body representation in the end-user interface. Post cut-scene, the player takes on a high-position camera, as though above the world.

FarmVille 3 also utilises the antithesis of cuteness as a prompt for end-user engagement. The opening cinematic highlights mundanity, chaos, and inhuman nature of the real-world, against the idyllic nature of the previous loading screen. The design of the environment and visual aids which an end user is exposed to, play a large part in not only world building, but also in seeking to link cuteness to a better life, where the end user can escape their dull and mundane life for an idyllic world. A recent YouGov poll found that 37% of British working adults believe that their job is not 'making a meaningful contribution to the world' (Walo 2023). This mundanity and lack of impact is shown by the environmental design of the real-world in the app. The washed-out hues of the dull greys and blues suggest a cold, lifeless, and unchanging environment. This idea is also apparent through the inclusion of a fog/smog layer, and a fade, which obscures not only the ground and the sky, but even close by buildings. Further, and in contrast to the soft visuals of the preceding loading screen, the world is made of buildings all of which are entirely composed of very sharp edges, with rectangles sat upon rectangles, and hard shadows fall upon the environment. Being unable to discern any other sign of human activity can conjure thoughts of isolation, anti-community, and anti-socialisation. Unlike the harmonious, communal displays of the loading screen, the city is a sprawling collection of haphazardly placed buildings. In contrast to the idyllic game world, which is saturated by meaningful social relationships, there is no implied connection or communication.

4. Pop-ups

Pop-up ads appear for in-game item packs at the start of the gameplay. This is a reoccurring step which locks gameplay until the end user manually selects each of the multiple offers and closes them. End users are presented with multiple, cute animals in a row, all posed to show excitement and alertness in response to the end user's return. The previously discussed cute features, expressed though Lorenz's work (1971), are present once again. However, these features combine with additional effects to create a level of anticipation not seen by the end user thus far. Characters are shown lent forward with their eyes open wide. This design harkens back to the original game, which was

> more than happy to bribe players for participating in its viral spread: cute lonely animals will show up on your farm periodically and as a player you face a dilemma in sentencing them to virtual abandonment and death unless you post on your Facebook wall that you need one of your friends to start playing *FarmVille* and 'adopt' the adorable little self-promoter. (Newheiser 2009)

In *FarmVille 3,* a one-time payment can save the animals and add them to the farm – or, should the user decide against it, then they consign the animal to 'virtual abandonment and death', although this is not shown visually. Violence, like slaughter of livestock (required to gain meat products from the animals, for example), is muted: unproductive animals are sent to a happy retirement on a commune. Much like Rose (2023, 5) identifies in the game *Animal Crossing: New Horizons*, the *FarmVille* games reproduce capitalist and post-industrial market dynamics present in the lives of the adult players, but 'cutified'. From a similar analytical conclusion, the soft and gentle environment of *FarmVille* appeals to the adult consumer in today's digital economy because it simplifies the productive burden, minimising punishment over failure, and maximising reward for mere engagement. It 'cutifies' the livestock handling process, to being a simply case of either they are producing, and therefore valuable, or not producing. In the game, the animals will then be sitting, with droopy ears, some showing fear or uncertainty in their behaviour, and lethargically staring. Their weakness to feed themselves is a clear prompt to the nurturer, i.e. the end user. This interaction will be rewarded, the end user will earn points that contribute to levelling up.

5. The game world

Upon loading the game, and until the farm is named, a large arrow points to the name of the farm, indicating urgency by its red colour. Once selected the end user is prompted to rename the farm. As previously discussed, Sherman and Haidt (2011) emphasised the importance of personalisation. Accordingly, Degges-White (2016) has suggested that there is 'great power in naming things'. Through the act of bestowing a name, the end user creates their own social experience and establishes ties and emotional bonds with people and things. In doing so, the end user brings the farm, and the virtual world, closer, be that to control, to care, or to bring it into part of an established social relationship. Additionally, the act of naming can change the end user's method of thinking towards the farm. Naming a possession not only indicates affection but also triggers further bonding with that object. The act of naming is also a claim and, as the end user has been placed in the nurturing position, they can assume that role.

As part of the gameplay, the end user gathers items or crops that were left to finish from the previous session. This adds to daily challenge goals for immediate non-premium currency rewards. When doing so, the end user completes delivery items via a board, each item rewards the player with non-premium currency, while also building a visible progress bar. Once the bar is filled the end user receives a loot box which contains a low value animal. After completing five bars the end user receives a loot box containing higher-value items. This is a timed challenge and will reset every twenty-four hours. In doing so, *FarmVille* normalises the concept of caring for the villagers, who depend on the end user for their needs, thus forming a sense of dependency and vulnerability. At first, goods are requested for the villagers, for which the end user is rewarded by game currency or random loot chests. As the player develops the farm, villagers begin appearing outside the farm, jumping up and down and waving their arms. The villagers are one of the few NPCs that directly gesture to the player, and their behaviour shows a sense of urgency. The end user is represented in the world through a God's eye view, looking down upon their realm of dependents.

In-game rewards, such as an upgrade or added game currency, are available to the end user. The Terms clearly state how this may occur:

> Sometimes we provide links in our games or on the Services to other third-party companies' websites or to companies who invite you to participate in a promotional offer and offer you some feature of the Services or upgrade (such as in-game currency) in exchange.

Although end-user engagement is clearly stimulated by the reward mechanism, responsibility is again shifted firmly to end-user decision-making:

> Any charge or obligation you take on in dealing with these other companies is your responsibility. We are not responsible for any third-party website that we link to in our Services, and such a link does not mean we endorse or approve that linked site or any information you obtain from it. We are not liable for any claim relating to any content, goods, and/or services of third parties.

This is echoed in the Privacy Policy:

> Our Services may direct you to third-party sites. If we link to another site, it is not an endorsement, authorization, or representation of our affiliation with that third party. Please review the privacy policy of the other site before you submit any of your personal information to that site.

The shifting responsibilities may appear odd, in that the links to third-party companies do not appear randomly or unintentionally in the company's product. With regard to data ownership, the end user is placed in another precarious position as stated in the Terms: 'Please also note that the linked third-party sites are not under our control and may collect data or ask you to provide them with personal or other information, or they may automatically collect information from you.' It is stated that those third parties 'may (or may not) ask you for permission' to collect that data. While it is indeed not Zynga's responsibility to monitor other companies' legal compliance, it is concerning that unlawful data harvesting is noted as a possibility. While the end user is responsible, they have also been powerfully influenced by the cute design of the game to engage (because the villagers are in need, because the real-world is undesirable, because the game world appears safe and happy, because the end user is the prime nurturer etc.). In compliance with their own legal responsibilities, Take-Two Interactive's Privacy Policy further details that third-party platforms may be a source for the information they collect, either by explicit consent, or automatically through tracking technologies, or via their own third-party information exchanges. There is no list provided about which third-party exchanges may take place, aligning with previously noted transparency concerns on the data mining practices (Willson and Leaver 2015). The only certainty appears to be that it will happen, but it is unclear exactly when, which data, why, to which companies, and for how long.

It is also noted as a possibility that other end users could seek to unlawfully gather or otherwise use personal data. The advice given in the Terms is as follows: 'If you have an idea or information that you would like to keep confidential and/or don't want others to use, don't post it.' In the Zynga Community Rules (a separate policy), it's also stated end users should not (A) try to unlawfully obtain login information or account access belonging to other players, (B) seek to harvest other otherwise use other player's data, either actively or (C) passively by spyware technologies. Again, agreement to the Community Rules remains implicit to playing the game. It is unclear whether or how monitoring these end user dynamics occur in practice. Although, as previously stated, the Terms clarify that there is no obligation for Zynga to monitor 'the conduct of other players, and we take no responsibility for such conduct'. Instead, 'You are responsible for your interactions with other players. If you have a problem with another player, we are not required to get involved, but we can if we desire.' While there is no obligation, they do maintain

> the right, in our sole discretion, to monitor, record, or store your interactions with the Services or your communications with Zynga or other player when you are using the Services (including without limitation your communications through in-game text or video chat), in accordance with applicable privacy law.

Notably, communication data was not listed as part of the Privacy Policy.

Data protection law such as the UK GDPR does state that end users can request deletion of their data at any time (Article 17), and that data controllers such as product companies should delete data automatically after a certain time when it is no longer needed (Article 5(1)(c)). However, the regulatory framework also leaves a crucial grey area for interpretation in that regard, which can be exploited by companies with an interest in data commodities. When *FarmVille* players request deletion of an account and related user content, Zynga's Terms state that:

> we will take reasonable steps to remove your User Content from active use, which may include suppression of your User Content in our systems. However, User Content may persist in our systems, including in back-up copies. We may also retain copies of User Content if we reasonably believe it is legally required.

The terminology of 'reasonable' decision and actions alongside tentative auxiliary verbs form a common approach to allow interpretive space. Requesting deletion is, however, listed as a data right in the Take-Two Interactive Privacy Policy, which (upon expansion of the collapsed text), links to a data rights request page (Last Amended: 30th May 2023). On this page, Zynga is listed as the sixth item on a page of thirteen data processors under the purview of Take-Two Interactive. The end user can either scroll down further and complete a form on this page, or continue to Zynga's own data request page.

Regulatory frameworks

Legislators have traditionally refrained from closely regulating digital design (Jarovsky 2022; Vanberg 2023) and there is no clear definition of dark patterns in English law. Yet OECD (2022, 19) concluded the rate of dark patterns to be very high across popular apps, including those accessed lawfully by children. Jibb et al. (2022) further point out that privacy policies are sometimes missing or lacking, and that legislation over (children's) personal data has not kept pace with the proliferation of commercial data handling.

Zynga's Terms of Service state that children cannot enter into a binding contract, with 'children' defined as 'someone (a) under 13 years old or, if older, (b) between 13 and 18 years old but under the age at which you can give valid consent to processing of your personal information under applicable data privacy laws'. In the UK children are considered to be any person under the age of eighteen, consistent with the UN Convention on the Rights of the Child. In the UK context, data protection law stipulates the age of thirteen years as the valid data consent threshold, awarding the same rights and responsibilities as adults (Article 8, UK GDPR). Historically, this coincides with previous *FarmVille* versions, available to play via the Facebook platform, to which the sign-up age is also thirteen years. The Terms also state that: 'If you are under the age of 18, or under the age of majority where you are located, you represent that your legal guardian has reviewed and agreed to these Terms.' This all aligns with the Privacy Policy, which states that the company will not 'knowingly collect personal information from children under thirteen years old', but also that 'We do not sell or share personal information about persons that we know are under the age of sixteen without their (or depending on age, their parent's) consent.' There is no age verification method and there is also uncertainty as to whether a child, or holder of parental responsibility has truly consented to the processing of data, raising queries as to the compatibility of *FarmVille 3* with Articles 7 and 8 of the UK GDPR with reference to the definition of consent as being 'freely given, specific, informed and unambiguous' (Article 4(11) GDPR).

Our analysis of *FarmVille 3* demonstrates that children are lawfully exposed to what we identify as cute but dark patterns. They are also engaging in a binding contract of personal data exchange. It is notable that considerable data has already been collected through previous *FarmVille* versions. As these were accessed through Facebook, the individual gameplay data pervasively linked to other personal data harvested through the social media profile. It is unclear what happened to the data assets in the product ownership transfer. Children who played the first *FarmVille* on Facebook in 2009 at age thirteen (and therefore are twenty-eight years old today) may have agreed to a personal data exchange with this company at that time, but their data may be owned by an entirely different company today. If so, it is also unclear how that data is being used today, and whether their adult identity is linked to other data sets. The nebulous nature of personal data transfers, links, and uses is a significant threat to individuals engaging with any online technologies.

In the UK, the regulatory approach to dark patterns is piecemeal. Various data protection and consumer regulations manage the protection of the UK consumer in the context of digital technologies, with some further specified to children, such as rules for advertising towards children and the design of online platforms for children. The interaction of different frameworks (some ratified in law and some posed as guidance) causes significant complexities which product companies can harness to their benefit. Much regulation, including the UK GDPR is silent about the concept of dark patterns and manipulative design tactics (Jarovsky 2022), including cute design – a notable absence. Jarovsky (2022) has identified that the GDPR may not provide sufficient protection from dark patterns. The GDPR is largely focused on the data processing phase, but dark patterns occur at the data collection phase and in the design interface (Jarovsky 2022).

The compatibility of dark patterns with elements of the UK GDPR (2016/679) framework is questionable. Influencing decisions by providing biased information can be considered contrary to the principle of fairness of processing and transparency of information (Article 5(1)(a), Article 12(1) UK GDPR). For the ICO (2023, 7), fairness involves handling 'personal data in ways that people would reasonably expect and not use it in ways that have unjustified adverse effects on them'. They advise that, personal data should not be collected by deception or by people being misled and suggest that individual and collective interests of the concerned data subjects should be considered. It could be deemed that dark patterns breach the principle of fairness and the impact on children is potentially even greater (OECD 2022). This highlights the need for frameworks to consider specific vulnerabilities, for example sociodemographic and culturally varied responses to cute design that may heighten the emotional steer. The response to cute design sits alongside other known vulnerabilities: for example, Jibb et al. (2022, 672) point out parents and children of lower socioeconomic status may more frequently engage with free apps, which more frequently contain in-app purchases or advertisements.

Dark patterns can also negatively impact a data subject from exercising their data protection rights (Article 12(2) UK GDPR). Rieger and Sinders (2020) have expressed key concerns posed by dark design including: the erosion of privacy; weakening of the protections afforded by the GDPR; challenges for consumer protection; advantages to be gained by dominant market players as well as particular issues for children. They do not propose new law-making, but instead that relevant consumer protection and data protection agencies should examine how current law applies to deceptive design and use this information to launch complaints or take legal action in the courts. Accordingly, they have suggested that policymakers and regulators should take action against serious forms of dark pattern, including those which systematically undermine the law (Rieger and Sinders 2020, 22–23). In recent years, regulatory bodies have published reports which specifically focus on dark patterns including the OECD (2022), the CMA (2021; 2022) and the FTC (2022). In February 2023, the European Data Protection Board published guidelines which aim to give end users control over their data. The guidelines explain that data protection authorities can sanction organisations if their use of dark patterns breaches the GDPR. Standards set out in the ICO's Age Appropriate Design Code (2020) should also go some way to limiting the dark patterns that can be used in digital technologies accessed by children, which include manipulation through interface design. Standard 13 specifically states that nudge techniques should not be used to lead or encourage children to provide unnecessary personal data or weaken or turn off their privacy protections. The code also mandates that the best interests of the child should be the primary consideration (standard 1) and endorses the principles of transparency (standard 4), data minimisation (standard 8) and privacy by default (standard 7).

In recent years, legislation has been developed in other jurisdictions which specifically addresses dark patterns. In the USA, the California Privacy Rights Act, which came into force in 2020, defined a dark pattern as 'a user interface designed or manipulated with the substantial effect of subverting or impairing user autonomy, decision making, or choice'. Accordingly, this jurisdiction can ban dark patterns which have 'the substantial effect of subverting or impairing a consumer's choice to opt-out'. Non-compliance results in companies being sent a 'notice to cure', whereby they are given thirty days to amend their services and, if changes are not made, they could face a penalty. The legislation further stipulates that 'agreement obtained through use of dark patterns does not constitute consent'. The EU's Digital Services Act defines dark patterns as 'practices that materially distort or impair, either purposefully or in effect, the ability of recipients of the service to make autonomous and informed choices or decisions'. Article 25(1) states that, 'Providers of online platforms shall not design, organise or operate their online interfaces in a way that deceives, manipulates or otherwise materially distorts or impairs the ability of recipients of their service to make free and informed decisions'. UK companies operating overseas therefore need to carefully consider their use of dark patterns.

Various consumer protection laws can also come into play in the regulation of dark patterns, including Consumer Contracts (Information Cancellation and Additional Charges) Regulations 2013, Consumer Protection from Unfair Trading Regulations, 2008, Consumer Rights Act 2015 and Unfair Terms in Consumer Contracts Regulations 1999. These pieces of legislation protect consumers by giving them *inter alia* rights to cancel contracts made via the internet, protecting consumer transactions and prohibitions on businesses using unfair contract terms or adopting unfair commercial practices that hamper informed decision-making when making purchases. Cuteness has been empirically established as applicable to marketing practices in steering consumer behaviour (Shin and Mattila 2021). However, because it powerfully impacts on the human psyche, and because it does not cause overt distress, it has not been explicitly considered in consumer protection frameworks. But cuteness can mask commodification of the end user. This necessitates critical consideration for the nature and form of the legal regulatory framework required to effectively manage it in light of consumer protection.

While our focus has been the data protection and consumer protection issues, it is a notable concern that children are also lawfully exposed to other potential online harms. The Terms for example clearly state convicted sex offenders cannot play *FarmVille 3*. There is no verification or monitoring of this, as stated: 'We have no obligation to monitor the Services for inappropriate or illegal User Content or the conduct of other players, and we take no responsibility for such conduct.' End users can report abuse, and the company reserves the right to delete accounts without notice or liability. These are different connotations to a darkness that might be masked by cuteness, much like the use of cuteness as a mask for gambling (Albarrán-Torres 2016). *FarmVille 3*'s current company owner also runs zyngapoker.com, running by the same Terms of Service.

Conclusion

Cute design is powerful. It is an intentional design choice, with an empirical foundation that shows its psychological impact on human feelings, decision, and behaviour. It pervades software for children and adults alike, manipulating end-user autonomy in light of personal data ownership and control. 'Cutification' of digital technologies can mask the dark pattern tactic that commodifies the end user as a data point. The cute aesthetic inherently carries a manipulative steer that aims to hook the end user. This raises concern over cute design as a potential dark pattern. However, cute design in digital technologies should not necessarily be instantly regarded as a dark pattern, as it is possible for cute design to be used without the presence of dark patterns. Nevertheless, where dark patterns are utilised, cute design is particularly effective to conceal yet simultaneously enhance consumer manipulation.

Cute design is not specifically acknowledged in the existing literature on dark patterns, although there are some known dark pattern features which often appear under the guise of cuteness such as emotional steering, behavioural rewards and loot boxes (OECD 2022; 5Rights Foundation 2023). Using *FarmVille 3* as a case study, this paper illustrates how cute design can materialise through a popular game application. The game design can be deemed dark, though our analysis also finds the game to be very cute. As these insights do not exclusively apply to *FarmVille 3*, but point out trends in online software more generally, we suggest that the notion of cute but dark design should be added to the mainstream critical discourse underpinning effective data protection.

This paper has provided a more extensive analysis of cute design than is offered in existing dark patterns literature, bringing together theoretical understandings of human behavioural responses to cute design. This is situated alongside a discussion of cute design as an established marketing tactic for both children and adults, and the steer of the cute aesthetic on consumer autonomy.

Terms of Service or other policies routinely waiver their own responsibilities with regard to other company policies, and firmly place sole responsibility with the end user. Legally, there is no issue in doing so. Yet the multitude of policies makes this a Machiavellian task, especially for children as the end user. The appeal of reading one or more Terms of Service, even if formally prompted to read and agree, is infinitely less than the appeal of cute design to engage with the product and begin play. More explicit reference to the dark patterns used in Terms of Service and Privacy Notices would go some way to achieving better compatibility with the principles fairness and transparency in the UK GDPR (Article 5(1)(a), Article 12(1)) but this does still place the burden on the end user, who might be resigned to the fact that there are dark patterns or have no choice but to accept them if they want to use a particular platform.

The cuteness of *FarmVille 3* appeals to many adults, but the application can be accessed lawfully by children from the age of thirteen, and there is evidence of children younger than thirteen engaging with the game. The legal frameworks do not sufficiently protect consumers (children or adults) against dark patterns masked by cute design. In the UK, there is no specific regulation on dark patterns. Part of the complexity is therefore pinpointing cute design within the various regulatory frameworks relating to data protection and consumer protection. A more streamlined approach to regulation, following the approach in some other jurisdictions, may offer greater protection to consumers but global regulation for internationally available technologies may not be effective due to cultural variations in the cute aesthetic.

We argue that, even in spite of dark pattern tactics, the human mind remains considerable force against the manipulative steer of persuasive design and thus regulators should empower this human element in end-user engagement with dark patterns, in light of cultural nuances and the vulnerabilities of certain consumer groups. Cute design in any guise is a widespread, powerful mechanism to enable dark patterns but until regulation is implemented or updated, to offer better protection or stricter rules for companies on their use of dark patterns, end users should be mindful that when they see or hear something cute, it might also be dark.

Disclosure statement

No potential conflict of interest was reported by the author(s).

References

5Rights Foundation. 2023. "Disrupted Childhood." https://5rightsfoundation.com/uploads/Disrupted-Childhood-2023.pdf.

Albarrán-Torres, César. 2016. "Kittens, Farms, and Wild Pandas: The Impact of Cuteness in Adult Gamble-Play Media." In *The Aesthetics and Affects of Cuteness*, edited by Joshua Paul Dale, Joyce Goggin, Julia Leyda, Anthony P. McIntyre, and Diane Negra, 245–262. New York: Routledge.

Anthony. 2010. "How Color Saturation Affects User Efficiency." *Uxmovement*. https://uxmovement.com/content/how-color-saturation-affects-user-efficiency/.

Brignull, Harry. 2010. "Dark Patterns: Dirty Tricks Designers Use to Make People Do Stuff." https://90percentofeverything.com/2010/07/08/dark-patterns-dirty-tricks-designers-use-to-make-people-do-stuff/.

Brown, Andy. 2023. "'Fortnite' Studio Hit with £201 Million Fine and Ordered to Stop Tricking Players." *NME*. https://www.nme.com/news/gaming-news/fortnite-studio-hit-with-201million-fine-and-ordered-to-stop-tricking-players-3413448.

California Privacy Rights Act. 2020. *California Consumer Privacy Act (CCPA)*. https://oag.ca.gov/privacy/ccpa.

Cauldwell, Catherine, and Cherie Lacey. 2020. "What Do Home Robots Want? The Ambivalent Power of Cuteness in Robotic Relationships." *Convergence: The International Journal of Research into New Media Technologies* 26 (4): 956–968. https://doi.org/10.1177/1354856519837792.

Competition and Markets Authority. 2021. *Algorithms: How They Can Reduce Competition and Harm Consumers*. https://www.gov.uk/government/publications/algorithms-how-they-can-reduce-competition-and-harm-consumers/algorithms-how-they-can-reduce-competition-and-harm-consumers.

Competition and Markets Authority. 2022. *Online Choice Architecture. How Digital Design Can Harm Competition and Consumers*. Discussion Paper. https://assets.publishing.service.gov.uk/government/uploads/system/uploads/attachment_data/file/1066524/Online_choice_architecture_discussion_paper.pdf.

Dale, Joshua Paul. 2017. "The Appeal of the Cute Object: Desire, Domestication, and Agency." In *The Aesthetics and Affects of Cuteness*, edited by Joshua Paul Dale, Joyce Goggin, Julia Leyda, Anthony P. McIntyre, and Diane Negra, 35–56. New York: Routledge.

Defend Digital Me. 2021. *A Reflection on the UNCRC Best Interests of the Child Principle in the Context of the Age Appropriate Design Code*. https://defenddigitalme.org/wp-content/uploads/2021/10/A-Reflection-on-the-Best-Interests-of-the-Child-in-the-context-of-the-Age-Appropriate-Design-Code-05102021-v2.0.pdf.

Degges-White, Suzanne. 2016. "Pet Names Between Couples Are a Very Good Sign." *Psychology Today*. https://www.psychologytoday.com/us/blog/lifetime-connections/201603/pet-names-between-couples-are-very-good-sign.

Digital Services Act: Regulation (EU) 2022/2065 of the European Parliament and of the Council of 19 October 2022 on a Single Market for Digital Services and Amending Directive 2000/31/EC (Text with EEA relevance).

European Data Protection Board. 2023. *Deceptive Design Patterns in Social Media Platform Interfaces: How to Recognise and Avoid Them*. https://edpb.europa.eu/our-work-tools/our-documents/guidelines/guidelines-032022-deceptive-design-patterns-social-media_en.

Federal Trade Commission. 2022. *Bringing Dark Patterns to Light*. https://www.ftc.gov/reports/bringing-dark-patterns-light.

Federal Trade Commission. 2023. *Fortnite Refunds*. https://www.ftc.gov/enforcement/refunds/fortnite-refunds.

GDPR: Regulation (EU) 2016/679 of the European Parliament and of the Council of 27 April 2016 on the Protection of Natural Persons with Regard to the Processing of Personal Data and on the Free Movement of Such Data, and Repealing Directive 95/46/EC (General Data Protection Regulation).

Glocker, Melanie L., Daniel D. Langleben, Kosha Ruparel, James W. Loughead, Jeffrey N. Valdez, Marl D. Griffin, Norbert Sachser, and Ruben C. Gur. 2009. "Baby Schema Modulates the Brain Reward System in Nulliparous Women." *Proceedings of the National Academy of Sciences of the United States of America* 106 (22): 9115–9119. https://doi.org/10.1073/pnas.0811620106.

Harris, Daniel. 2000. *Cute, Quaint, Hungry and Romantic: The Aesthetics of Consumerism*. Boston: De Capo Press.

Hartzog, Woodrow. 2018. "The Case Against Idealizing Control." *European Data Protection Law Review* 4 (4): 423–432. https://doi.org/10.21552/edpl/2018/4/5.

Hellén, Katarina, and Maria Sääksjärvi. 2013. "Development of a Scale Measuring Childlike Anthropomorphism in Products." *Journal of Marketing Management* 29 (1–2): 141–157. https://doi.org/10.1080/0267257X.2012.759989.

Hildebrandt, K. A. 1983. "Effect of Facial Expression Variations on Ratings of Infants' Physical Attractiveness." *Developmental Psychology* 19 (3): 414–417. https://doi.org/10.1037/0012-1649.19.3.414.

House, James S., Karl R. Landis, and Debra Umberson. 1988. "Social Relationships and Health." *Science* 241 (4865): 540–545. https://doi.org/10.1126/science.3399889.

Huron, David. 2015. "Affect Induction Through Musical Sounds: An Ethological Perspective." *Philosophical Transactions of the Royal Society*. 370 (1664): 20140098. https://doi.org/10.1098/rstb.2014.0098.

Information Commissioner's Office. 2020. *Age Appropriate Design: A Code of Practice for Online Services*. https://ico.org.uk/for-organisations/uk-gdpr-guidance-and-resources/childrens-information/childrens-code-guidance-and-resources/introduction-to-the-childrens-code/.

Information Commissioner's Office. 2023. *A Guide to the Data Protection Principles*. https://ico.org.uk/media/for-organisations/uk-gdpr-guidance-and-resources/data-protection-principles/a-guide-to-the-data-protection-principles-0-0.pdf.

Jarovsky, Luiza. 2022. "Dark Patterns in Personal Data Collection: Definition, Taxonomy and Lawfulness." https://papers.ssrn.com/sol3/papers.cfm?abstract_id=4048582.

Jibb, Lindsay, Elsie Amoako, Melissa Heisey, Lily Ren, and Quinn Grundy. 2022. "Data Handling Practices and Commercial Features of Apps Related to Children: A Scoping Review of Content Analyses." *Archives of Disease in Childhood* 107 (7): 665–673. https://doi.org/10.1136/archdischild-2021-323292.

Kennedy, Ann-Marie, Katharine Jones, and Williams Janine. 2019. "Children as Vulnerable Consumers in Online Environments." *Journal of Consumer Affairs* 53 (4): 1478–1506. https://doi.org/10.1111/joca.12253.

Kumagai, Gakuji. 2022. "What's in a Japanese *Kawaii* 'Cute' Name? A Linguistic Perspective." *Frontiers in Psychology* 13:1–9. https://doi.org/10.3389/fpsyg.2022.1040415. PMID: 36438396; PMCID: PMC9683379.

Lorenz, Konrad. 1971. *Studies in Animal and Human Behavior*. Cambridge: Harvard University Press.

Lv, Xingyang, Jingjing Luo, Yuqing Liang, Yuqing Liu, and Chunxiao Li. 2022. "Is Cuteness Irresistible? The Impact of Cuteness on Customers' Intentions to Use AI Applications." *Tourism Management* 90:104472. https://doi.org/10.1016/j.tourman.2021.104472.

Mara, Martina, and Markus Appel. 2015. "Effects of Lateral Head Tilt on the User Perceptions of Humanoid and Android Robots." *Computers in Human Behaviour* 44:326–334. https://doi.org/10.1016/j.chb.2014.09.025.

Massot, Dolors. 2019. "6 Reasons Why Childhood Friends are so Valuable When We're Adults." *Aleteia*. https://aleteia.org/2019/05/14/6-reasons-childhood-friends-are-so-valuable-when-were-adults/.

Mathur, Arunesh, Gunes Acar, Michael J. Friedman, Eli Lucherini, Jonathan Mayer, Marshini Chetty, and Arvind Narayanan. 2019. "Dark Patterns at Scale: Findings from a Crawl of 11 K Shopping Websites." In *Proceedings of the ACM on Human-Computer Interaction*, 3 (CSCW). Article 81. https://doi.org/10.1145/3359183.

Mathur, Arunesh, Jonathan Mayer, and Mihir Kshirsagar. 2021. "What Makes a Dark Pattern … Dark? Design Attributes, Normative Considerations, and Measurement Methods." In *CHI Conference on Human Factors in Computing Systems (CHI '21)*, May 8–13, 2021, Yokohama, Japan. New York: ACM.

McSpadden, Kevin. 2015. "You Now Have a Shorter Attention Space Than a Goldfish." *TIME*. https://time.com/3858309/attention-spans-goldfish/.

Newheiser, Mark. 2009. "FarmVille, Social Gaming, and Addiction." *GameDeveloper*. https://www.gamedeveloper.com/design/farmville-social-gaming-and-addiction.

Newzoo. 2022. "Newzoo Global Gamers Market Report 2022." https://newzoo.com/resources/trend-reports/newzoo-global-games-market-report-2022-free-version.

Ngai, Sianne. 2012. *Our Aesthetic Categories: Zany, Cute, Interesting*. Cambridge: Harvard University Press.

Nodder, C. 2013. *Evil by Design: Interaction Design to Lead Us into Temptation*. Indianapolis: Wiley and Sons.

OECD. 2022. *Dark Commercial Patterns*. OECD Digital Economy Papers, No. 336. https://www.oecd.org/digital/dark-commercial-patterns-44f5e846-en.htm.

Poutvaara, Panu, Henrik Jordahl, and Niclas Berggren. 2009. "Faces of Politicians: Babyfacedness Predicts Inferred Competence but not Electoral Success." *Journal of Experimental Social Psychology* 45 (5): 1132–1135. https://doi.org/10.1016/j.jesp.2009.06.007.

Radesky, Jenny, Alexis Hiniker, Caroline McLaren, Eliz Akgun, Alexandria Schaller, Heidi M. Weeks, Scott Campbell, and Ashley N. Gearhardt. 2022. "Prevalence and Characteristics of Manipulative Design in Mobile Applications Used by Children." *Jama Network Open* 5 (6): 1–11.

Rieger, Sebastian, and Caroline Sinders. 2020. "Dark Patterns: Regulating Digital Design." *Stiftung Neue Verantwortung*. https://www.stiftung-nv.de/sites/default/files/dark.patterns.english.pdf.

Rose, Megan C. 2023. "Playful, Sociable, Cute, Quarantine – Interactions with Kawaii Characters in Animal Crossing: New Horizons During COVID-19." *Japanese Studies* 43 (3): 297–311. https://doi.org/10.1080/10371397.2023.2211944.

Shaul, Brandy. 2015. "Report: 92% of Online Consumers Use Emoji (Infographic)." *Adweek*. https://www.adweek.com/performance-marketing/report-92-of-online-consumers-use-emoji-infographic/.

Sherman, Gary D., and Jonathan Haidt. 2011. "Cuteness and Disgust: The Humanizing and Dehumanizing Effects of Emotion." *Emotion Review* 3 (3): 245–251. https://doi.org/10.1177/1754073911402396.

Sherman, Gary D., Jonathan Haidt, and James A. Coan. 2009. "Viewing Cute Images Increases Behavioral Carefulness." *Emotion* 9 (2): 282–286. https://doi.org/10.1037/a0014904.

Shin, Joongwon, and Anna S. Mattila. 2021. "Aww Effect: Engaging Consumers in 'Non-Cute' Prosocial Initiatives with Cuteness." *Journal of Business Research* 126:209–220. https://doi.org/10.1016/j.jbusres.2020.11.046.

Statista. 2023. "Average Monthly Active Users (MAU) of Zynga Mobile Games from 4th Quarter 2012 to 1st Quarter 2022." https://www.statista.com/statistics/273569/monthly-active-users-of-zynga-games/.

Stockman, Caroline. 2019. *Decoding Technology Acceptance in Education*. London: Routledge.

Thaler, Richard H., and Cass R. Sunstein. 2013. "Choice Architecture." In *The Behavioral Foundations of Public Policy*, edited by E. Shafir, 428–439. Princeton: Princeton University Press.

Turkle, Sherry. 2010. "In Good Company? On the Threshold of Robotic Companions." In *Close Engagements with Artificial Companions: Key Social, Psychological, Ethical and Design Issues*, edited by Yorick Wilks, 3–10. Amsterdam: John Benjamins. https://doi.org/10.1075/nlp.8.03tur.

Vanberg, Aysem Diker. 2023. "Coordinating Digital Regulation in the UK: Is the Digital Regulation Cooperation Forum (DRCF) up to the Task?" *International Review of Law, Computers and Technology* 37 (2): 128–146. https://doi.org/10.1080/13600869.2023.2192566.

Walo, Simon. 2023. "'Bullshit' After All? Why People Consider Their Jobs Socially Useless." *Work, Employment and Society* 37 (5): 1123–1146. https://doi.org/10.1177/09500170231175771.

Webber, Pam. 2018. "How Color Impacts Your Retail Brand." *MyTotalRetail*. https://www.mytotalretail.com/article/how-color-impacts-your-retail-brand/.

Willson, Michele, and Tama Leaver. 2015. "Zynga's FarmVille, Social Games, and the Ethics of Big Data Mining." *Communication Research and Practice* 1 (2): 147–158. https://doi.org/10.1080/22041451.2015.1048039.

Workerbee. 2017. "How to Design an App Icon: The Ultimate Guide." *99Designs*. https://99designs.com/blog/web-digital/how-to-design-app-icons/.

Xie, Zhipeng, Tao Wang, Jing Zhao, and Huanyu Qin. 2023. "Too Thin to be Cute: The Influence of Letter Height-to-Width Ratio on Consumer Perception." *Journal of Product and Brand Management* 32 (6): 789–798. https://doi.org/10.1108/JPBM-05-2022-3977.

Zagal, José P., Staffan Bjork, and Chris Lewis. 2013. "Dark Patterns in the Design of Games." In *Foundations of Digital Games Conference*, FDG 2013, 14–17 May, Chania, Greece. http://www.fdg2013.org/program/papers/paper06_zagal_etal.pdf.

Getting global cooperation right on internet governance: strategic roadmaps for the future

Miriam F. Weismann

ABSTRACT

Except for a single cybercrime treaty, there are no international binding treaties governing nation state relations in cyberspace. The reasons include the challenges of fragmentation, interoperability, and localization. These challenges are compounded by treaty harmonization issues where many countries have yet to enact domestic legislation prohibiting the targeted conduct or disagree about the protection of human rights and privacy. Mistrust between nation states and the growing wariness of diminished sovereignty create political roadblocks to multilateral partnerships and treaty agreements as well. Extensive research has investigated global approaches to cybersecurity cooperation with mixed results. Literature addressing the legal complexities of treaty negotiation is sparse and falls short of providing meaningful insight into the current combined effects of the global legal, cultural, economic, and political challenges that form a roadblock to meaningful treaty cooperation. This study contributes to global cybersecurity governance literature by investigating and analyzing not only the diverse views regarding the appropriate breadth and expanse of future global cybersecurity agreements but also considers current strategic global recommendations for increased cooperation to achieve internet governance by treaty and otherwise. The results show one common thread uniting these strategies: The need for a collective global response.

1. Introduction

'There is a real risk that, in an attempt to entice all States to sign a proposed UN cybercrime convention, bad human rights practices will be accommodated, resulting in a race to the bottom' (Letter to the United Nations to Include Human Rights Safeguards in Proposed Cybercrime Treaty) (Joint Letter 2021).

1.1. Defining the problem

Currently, there is no unified global response to the problem of cybersecurity and there is a need for it. Except for a single cybercrime treaty, there are no international binding treaties governing nation state relations in cyberspace. The reasons are many and complex. They include the challenges of fragmentation, interoperability, and localization. These challenges are compounded by treaty harmonization issues where many countries have yet to enact domestic legislation prohibiting the targeted conduct or disagree about the protection of human rights and privacy. These challenges are compounded by mistrust between nation states and the growing wariness of diminished sovereignty create political roadblocks to multilateral partnerships and treaty agreements as well.

This study examines the reasons that nations states cannot come to terms on cybercrime negotiations and the attendant consequences both in terms of cost and lack of internal national security. The study goes on to explain the provisions of the only existing treaty to date, The Council of Europe Cybercrime Convention [the 'CoE Convention'], entered into force in 2004, and to examine its relative advantages and weaknesses. Next, the study addresses multiple current global initiatives or 'roadmaps' designed to address these challenges and whether the roadmaps are adequate to address the identified challenges and current regulatory fragmentation attendant to the CoE. Finally, the study concludes that the complexity of the problem of cogent internet governance, as reflected in the analysis of the multiple approaches taken by these various global roadmaps, cannot be resolved by reliance on scientific advances in digital technological development. Instead, this study shows that the solution lies in collective action and multilateral cooperation among stakeholders in both the government and the private sectors. However, this goal may be severely hindered by the lack of mutual trust between nation states. The remedy for mistrust depends upon global recognition of human rights and privacy concerns to protect national sovereignty. No single sector has the capacity to control cybercrime and cyber insecurity. A collective response is required.

Notably, extensive research has investigated global approaches to cybersecurity cooperation with mixed results. Literature addressing the legal complexities of treaty negotiation is sparse and falls short of providing meaningful insight into the current combined effects of the global legal, cultural, economic, and political challenges that form a roadblock to meaningful treaty cooperation. This study contributes to global cybersecurity governance literature by investigating and analyzing not only the diverse views regarding the appropriate breadth and expanse of future global cybersecurity agreements but also considers current strategic global recommendations for increased cooperation to achieve internet governance by treaty and otherwise. Again, the results show one common thread uniting these strategies: The need for a collective global response.

1.2. Empty cyberspace: the problem of regulating at the international level

Cybercrime operates outside of any geographical constraints and light years ahead of national planning and implementation. The laws, criminal justice systems, and levels of international cooperation have failed to keep pace with the escalating unlawful conduct, increasing the continued threat to cybersecurity, despite the concerted efforts of the United Nations and the Council of Europe (CoE). In part the explanation for this lies in the magnitude and complexity of the problem when elevated from the national arena to the international venue, particularly where many countries have yet to enact domestic legislation prohibiting the targeted conduct or disagree about the protection of human rights and privacy. Except for a single cybercrime treaty, there are no other international legally binding treaties explicitly governing internet governance in cyberspace. Radu recognizes that

> '[w]hat is at stake for how the internet continues to evolve is the preservation of its integrity as a single network. In practice, however, its governance is neither centralized nor unitary. It is piecemeal and decentralized, with authoritative decision-making coming from different sources simultaneously' (Radu 2019, 9)

Moreover, it is important to distinguish between the types of conduct sought to be controlled at the global level. There is a distinction between cybercrime, cybersecurity, national security, and cyberwarfare (Blank 2015). These distinctions are important for, as explained in greater detail below, not all countries agree that treaty provisions should be expansive enough to include all forms of cyber threats. Some countries advocate for narrower global treaty cooperation leaving to their own domestic legal infrastructure the task of preventing cybersecurity threats to domestic national security.

To distinguish between the types of conduct that are the focus of a global response, the cyber terms require definitions, and the class of cyber actors needs to be identified. This is perhaps the first barrier to treaty accession (Li and Liu 2021). The Congressional Research Service (CRS), a legislative research branch of the U.S. Congress, observes that in the first instance there is a lack of international consensus on what constitutes a cyberattack, an act of war in cyberspace or cyberterrorism (Theohary and Rollins 2015). Generally, cyberwar is defined as 'state-on-state action equivalent to an armed attack or use of force in cyberspace that may trigger a military response with a proportional kinetic use of force. Cyberterrorism can be considered 'the premeditated use of disruptive activities, or the threat thereof, against computers and/or networks, with the intention to cause harm or further social, ideological, religious, political or similar objectives, or to intimidate any person in furtherance of such objectives.' Cybercrime includes unauthorized network breaches and theft of intellectual property and other data; it can be financially motivated, and response is typically the jurisdiction of law enforcement agencies' (Theohary and Rollins 2015, 2). Within these distinct offense categories, various types of actors with different motivations and end goals further complicate a definitional consensus.

The class of actors includes both private and state-sponsored criminals, terrorists and spies utilizing cyber based technologies to accomplish organizational goals and objectives. These actors do not necessarily share the same motivations. For example, cyberthieves typically engage in cyberattacks for monetary profit. Cyberactivists may engage in similar behavior for economic or non-economic political reasons. Cyberspies, who threaten classified or proprietary information, aim to gain some form of competitive strategic, security, financial, or political advantage. Cyberterrorists can be state-sponsored or private actors engaging in cyberattacks to pursue their own political or ideological objectives. Cyberwarriors can be agents of nation states who engage in cyberattacks to support a country's strategic agenda. A summary of these actors and their strategic motives is summarized by the European Systemic Risk Board in Table 1 below (ESB 2020).

While these various characterizations provide a better theoretical understanding of the players and their respective motivations, it is sometimes difficult to tell them apart. This underscores the fact that currently, there are no international legal criteria for determining who the actors are, whether a particular cyberattack is illegal, whether the conduct is the act of a private hacker, whether it is terrorism, or a state declaration of force equivalent to an armed attack. A collateral consequence is the absence of a global consensus regarding the conditions for individual or nation state accountability. Likewise, there is an absence of individual nation state due diligence efforts to meet the collective challenges of cybersecurity at the global level (Shrivastava and Lakra 2022).

1.3. Assessing the financial impact of the threat

Quantifying the cyber problem is also not a simple data collections exercise as cybersecurity can infiltrate every industry, market, and country. As more people are brought online, new vulnerabilities arise. The United Nations estimates that the potential cost of worldwide data breaches will be more than $5 trillion by 2024 (U.N. Report 2020).

Table 1. Systemic Cyber Risk.

A closer look at cyberattacks

The actors behind these incidents include not only increasingly daring criminals but also states and state-sponsored groups, with diverse goals and motivations.

THREAT ACTOR	MOTIVATIONS	GOALS	EXAMPLES
 **Nation-states, state-sponsored groups**	Geopolitical, ideological	Disruption, destruction, damage, theft, espionage, financial gain	Permanent data corruption, targeted physical damage, power grid disruption, payment system disruption, fraudulent transfers, espionage
 **Cybercriminals**	Enrichment	Theft/financial gain	Cash theft, fraudulent transfers, credential theft
 **Terrorist groups, hacktivists, insider threats**	Ideological, discontent	Disruption	Leaks, defamation, distributed denial-of-service attacks

Source: European Systemic Risk Board. 2020. 'Systemic Cyber Risk.'
https://www.esrb.europa.eu/pub/pdf/reports/esrb.report200219_systemiccyberrisk ~101a09685e.en.pdf

While the data may be difficult to accurately track, the assessment of a potential cyberthreat to the current financial markets is not. The International Monetary Fund (IMF) observed that it is a 'given' that a major cyberattack to the global financial system poses a threat to financial stability. It is no longer a question of 'if' but 'when' (Maurer and Nelson 2020a). In April 2020, the Financial Stability Board (FSB) warned that 'a major cyber incident, if not properly contained, could seriously disrupt financial systems, including critical financial infrastructure, leading to broader financial stability implications. The potential economic costs of such events can be immense and the damage to public trust and confidence significant.' (FSB Report 2020).

The global financial system is experiencing an unprecedented digital transformation (Kobrin 2001). Yet, governments and companies continuously struggle to prevent breaches of cybersecurity because it is unclear who is responsible for protecting the global system. The IMF urges global stakeholders to accept that the central security issue response should be treated as a 'collective action problem' (Maurer and Nelson 2020a). However, how best to organize system protections across governments, financial authorities, and industries and how to leverage these resources effectively are the principal challenges. As discussed in greater detail below, countries know what must and should be done but seemingly cannot agree about how to do it. There is a consensus, however, that there cannot be two sets of rules for the real world and the virtual world (Kobrin 2001).

Additionally, global mistrust and fragmentation of interests among the various stakeholders serve as further barriers to global cooperation. The FSB and the IMF recognize that the disconnect between financial authorities, the national security and the diplomatic communities is problematic. Notably, the relationship between financial authorities facing cyber-insecurity and national security agencies, whose involvement is necessary to prevent and detect these threats, is strained and undefined. This creates what is referred to as the 'responsibility gap' (Maurer and Nelson 2020a). Here, continued uncertainty about stakeholder roles, accountability, and global treaty mandates to protect the global financial system increase risk exposure. As further discussed below, part of this uncertainty is due to the current geopolitical environment characterized by high levels of mistrust which impede global collaboration. As Zander, Mockaitis, and Butler observe, 'leveraging cultural differences suffers from temporal limitations, which could reinforce polarization and negative stereotyping, instead of creating a mutually permanent functioning work environment' for the necessary stakeholders (Zander, Mockaitis, and Butler 2012).

2. The convention against cybercrime

2.1. 2004 treaty

The Council of Europe Cybercrime Convention [the 'CoE Convention'] is the first and only multilateral treaty to address computer-related crime and evidence gathering (CoE 2004). In 2004, the CoE Convention entered into force. As of 2020, 65 countries, including the U.S., ratified the treaty with four additional countries that have signed but not ratified the treaty (CoE 2022). The treaty represents the current normative baseline for internet governance in the field of cybercrime.

The Official Explanatory Report, accompanying the CoE Convention, was formally adopted by the CoE's Committee of Ministers on November 8, 2001. The CoE Explanatory Report provides an analysis of the CoE Convention. Under established CoE practice, such reports reflect the understanding of the parties in drafting treaty provisions and are accepted as fundamental bases for interpretation of CoE principles. Explanatory Reports are analogous to the legislative history that typically accompanies legislation in the United States.

The CoE Convention provides a treaty-based framework that imposes three necessary obligations on the participating nations to:

- enact domestic legislation criminalizing certain conduct related to computer systems to ensure treaty harmonization with domestic legislation.
- create investigative procedures and ensure their availability to domestic law enforcement authorities to investigate cybercrime offenses, including procedures to obtain electronic evidence in all forms; and,
- create a regime of broad international cooperation, including assistance in extradition of fugitives sought for crimes identified under the CoE Convention.

The United States did not require implementing domestic legislation upon ratification in 2006, as existing domestic federal law was adequate to meet these treaty requirements. However, the challenge of achieving uniform cross-border treaty harmonization through varying domestic legislation in 65 countries may also create a barrier to global treaty accession and implementation (Weismann 2005). Institutional differences between countries are also important because they determine how the private sector will internationalize as well (Pedersen and Tallman 2022).

In summary, the CoE Convention consists of forty-eight articles[1] divided among four chapters: (I) Use of terms; (II) Measures to be taken at the national level; (III) International cooperation; and (IV) Final provisions. The following is a brief outline of the conduct regulated by the treaty.

Chapter II, Section 1, Articles two through thirteen address substantive law issues and include criminalization provisions and other related provisions in computer or computer-related crime. Specifically, they define nine offenses grouped into four different categories. The offenses include illegal access, illegal interception, data interference, system interference, misuse of devices, computer-related forgery, computer-related fraud, offenses related to child pornography and offenses related to copyright.

Chapter II, Section 2, Articles fourteen through twenty-one address procedural law issues. Section 2 applies to a broader range of offenses than those defined in Section 1, including any offense committed by means of a computer system or evidence of which is in electronic form. Specifically, Article 15 requires the parties to provide for safeguards that are adequate for the protection of human rights and liberties. According to the CoE Explanatory Report, the substantive criteria and procedure authorizing an investigative power may vary according to the sensitivity of the data being sought in the investigation.

The procedural powers include expedited preservation of stored data, expedited preservation and partial disclosure of traffic data, and interception of content data. Traditional application of search and seizure methodology is provided for within a nation's own territory along with other procedural options, including real-time interception of content data. As explained in greater detail below, human rights organizations and countries have questioned the adequacy of the Section II, Article 15 requirements that countries provide for safeguards for the protection of human rights and liberties.

Chapter III addresses traditional and cybercrime-related mutual assistance obligations as well as extradition rules. Traditional mutual assistance is covered in two situations: where no legal treaty, reciprocal legislation or other such agreement exists between the countries; and where such pre-existing legal relationship exists between countries. In the former situation, the provisions of the CoE Convention apply. In the latter situation, however, pre-existing legal relationships apply 'to provide further assistance' under the CoE Convention. It bears emphasizing that the three general principles of international cooperation in Chapter III do not supersede the provisions on international agreements on mutual legal assistance (MLATs) and extradition, reciprocal agreements between parties, or relevant provisions of domestic law applying to international cooperation.

Finally, Chapter III provides transborder access to stored computer data not requiring mutual assistance because there is either consent or the information is otherwise publicly available. This self-help provision has stirred much controversy being viewed as an infringement of national sovereignty. There is also provision for the establishment of a '24/7 network' for ensuring speedy assistance between countries.

2.2. 2022 CoE second additional protocol

With the huge and unanticipated influx of cross border requests for data after the CoE Convention entered into force, countries agreed on the need for treaty revisions to modernize and streamline the process (CTED 2022). In 2012, the Cloud Evidence Group, comprised of global experts in the field, studied the problem and drafted a Second Additional Protocol on Enhanced Cooperation and Disclosure of Electronic Evidence (Protocol) (Summary, 2019). The Protocol has been advanced as a new tool for promoting greater global cooperation under the treaty. Several changes made by the Protocol are significant in terms of streamlining and expediting data access on a global level. After four years of intense negotiations, the Protocol was opened for signature in 2022. On May 12, 2022, it was signed by the United States (Protocol 2021).

The most salient features of the Protocol include a legal basis for direct request and disclosure of domain name registration information and for direct cooperation with service providers for subscriber information, effective means to obtain subscriber information and traffic data, immediate cooperation in emergencies, mutual assistance tools, as well as personal data protection safeguards. Most importantly, it alters how law enforcement requests for data occur between nation states. Nations are now empowered to make direct requests to a service provider for subscriber information, even if that service provider is in another country. Subscriber information is defined to include 'any information contained in the form of computer data [...] relating to subscribers of its services other than traffic or content data,' which includes subscriber identity, location, telephone and other contact details, payment information, and more (Protocol 2021, para 93). The collateral consequence is broader access for investigators allowing them to bypass the formal multi-lateral assistance treaty processes (MLATs) and make direct requests to foreign technology companies.

Furthermore, the Protocol expedites requests for both basic subscriber information and traffic data by characterizing the request as a domestic request of the receiving country (Protocol 2021, Art. 3(2)(c)). A properly documented request is not made directly to foreign technology service providers but rather to the competent country authority to compel the targeted service provider to produce the relevant data. The receiving country must order the service provider in its jurisdiction to produce the relevant data in 20 days (for basic subscriber information) or 45 days (for traffic data). The Protocol also allows for expedited requests in cases of emergency, which are defined as 'a situation in which there is a significant and imminent risk to the life or safety of any natural person' (Protocol 2021, Art. 8). As of 2022, only 24 nations have signed the Protocol (CoE 2022). The current signatories do not include Russia or India (Protocol 2021).

2.3. Implementation of The European Production Order

In addition to European accession to the CoE, the European Union has also promoted a separate regional reform effort to implement a unified pan-European approach to electronic evidence which is somewhat broader in scope than the Protocol. In April 2018, the European Commission proposed the European Union e-Evidence Regulation (E Reg. 2018) and a Directive (E.U. Directive 2018). These rules are designed '[t]o make it easier and faster for law enforcement and judicial authorities to obtain the electronic evidence they need to investigate and eventually prosecute criminals and terrorists' (E Reg. 2018). Specifically, the regulation was drafted to include various tools to expedite production requests including a European Production Order, a European Preservation Order, and other safeguards for protection of personal data.

The European Production Order (EPO) allows 'a judicial authority in one Member State to obtain electronic evidence (such as emails, texts or messages in apps, as well as information to identify a perpetrator as a first step) directly from a service provider or its legal representative in another EU country.' (EPO 2018; Wahl 2018). It is useful to compare and contrast the EPO regime with that of the Protocol. Whereas, the Protocol allows direct requests for subscriber information only, the EPO is broader and allows for direct requests of stored content and non-content data, including traffic data. The Directive also obligates service providers to designate a legal representative in the European Union for the receipt of, compliance with, and enforcement of decisions and orders.

In February 2019, the European Council opened negotiations between the United States and the European Union for simplified transatlantic law enforcement requests. One of the barriers to finalizing this agreement is the need to ensure the viability of domestic treaty harmonization; namely, that any transatlantic deal meets both the domestic requirements in the U.S. CLOUD Act, (Clarifying Lawful Overseas Use of Data) (Cloud Act 2018) and in the e-Evidence Regulation (E Reg. 2018, Art. 23). Notably, the U.S. CLOUD Act has two critical provisions that must be harmonized with the proposed EU treaty: (1) the authority it gives U.S. law enforcement over foreign-held data, and (2) the authority it gives (or denies) foreign entities over U.S.-held data.

3. Global treaty acceptance and rejection

3.1. Understanding the disagreement over the CoE convention

Several countries including Russia, Brazil and India declined to adopt the CoE Convention on grounds that they had not been included in its drafting and that several provisions violated nation state sovereignty. The real sticking point for Russia involved disagreement over the authority of foreign nations to enter domestic borders to obtain evidence and conduct criminal investigations as provided for in Chapter III of the treaty. For example, Russia firmly opposed the CoE Convention provision that offers law enforcement agencies the power to access computers in other countries with owner permission but without the approval of national authorities. Utilizing that provision in 2000, FBI agents accessed the computers of two Russians who had been defrauding American businesses leading to their prosecution and conviction in U.S. courts. Russia expressed public offense at the intrusion over Russian borders and claimed that the seizure of stored information violated Soviet law (Brenner and Schwerha 2002).

Brazil considered signing the CoE Convention, but then declined to do so, expressing reservations about the provisions relating to the criminalization of intellectual property infringements. Later, on December 15, 2021, Brazil changed its position and signed on to the treaty. As discussed in further detail below, Brazil has since enacted extensive domestic legislation to control cybercrime.

In 2018, India's foreign minister had second thoughts about its refusal to sign when cybercrime rates surged in India. However, the move to join the CoE was opposed by the Indian Intelligence Bureau on the grounds that sharing data with foreign law enforcement agencies infringed on national sovereignty and could jeopardize the rights of individuals (Tripathi 2018).

However, Russia and India are not alone in their human rights and privacy concerns surrounding the CoE. Sometimes referred to as the 'gold standard,' the CoE Convention has still been criticized since its inception for not having stronger safeguards for human rights (Weismann 2005). The initial concern regarding the absence of due process and privacy protections has morphed into a much broader concern given the unforeseen consequences of the treaty's application over the last decade. Specifically, more recent concerns focus on the enactment of domestic legislation in several countries that curtail freedom of speech and expression under the false guise of regulating cybersecurity in harmony with the CoE. For example, some countries continue to argue for greater inclusion of content related conduct in the CoE, which could otherwise result in the criminalization of protected expression in violation of international human rights law. This problem was underscored in 2019 by the UN special envoy, Clément Nyaletsossi Voule who stated that '[a] surge in legislation and policies aimed at combating cybercrime has also opened the door to punishing and surveilling activists and protesters in many countries around the world' (Joint Letter 2021). Voule was joined by the U.N. General Assembly at large in expressing concerns that cybercrime legislation was being misused to target human rights defenders or interfere with their work and endanger their safety in a manner contrary to international law stemming from overbroad domestic cybercrime laws.

There exist due process criticisms as well. The CoE Convention addresses the complicated problem of guaranteeing civil rights protection to citizens living in different cultures and political systems, yet it did not detail all the conditions and safeguards necessary to circumscribe each power and procedure provided for in the treaty. Instead, Article 15 was limited providing only 'the common standards or minimum safeguards to which Parties to the Convention must adhere.' These minimum safeguards reference certain applicable human rights instruments including: the 1950 European Convention for the Protection of Human Rights and Fundamental Freedoms ('ECHR') and its additional Protocols No. I, 4, 6, 7 and 12; the 1966 United Nations International Covenant on Civil and Political Rights; and 'other international human rights instruments, and which shall incorporate the principle or mandates that a power or procedure implemented under the Convention shall be proportional to the nature and circumstances of the offense' (U.N. Manual 1994). Thus, it is left to the process of treaty harmonization through the enactment of domestic laws to determine the limits on the overbreadth of protection orders authorized, provide reasonableness requirements for searches and seizures, and minimize intrusion regarding interception measures taken with respect to the wide variety of offenses. Given the inability of nations to agree on offense definitions and cyberactor accountability, there has been little cross-border uniformity in due process legislation. The problem may lie in the intentional ambiguity of the treaty couched in aspirational goals. In January 2023, The U.N. Cybercrime Ad Hoc Committee of the U.N. General Assembly met to negotiate a proposed set of 55 articles called the General Provisions, Criminalization, and Procedural Measures and Law Enforcement document in attempt to remedy these ambiguities. The articles include 28 proposed crimes. Still, numerous states objected to the majority of these proposals (Bannelier 2023). The proceedings remain subject to the same earlier criticisms of the CoE Convention and have been marked by the same disagreements and controversies about the objectives and scope of the Convention. Likewise, states continue to strongly disagree about what cybercrime means and concerns about the adequacy of human rights safeguards persist (Bannelier 2023).

For example, the CoE Explanatory Report loosely identifies due process procedural safeguards 'as [those] appropriate in view of the nature of the power or procedure, judicial or independent supervision, grounds justifying the application of the power or procedure and the limitation on the scope or duration thereof'. It is by design that '[n]ational legislatures were charged under the treaty to determine, in applying binding international obligations and established domestic principles, which of the powers and procedures are sufficiently intrusive in nature to require implementation of particular conditions and safeguards.' Other than this aspirational language, couched in terms of legally non-binding human rights instruments, CoE offers no specific minimal procedural guarantees of due process incident to treaty implementation (Weismann 2005).

In response to these various due process criticisms, and only after a highly contentious vote, the U.N. approved a Russian driven resolution to reopen treaty negotiations in 2022 to garner global support for a new treaty (U.N. General Assembly resolution 74/247; December 27 2019). The U.N. Ad Hoc Committee to Elaborate a Comprehensive International Convention on Countering the Use of Information and Communication Technologies for Criminal Purposes (Ad Hoc Committee) was set up to conduct the negotiations. Nations opposed to these new negotiations have expressed concerns that the new treaty might be too expansive, ultimately including everything from cyberwarfare to national security, to a new set of rules for internet governance. In an interesting twist, countries expressed reservations about acceding to global internet governance. Again, countries expressed concern that overly broad treaty provisions would provide an imprimatur to countries to misuse the treaty by targeting protected expression in the form of new domestic legislation. While there was uniform sentiment expressed that cybercrime damaged economies and State credibility, impeding national development, member nations remained undecided over the required response. The debate centered upon accession to the current 'gold standard' CoE Convention with its privacy and due process flaws or the need to negotiate a 'fresh' UN multilateral agreement that might lead to even greater human rights abuses (Rodriguez and Baghdasaryan 2022).

One response came in a joint letter signed off by 130 human rights organizations and experts titled, 'Letter to the United Nations to Include Human Rights Safeguards in Proposed Cybercrime Treaty' (Joint Letter 2021). The letter was sent to the Ad Hoc Committee with the request that 'any proposed convention include human rights safeguards applicable to both its substantive and procedural provisions.' The joint letter further recognizes that there is no consensus on how to tackle cybercrime at the global level or a common understanding or definition of what constitutes cybercrime. It warns that domestic legislation has been manipulated to target digital security researchers, whistleblowers, activists, and journalists. The letter concludes that '[f]rom a human rights perspective, it is essential to keep the scope of any convention on cybercrime narrow. Just because a crime might involve technology does not mean it needs to be included in the proposed convention' (Joint Letter 2021).

The Joint Letter also addresses the need to preserve individual privacy rights. The letter asserts that police in various countries have used intrusive investigative tools to access digital evidence. It is claimed that in some instances, cross-border investigations proceeded without proper safeguards and bypassed legal protections previously negotiated in mutual legal assistance treaties (MLATs). The Joint Letter further details instances where there is a complete absence of judicial oversight, and the role of independent data protection regulators was undermined. In the closing paragraph, the signatories warn that '[t]here is a real risk that, in an attempt to entice all States to sign a proposed UN cybercrime convention, bad human rights practices will be accommodated, resulting in a race to the bottom' (Joint Letter 2021).

In the meantime, the Protocol, designed to modernize the CoE Convention, has done little to assuage these specific criticisms. The human rights and privacy concerns have only increased with the opening for signature of the Protocol. This time the pushback is from inside the EU as well. The European Data Protection Board, the EU Fundamental Rights Agency, and the Council of Bars and Law Societies of Europe also called for stronger protections of fundamental rights in response to the Protocol (Kabelka 2022). These critics point to the expansion of law enforcement powers without a corresponding provision detailing data protection, privacy, and procedural rights safeguards. One major issue concerns the Protocol provision authorizing direct transfers of personal data from service providers in the EU to law enforcement authorities in third countries without a mandatory notification to the authorities in the country where the provider is based. Andreas Gruber, legal counsel at the non-profit Internet Service Providers Austria (ISPA), stated that '[t]he legal assessment and proportionality assessment should not be the task of private companies' (Kabelka 2022).

The increasing tension between national sovereignty and multilateral treaty accession, as an impediment to implementation of a multilateral agreement providing internet governance tends to delay the curative process and may magnify the problem. Data safe havens continue to flourish for potential offenders. The existence of these data safe havens which undermine the effectiveness of global enforcement serves to drive a bigger wedge between treaty participating and non-participating countries as evidenced by the contentious U.N. debate over Russia's proposal to replace the CoE with a new treaty (Joint Letter 2021).

3.2. The problem of treaty harmonization

Harmonization, also referred to as unification or uniformity, can be defined as the process of identifying and reconciling differences in legal systems and cultures to create domestic instruments that standardize terms and practices of cross-border agreements (Turner 2022). Generally, harmonization can be accomplished (i) by replacing existing domestic rules with an internationally agreed rule or (ii) by supplementing domestic law with an internationally agreed rule applicable only to international dealings (Twigg-Flesner 2021, 62).

Harmonization may result in instruments that establish binding legal obligations, referred to as 'hard law,' or non-binding norms, referred to as 'soft law.' The idea is to standardize cross-border dealings by treaty and the subsequent implementation of domestic legislation to provide better global cooperation and efficiency (Gopalan 2003). While in theory, the idea of ratifying an international agreement and then implementing it by passing domestic legislation consistent with broad treaty obligations is a good idea, it is much more difficult to translate into practice. Experience in global treaty harmonization has demonstrated that blending different economic and legal systems and cultures is difficult and, when attempted, has sometimes resulted in watered-down standards (Austen-Baker 2018; Joint Letter 2021).

Nonetheless, treaty harmonization is an established international law principle which operates independent of any international court or other means to guarantee enforcement. Harmonization, like treaty ratification, happens through nation state voluntary accession (Weismann 2005). For example, treaty harmonization has been applied in the field of commercial transactions including General International Commercial Contract Law; E-Commerce; Private International Law; Conflicts of Laws; International Sale of Goods; International Transportation of Goods; International Finance & Secured Transactions; International Payments; Debt Collection & Insolvency; Dispute Resolution; and Judgment Enforcement to name a few (Turner 2022). Likewise, international organizations participating in the process of treaty harmonization projects include The Hague Conference on Private International Law (HCCH); The International Institute for the Unification of Private Law (UNIDROIT); The United Nations Commission on International Trade Law (UNCITRAL);The International Chamber of Commerce (ICC);The Organization for the Harmonization of Business Laws in Africa (OHADA); The European Union ('EU'); The Commission on European Contract Law (CECL); The Research Group on the Existing EC Private Law (Acquis Group); The Academy of European Private Lawyers (Academia dei Giusprivatisti Europei); The Organization of American States (OAS); and the Fundación Fernando Fueyo at Diego Portales University & Fondation pour le droit continental (Turner 2022).

Despite the universal application of treaty harmonization, treaty outcomes vary depending on the support and political will of countries in the domestic ratification process after signing a global treaty. Another barrier to cyber cooperation arises because unlike traditional economic cooperation treaties, some of the misconduct in the field of cybersecurity may originate inside of governments by such means as espionage or theft of intellectual property, for example. It is a challenge then to draft treaty provisions broad enough to outlaw the very conduct engaged in by rogue countries who also act as signatories on the treaty and are then tasked to enforce the treaty by enacting domestic laws aimed at the government's own conduct (Cybersecurity Infrastructure Security Agency, CISA 2020).

4. The Russian proposal: maybe not the best timing

It has been reported that the very same day that the United Nations General Assembly convened an emergency special session to respond to Russia's full-scale invasion of Ukraine in early March 2022, the Ad Hoc Committee held its first session in another conference room (Falchetta, Brown, and Rodriguez 2022). The Ad Hoc Committee, formed after a contentious vote passing Russia's resolution for a new treaty, conducted the first of several planned negotiation sessions. The goal is to complete a global agreement by early 2024 that facilitates international coordination on cybercrime.

Russia did submit a draft treaty proposal to the Ad Hoc Committee for consideration in these negotiations (Russian Proposal, June 29 2021).[2] The Russian Proposal departs from the CoE Convention in several significant ways including expanding the types of conduct that should be criminalized, replacing well established definitions with vague and undefined terms, and including restrictions on international cooperation. For example, the draft includes a more extensive list of crimes than the CoE including encouragement of or coercion to suicide, offenses related to the involvement of minors in the commission of unlawful acts that endanger their life or health, terrorism, and extremism related offences, to name a few. The proposed expansion of offense conduct exacerbates the debate because in Article 86 of the Russian Proposal, the language does not allow signatories to make reservations concerning the offenses included in some of its articles including but not limited to child pornography, encouragement, or coercion to suicide, offences that endanger the life or health of minors (Articles 15–17) and incitement to subversive activity and terrorism related offenses (Articles 19, 22-26). Reservations are also not allowed in relation to extradition related provisions (Article 47, para 11). Simply put, any nation state signing the agreement must agree to the addition of all offense conduct revisions and cannot make a reservation to opt out of select portions of the treaty. A reservation is generally standard procedure in treaty negotiations on the assumption that no treaty is ever perfect and there must be some room for countries to agree to most but not all provisions when signing a treaty.

With these wiggle room reservations removed, critics observe the further problem of vague offense conduct definitions for the new crimes. For example, Article 18 on 'the creation and use of digital data to mislead the user' is open to various interpretations and could be used to outlaw dissent, parody, and other forms of expression. The most serious concern is that vague laws enable arbitrary interpretation and the use of criminal law for prosecution of political opponents, journalists, and human rights defenders.

Combined with other language in the draft treaty to ban refusal of mutual legal assistance and extradition on the grounds of considering an offense a political offense (Article 46.4), the draft creates the potential for using cybercrime investigations, both nationally and across borders, as an instrument for political oppression.

Likewise, the draft language omits traditional international human rights norms and standards. For example, Article 21.1 includes the crime of 'extremism.' The crime focuses on 'unlawful acts motivated by political, ideological, social, racial, ethnic, or religious hatred or enmity, advocacy and justification of such actions or the provision of access to them.' There are no definitions specifying the nature of the illegal conduct or who is in the class of persons covered by the crime of extremism. The Article goes so far as to define extremism as mere 'humiliation by means of ICTs.' Humiliation is not defined nor is it thought to be susceptible to clear definition for purposes of giving notice as to the conduct that constitutes the crime which is a key requirement of due process of law. The fear is that including new crimes like extremism may allow governments to target otherwise protected political views, ideologies, and identities simply to silence opposition to the government.

The sticking point in negotiations remains the inability of nation states to agree on a universal standard that reflects a consensus on human rights and privacy. Because respect for human rights varies widely among nation states, and because there is no current universal agreement on a set of common exacting standards for accessing private data, it is predicted that any new treaty standards adopted will represent the lowest common denominator for due process of law and individual privacy rights between nation states (Joint Letter 2021).

5. The BRICs approach to cybersecurity

In 2001 a chief economist at Goldman Sachs, Jim O'Neill, theorized that by 2035, the combined GDP of the BRIC economies, Brazil, Russia, India, and China, would exceed the combined GDP of the G7 countries (Canada, France, Germany, Italy, Japan, U.K., and the U.S.) (O'Neill 2001). The BRIC countries, including Brazil, Russia, India, and China, have recently expanded to include South Africa. The BRICs' rejection of the CoE was viewed as significant given their combined political and economic market power. Likewise, cybersecurity in the BRIC countries has long been a topic of concern for businesses operating in these countries given BRIC non accession to the CoE (with the recent exception of Brazil) and the increased threat of theft of intellectual property (Buscaglia and Weismann 2012).

While India and Brazil have lent support to Russia's call for a replacement of the CoE, the prospect for cooperation even among BRIC nations in resolving cybersecurity issues remains at an impasse without many prospects for a unified response on internet governance or cyber security. In a recent study conducted by Ignatov, the data showed that conflicting cultural and structural views continued to divide the BRIC nations regarding managing cyber content, cyberterrorism, and extremism (Ignatov 2022). This study is consistent with the following analysis of recent domestic legislative initiatives by both India and Brazil. Both countries have designed their own respective domestic data privacy and security legislation and proposed regulations using EU guidance as opposed to the current Russian Proposal. Specifically, both countries modeled their respective legislative drafts on the EU's GDPR and/or the European Union's e-Evidence regulation.

5.1. India's legislation

In December 2019, India introduced the Personal Data Protection Bill (PDPB 2019), which underwent 81 proposed amendments and 12 recommendations in a Joint Committee of Parliament (JCP) review process. The JCP adopted the final report on the Bill in late November 2021. The Bill had long been anticipated, given India's massive on-line market. The PDPB 2019 was a comprehensive privacy law which covers a range of issues and aims to align India's data-protection regime with the European Union General Data Protection Regulation (GDPR) (GDPR. EU 2016). For example, the Bill established protections on the cross-border flow of data and includes the creation of a Data Protection Authority (DPA) (Arindrajit & Justin 2021). However, there were some key differences from the GDPR. The PDPB 2019 would require only 'significant' data fiduciaries (data controllers), instead of all data controllers and processors, to maintain records of processing activities. On the other hand, the scope of the Bill was broader than the GDPR as it would 'include the processing of personal data by the State, any Indian company, any citizen of India, or any person or body of persons incorporated or created under Indian law' (PDPB 2019).

After a lengthy five-year period of negotiations, the Bill was withdrawn in August 2022 from the JCP reportedly in response to industry backlash from industry titans like Meta and Google aimed at the DPA along with criticism from the New Delhi based privacy advocacy group Internet Freedom Foundation (Singh 2022).

However, India succeeded in its mission to regulate data privacy and passed the Digital Personal Data Protection Bill 2023 (DPDP 2023). The DPDP regulates personal data collection, processing, and sharing. The Bill includes several salient features. It empowers individuals, referred to as Data Principals, to control their personal data by providing the right to access data summaries, update information, nominate fiduciaries in the event of death or incapacity, correct data inaccuracies and erase data under certain circumstances. Second, the Bill regulates Data Processors referred to as Data Fiduciaries. These are the organizations responsible for processing personal data. The new stringent obligations are subject to monetary penalties. Processors are obliged to design grievance procedures to process complaints. Additionally, they must implement appropriate technical and organizational measures for compliance with the Bill.

Third, the Bill addresses cross border data transmission and data localization rules. Cross-border transfers of personal data is permitted to all countries or territories except those specifically blacklisted by the Central Government. Further, unlike the 2019 proposed Bill, it does not regulate local storage or localization requirements in an effort to assist businesses reduce storage infrastructure costs.

The governance structure of the Bill creates The Data Protection Board of India which has the power to direct remedial measures, inquire into personal data breaches, and impose penalties. The Data Protection Board works with newly created Consent Managers. Consent Managers are the contact point for users to offer, withdraw and manage their consent regarding data usage using an 'accessible, transparent and interoperable' platform. Consent Managers must be registered with the Data Protection Board and are authorized to file complaints on behalf of users streamline the consent management operation.

Finally, the Bill authorizes appeals to the Appellate Courts and introduces the options for mediation and voluntary undertakings, providing alternative resolution mechanisms in data disputes. The Bill does not include any cybercrime provisions.

However, the 2013 Jurisdiction of Information Technology Rules was amended in 2022 to include stricter cybersecurity reporting guidelines (Cybersecurity Laws and Regulations, India 2024 2023). As per India's IT Act of 2000, the Computer Emergency Response Team – India (CERT-In) is responsible for providing guidelines for monitoring, detecting, preventing, and managing cybersecurity incidents. Cert-In now requires organizations to deliver a detailed report within six-hours after an incident occurs. This changes the previous rule that a cyber incident had to be reported 'within a reasonable time' after being identified. Accompanying the six-hour reporting rule, is a list prepared by Cert-In of twenty cyber incident types that must be reported by service providers, intermediaries, data center operators, companies, and government organizations within the six-hour period (Sukianto 2023).

5.2. Brazil's legislation

In 2014 Brazil passed Federal Law No. 12.965/2014, the Brazilian Civil Rights Framework for the Internet (Marco Civil da Internet), which '[e]stablishes the principles, guarantees, rights and obligations for the use of Internet in Brazil' (Marco Civil 2014). The Marco Civil, referred to as Brazil's 'Internet Constitution,' provides certain rights and guarantees for Internet users and guidelines for State enforcement action. The law is similar in design to the European Union's e-Evidence regulation, discussed above, in that it authorizes law enforcement to make direct requests to service providers operating in the country. The Act has been used to require foreign Internet Service Providers (ISPs) to provide relevant criminal evidence to law enforcement, and fines have been levied against foreign service providers for noncompliance. One of the more controversial court cases involved Facebook's challenge to the constitutionality of the Marco Civil Act after itself having been fined $1.6 million dollars for privacy leaks. This included leaking data from 443,000 Facebook users to developers of an App called 'thisisyourdigitallife' (Brito 2019).

Most recently, Brazil's first general data protection law, the Lei Geral de Proteção de Dados (LGPD), entered into effect on 18 September 2020, with administrative sanctions for noncompliance (LGPD English version, 2020). The law covers the activities of data controllers and processors and creates requirements for the processing of information of data subjects. The LGPD modeled its own design on the European Union's General Data Protection Regulation (Koch 2020). User rights provided by the LGPD go beyond those provided in the GDPR with respect to user access to information about who holds and has received their data. Interestingly, the LGPD has extraterritorial effect and therefore, companies do not need to have a physical presence in Brazil for the law to apply.

The LGPD also includes provisions on the appointment of Data-Protection Officers, Data Protection Impact Assessments, record-keeping, data breaches, and the establishment of the Brazilian Data Protection Authority (ANPD), tasked with the formulation of guidelines for the application of the data protection rules. It mandates several requirements for the transfer of data using valid legal transfer mechanisms.

Although organizations may transfer personal data to other States that provide an 'adequate level of data protection,' Brazil has not yet defined this. The two main ways in which organizations can transfer data are: (i) with the specific and express consent of the individual, and (ii) through contractual instruments which commit the organization to comply with the LGPD principles, individual rights, and the Brazilian data-protection regime.

6. Cyber insecurity continues to proliferate: challenges to future cooperation

One thing that countries can agree on is that cyber-insecurity continues to increase at an alarming pace (U.N. Report 2020). This paper has identified several challenges to global cooperation which impede the prospect of a unified response to cyber insecurity including barriers to effective treaty harmonization, defining the expanse of proposed regulated conduct, defining the responsible actors, bridging the responsibility gap, and gaining a consensus on the depth and breadth of treaty content. Other practical barriers to global cooperation and reform exist as well including the challenges of fragmentation, operability, and localization.

6.1. Fragmentation: getting everyone on the same page

The well-intended development of treaty reform initiatives is designed to solve cyber-insecurity and standardize the cross-border data problem. There is the risk, however, that multiple treaties combined with the unique regulatory systems in each country will cause the global regulatory regime to become fragmented and increasingly complex. Countries may elect to support one reform effort and not another. This leaves law enforcement in a quandary in determining which, if any, country's rules or which global treaties will apply in a particular case. The problem of fragmentation is not new and has been the subject of international legal debate for many decades (Agon 2022; Ajevski 2014; Benvenisti and Downs 2007).

This problem was initially studied by the International Law Commission of the U.N. General Assembly which issued a report in 2006 (International Law Commission 2006). The Fragmentation Study engages in a lengthy and complex legal discussion of procedural treaty rules, hierarchy of treaty agreements, conflicts of law and harmonization principles. It makes recommendations regarding how conflicts and fragmentation in legal reforms should be addressed but the complexity of this proscribed treaty resolution process only adds to the complexity of fragmentation in the first instance.

Johnston and Trebilcock (2013) have suggested the use of treaty provisions in trade agreements such as most favored nation status clauses (MFNs) to speed up cooperation and harmonization in other global treaty contexts. MFN clauses do promote greater uniformity in multi-country regulation because countries who accede to the same terms earn economic benefits. The idea of tying standardization in e-commerce to favorable economic treatment is yet untried in the field of internet governance and cybersecurity but remains a promising opportunity. In any case, there does not appear to be a simple roadmap for getting all countries on the same page when addressing reform. Likewise, the fragmentation problem overlaps with the operability challenge.

6.2. Operability: standardization for cooperation

Multiple treaty reform efforts might be seen as better than none or even one. Reform is a good thing. However, multiple reform proposals challenge nations to create processes and cross-border procedures that offer enough comparability to enable law enforcement to move seamlessly throughout the globe, at least as seamlessly as the cyber actors threatening global security. The thinking is that the concurrent implementation of cyber reform regimes creates increased challenges in homogenizing processes for cross-border access. Depending upon which countries are governed by the CoE, the Protocol or the EU regulations, when a conflict between the treaty regimes arise, which takes precedence? The U.N Fragmentation Study does attempt to provide the answer, but it is a very complex legal document requiring interpretation in many of its provisions (International Law Commission 2006). It appears unlikely that law enforcement conflicts could be resolved in an expeditious fashion under this complex regime.

Sverdup observes that in the treaty context, 'institutional design is a complex process of matching existing institutions, actions and contexts in ways that are complicated and of long duration (Sverdrup 2002). An example of this matching principle designed to create long term treaty interoperability has been a challenge in the implementation of multilateral defense treaties such as NATO. NATO defines 'interoperability' in the treaty context as the 'ability for Allies to act together coherently, effectively, and efficiently to achieve tactical, operational, and strategic objectives. Specifically, interoperability enables forces, units and/or systems to operate together, allowing them to communicate and to share common doctrine and procedures, along with each other's infrastructure and bases' (NATO 2022). For NATO, the challenge to achieving interoperability was to reduce duplication, effectively pool global resources and produce synergies among allied nations. In identifying the specific mechanisms to achieve interoperability, NATO concludes that interoperable solutions can only be achieved through the effective employment of standardization, training, exercises, lessons learned, demonstrations, tests and trials. While favored, standardization of domestic legislative regimes remains a complex challenge.

6.3. Localization: data residency

The reasoning behind the implementation of a system of data localization has some attraction. The idea is that nation states can seek to eliminate the 'borderless' nature of cloud storage by controlling data residency. Typically, nations do this by requiring data providers to localize legal representation by opening a local office or appointing local staff to supervise the handling of data.

Law enforcement regulation is easier when foreign providers are required to localize data storage and the incidences of cross-border disputes are also reduced.

However, forced data localization and mandated local legal representation have been criticized by civil society groups and service providers. The critics observe that localized data storage is often implemented under 'shaky' national security pretenses where the real intent is to reduce barriers to access of otherwise unavailable user data (Sheppard, Yayboke, and Ramos 2021). In a study conducted at the Center for Strategic and International Studies, Sheppard, Yayboke & Ramos examined how established democracies have struggled to balance the attraction of the so-called digital sovereignty afforded by data localization with the economic and national security arguments against such policies. The study concludes that one size does not fit all, and each country will have its own regulations regarding data localization, again giving rise to the fragmentation and interoperability concerns. Distinct policies addressing each data localization concern require investigation into data localization's potential to impact and/or manipulate multiple facets of national security. The study warns that 'policymakers must be wary of fragmenting the internet, especially if the result is increased vulnerability to manipulation and coercion' (Sheppard, Yayboke, and Ramos 2021).

In conclusion, a theme that permeates the challenges of fragmentation, operability, localization, and other barriers to internet governance reform is the elephant in the room–the problem of mutual mistrust among global stakeholders. In theory, many of the ideas to increase global cooperation in the name of internet governance and cybersecurity make sense but in practice nations, civil organizations and market participants worry about manipulation, national security threats, breach of sovereignty, and unwanted increased cross-border information access. The importance of the development and management of 'relationship capital' or trust in global alliances cannot be minimized. Cullen, Johnson & Sackano observe that relationship capital cannot be established without mutual trust and commitment which are central for international strategic alliances (Cullen, Johnson, and Sackano 2000). Arguably the lack of global trust is perhaps the most significant barrier to getting global internet governance right. But there is no shortage of proposals aimed at achieving a model of internet governance and cybersecurity.

7. Getting it right: three strategic global options

In 2001, pre-CoE, Kobrin made several policy recommendations that continue to resonate in the present. The most important recommendation being that nation state self-governance is inadequate to resolve the complexity of internet governance and that the resolution requires a unified global response (Kobrin 2001). Indeed, Kobrin's early policy recommendations are consonant with the current IMF position. As stated above, the IMF has described the response to cyber insecurity as a collective action problem. Collective action problems require collective action solutions. Several global organizations have met recently to design collective action regimes or 'roadmaps' to respond to many of the issues and challenges to global internet governance described in this paper. Three of these initiatives are discussed here. All three proposals are in the embryonic stage and will require time to develop into concrete initiatives.

First, in July 2018, the Secretary-General of the United Nations convened a panel on digital cooperation. The Panel completed its deliberations and submitted its final report, entitled 'The Age of Digital Interdependence' (U.N. Report 2020). Second, The Carnegie Endowment for International Peace (CEIP) released a report in November 2020 titled 'International Strategy to Better Protect the Global Financial System against Cyber Threats' developed in collaboration with the World Economic Forum (CEIP Report 2020). Finally, the U.N. Security Council Counter Terrorism Committee Executive Directorate (CTED) released a report in 2022 addressing the state of international cooperation for lawful cross-border access to digital evidence of crimes (CTED Report 2022). All three provide guidance for nation states to enter into multilateral partnerships and agreements aimed at combating cyber insecurity and achieving some measure of internet governance through global partnerships.

7.1. Roadmap for digital cooperation UN Secretary-General (2020)

In July 2018, the Secretary-General of the United Nations convened a panel on digital cooperation. The central purpose was to advance proposals to strengthen cooperation in the digital space among Governments, the private sector, civil society, international organizations, academic institutions, the technical community, and other relevant stakeholders. The Panel completed its deliberations and submitted its final report, entitled 'The Age of Digital Interdependence' (U.N. Report 2020). In the report, the Panel included five recommendations on how the international community could work together to optimize the use of digital technologies and mitigate cyber security risk:

1. Build an inclusive digital economy and society.
2. Develop human and institutional capacity.
3. Protect human rights and human agency.
4. Promote digital trust, security, and stability.
5. Foster global digital cooperation.

The first two recommendations deal with user data and technological capacity. The last three recommendations are relevant to solving the barriers to global cooperation identified in this paper. In terms of protecting human rights and human agency, the first key principle is the recognition that the internet cannot be an ungoverned or ungovernable space – human rights exist online as they do offline and have to be respected in full (U.N. Report 2020).

Because new technologies have often been used for surveillance, repression, censorship, and online harassment, especially of vulnerable people and human rights defenders, development of further formal guidance on how human rights standards apply in the digital age is required. The Guiding Principles on Business and Human Rights provide a useful tool. The U.N. also identifies the significant stakeholders in this process to include the Human Rights Council, treaty organizations, the Office of the United Nations High Commissioner for Human Rights (OHCHR) and diverse community stakeholders.

Finally, the U.N. criticizes and discourages future blanket internet shutdowns and generic blocking and filtering of services which are considered by U.N. human rights mechanisms to be in violation of international human rights law. Countries need to do more than simply rely on law enforcement or using disruptive blanket internet shutdowns to deal with the spread of disinformation and harmful, life-threatening content.

The way forward under this proposal first requires digital cooperation involving global stakeholders. While Governments remain at the center of the effort, the involvement of the private sector, technology companies, civil society and other stakeholders is essential to making realistic and effective decisions and policies. Second, it will be important for the international community to also prioritize broader issues of trust and security to achieve Sustainable Development Goals. Thus, a universal statement, endorsed by nation states, which describe elements of common understanding, could facilitate a shared vision for digital cooperation based on core values.

To address gaps in global digital cooperation, the report suggests three potential models: a strengthened and enhanced Internet Governance Forum Plus, a distributed co-governance architecture and a digital commons architecture. The report underscores the point that the existing digital cooperation architecture is highly complex and not necessarily effective. This situation is exacerbated by the lack of a common entry point into the global digital architecture, which makes it especially hard for developing countries, small and medium-sized enterprises, marginalized groups and other stakeholders with limited budgets and expertise to make their voices heard in the global dialogue.

As an epilogue, discussions among relevant stakeholders on the report's three proposed models are ongoing, given the complexity and significance of the issues and the need to ensure global inclusivity of all nation states. Several nation states are considering working with a multi-stakeholder task force to pilot the distributed co-governance model at the national or regional levels.

7.2. Roadmap for digital cooperation: world economic forum/Carnegie Endowment for National Peace (2020)

The Carnegie Endowment for International Peace (CEIP) released a report in November 2020 titled 'International Strategy to Better Protect the Global Financial System against Cyber Threats' (CEIP Report 2020). Developed in collaboration with the World Economic Forum, the report recommends specific actions to reduce global fragmentation by fostering more collaboration, both internationally and among government agencies and the private sector. The data in the report was gathered based on consultations with more than 200 key stakeholders in government, the central bank and financial supervisory community, industry, and other relevant organizations. It also incorporates insights gained through a cyber war game convened by the CEIP at the 2020 Munich Security Conference simulating a cyberattack against the financial system, and a high-level roundtable co-hosted with the IMF for central bank governors focusing on cybersecurity and the financial system (Mauer and Nelson 2021b).

The resulting recommendations for a global strategy are based on four principles: first, greater clarity about roles and responsibilities is required. The report acknowledges the tenuous connection between law enforcement and financial markets observing that only a handful of countries have built effective domestic relationships among their financial authorities, law enforcement, diplomats, other relevant government actors, and industry. Thus, existing fragmentation hampers international cooperation and weakens the international system's collective resilience, recovery, and response capabilities. Echoing the U.N. and IMF sentiments, the report underscores the critical importance of international collaboration. Described as 'necessary and urgent' given the scale of the threat and the system's globally interdependent nature, it concludes that individual governments, financial firms, and the private sector are ill equipped to unilaterally face the challenge.

Third, reducing fragmentation can free up capacity to tackle the problem. The report emphasizes that initiatives to better protect financial institutions tend to be siloed. The consequences of this includes duplication of effort and increased transaction costs.

Fourth, protecting the international financial system can be a model for other sectors. The idea is that the financial system is one of the few areas in which countries have a clear shared interest in cooperation, even when geopolitical tensions are high. Focusing on the financial sector provides a starting point and could provide better protection of other sectors in the future. Specific recommendations for strengthening cyber resilience include the development by the FSB of a basic framework for supervising cyber risk management at financial institutions. Governments and private industry should strengthen security by sharing information on threats and by creating financial computer emergency response teams (CERTs), modeled on Israel's FinCERT. Financial authorities should also prioritize increasing the financial sector's resilience against attacks targeting data and algorithms. Here, initiatives might include secure, encrypted data vaulting that allows nightly secure back up of customer account data. Regular exercises to simulate cyberattacks should be employed to identify weaknesses and develop action plans.

The report also focuses on the importance of cross-border standardization in the application of these recommendations. To reinforce international norms, the report recommends that governments make clear how they will apply international law to cyberspace and strengthen norms to protect the integrity of respective domestic financial systems. The specific recommendations include strengthened international norms to facilitate collective response through law enforcement actions which can include sanctions, arrests, and asset seizures. However, no particulars are articulated to solve the current mistrust surrounding cross-border law enforcement cooperation.

Another focus is directed at intelligence gathering. Again, the recommendations urge cross-border sharing of such intelligence by governments with allies and like-minded countries. The report concludes that '[b]etter protecting the global financial system requires international collaboration and creative thinking' (CEIP Report 2020).

7.3. Roadmap for digital cooperation: United Nations CTED (2022)

The U.N. Security Council Counter Terrorism Committee Executive Directorate (CTED) released a report in 2022 addressing the state of international cooperation for lawful cross-border access to digital evidence of crimes (CTED Report 2022). The Report focuses on the two problems: interoperability and capacity building.

The first recommendation is to increase interoperability by seeking to clarify where one infrastructure is or is not interoperable with another. Interoperability also requires ensuring that the same point of contact (whether an office or a person) is used for each infrastructure or regime. Universal request forms should be designed to manage requests. The problem of fragmentation could be ameliorated, and capacity building efforts greatly enhanced if a shared request form could be used by all law enforcement agencies. A single form could guide law enforcement agencies towards one set of standards and would be understandable and actionable regardless of the legal authority invoked. To the extent that private service providers are affected, guidance should be provided in the private sector on how to handle requests.

To ensure that privacy rights are recognized, the Report concludes that in terms of human rights, in the context of requesting cross-border electronic evidence, the United Nations International Covenant on Civil and Political Rights (ICCPR) Article 17 and the Universal Declaration of Human Rights (UDHR) Article 12 should serve as the benchmark to ensure a clear baseline on privacy matters.

The second recommendation in the Report focuses on the need for capacity building. Capacity building has been identified as a key policy issue (Antonova 2011). Here, the CTED relates that its dialogue with nation states has revealed that significant portions of the world's law enforcement establishments continue to have little or no training on the basic rules governing the kind of process required for each type of digital evidence. Thus capacity-building efforts should be guided by interoperability guidelines. While there are guides that currently exist for law enforcement agencies making requests of one country or another, there is a need to develop guidelines for law enforcement agents making a request under one of several overlapping regimes, as well as guidance for the different types of data requested, depending on the nature of the data and where it is held. Again, this requires cross-border cooperation in the form of regional and cross-regional partnerships as avenues to facilitate capacity building.

Capacity building efforts should also focus on the private sector. Smaller service providers may lack the necessary resources to manage global law enforcement. CTED suggests that larger firms could help smaller firms with training materials and tools for managing incoming law enforcement requests. The Report identifies many examples of this kind of private sector capacity-building. One such example is the Global Internet Forum to Counter Terrorism (GIFCT), which was formed in 2017 with funding from Microsoft, Twitter, Facebook, and YouTube. The GIFCT has provided a forum for regular information sharing across firms, developing technological solutions for the responsible management of violent extremist content, and developing industry best practices.

8. Conclusion

Except for a single cybercrime treaty, there are no international legally binding treaties explicitly governing nation state relations in cyberspace. The reasons include the challenges of fragmentation, interoperability, and localization. These challenges are compounded by treaty harmonization issues where many countries have yet to enact domestic legislation prohibiting the targeted conduct or disagree about the protection of human rights and privacy. Mistrust between nation states and the growing wariness of diminished sovereignty create political roadblocks to multilateral partnerships and treaty agreements as well.

The complexity of solving these barriers to agreement is reflected in the respective roadmap proposals discussed above. However, noticeable common threads run through each of these proposals. First, and perhaps most significant, is the call for collective action and multilateral cooperation among stakeholders in government and the private sector. Second, cooperation agreements must account for human rights and privacy concerns to protect the interests of sovereign nations and their people. Finally, the development of digital technology and advances will not solve the problem of internet governance. No single sector has the capacity to control cybercrime and cyber insecurity. A collective response is required.

Notes

1. All treaty references are to the CoE 2004.
2. All references to Articles in the Russian Proposal are to Russian Proposal, June 29, 2021.

Disclosure statement

No potential conflict of interest was reported by the author(s).

ORCID

Miriam F. Weismann http://orcid.org/0000-0002-6354-7068

References

Agon, S. 2022. "Farewell to the F-Word? Fragmentation of International law in Times of the Covid-19 Pandemic." *University of Toronto Law Journal* 72 (1): 1–49.

Ajevski, M. 2014. "Fragmentation in International Human Rights Law – Beyond Conflict of Laws." *Nordic Journal of Human Rights* 32 (2): 87–98. https://doi.org/10.1080/18918131.2014.897795.

Antonova, S. 2011. "Capacity-building" in Global Internet Governance: The Long-Term Outcomes of "Multistakeholderism." *Regulation & Governance* 5 (4): 425–445.

Arindrajit, B., and S. Justin. 2020. "Key Global Takeaways from India's Revised Personal Data Protection Bill." *LAWFARE*, January 23. https://www.lawfareblog.com/key-global-takeaways-indias-revised-personal-data-protection-bill/.

Austen-Baker, R., ed. 2018. "Harmonization and Contract in a Globalized World." In *Essays in Memory of Professor Jill Poole: Coherence, Modernisation, and Integration in Contract, Commercial, and Corporate Laws*, chap. 4, p. 1. London, UK: Routledge Publishing.

Bannelier, Karine. 2023. "The U.N. Cybercrime Convention Should Not Become a Tool for Political Control or the Watering Down of Human Rights." *LAWFARE*, January 31. https://www.lawfaremedia.org/article/the-u.n.-cybercrime-convention-should-not-become-a-tool-for-political-control-or-the-watering-down-of-human-rights.

Benvenisti, E., and G. Downs. 2007. "The Empire's New Clothing: Political Economy and Fragmentation of International law." *Stanford Law Review* 60: 595–632.

Blank, L. 2015. "Cyberwar Versus Cyber Attack: The Role of Rhetoric in the Application of Law to Activities in Cyberspace." In *Cyber War: Law and Ethics for Virtual Conflicts*, edited by J. D. Ohlin, K. Govern, and C. Finkelstein, 76–101. Oxford, UK: Oxford University Press. https://doi.org/10.1093/acprof:oso/9780198717492.003.0006.

Brazilian General Data Protection Law (LGPD, English version). 2020, October. https://iapp.org/resources/article/brazilian-data-protection-law-lgpd-english-translation/.

Brenner, S., and J. Schwerha. 2002. "Transnational Evidence Gathering and Local Prosecution of International Cybercrime." *J. Marshall J. Computer & Info. L.* 20: 347–395.

Brito, R. 2019. "Brazil Fines Facebook $1.6 Million for Improper Sharing of User Data." *Reuters*, December 30. https://www.reuters.com/article/us-facebook-brazil-fine/brazil-fines-facebook-1-6-million-for-improper-sharing-of-user-data-idUSKBN1YY0VK.

Buscaglia, C., and M. Weismann. 2012. "How Cybersafe are the BRICs?" *Journal of Legal, Ethical and Regulatory Issues* 15: 61–92. https://www.academia.edu/10165520/Volume_15_Number_2_JOURNAL_OF_LEGAL_ETHICAL_AND_REGULATORY_ISSUES?email_work_card=view-paper.

CEIP Report, The Carnegie Endowment for International Peace. 2020. International Strategy to Better Protect the Financial System Against Cyber Threats, November 18. https://carnegieendowment.org/2020/11/18/international-strategy-to-better-protect-financial-system-against-cyber-threats-pub-83105.

CISA (Cybersecurity Infrastructure Security Agency). 2020. Insider Threat Mitigation Guide, November. https://www.cisa.gov/sites/default/files/2022-11/Insider%20Threat%20Mitigation%20Guide_Final_508.pdf.

CLOUD Act. 2018. https://www.congress.gov/bill/115th-congress/house-bill/4943.

CoE (Council of Europe). 2004. The Convention Against Cybercrime, ETS No. 185 (2004). https://www.coe.int/en/web/cybercrime/the-budapest-convention.

CoE (Council of Europe). 2022. Chart of Signatures and Ratification of the Treaty, November 17. https://www.coe.int/en/web/conventions/full-list?module=signatures-by-treaty&treatynum=224.

Council of Europe (Protocol 2021). 2021. Second Additional Protocol to the Convention on Cybercrime on enhanced co-operation and disclosure of electronic evidence CETS No.224., May 28. https://www.coe.int/en/web/cybercrime/the-budapest-convention.

Council of Europe (Summary, 2019). 2019. Enhanced International Cooperation on Cybercrime and Electronic Evidence: Towards a Protocol to the Budapest Convention, September 5. https://rm.coe.int/summary-towards-a-protocol-to-the-budapest-convention/1680972d07.

CTED Report, United Nations Security Council Counter Terrorism Committee Executive Directorate. 2022. The state of international cooperation for lawful access to digital evidence, January. chrome-extension://efaidnbmnnnibpcajpcglclefindmkaj/https://www.un.org/securitycouncil/ctc/sites/www.un.org.securitycouncil.ctc/files/files/documents/2022/Jan/cted_trends_report_lawful_access_to_digital_data_.pdf.

Cullen, J., J. Johnson, and T. Sackano. 2000. "Success Through Commitment and Trust: The Soft Side of Strategic Alliance Management." *Journal of World Business* 35 (3): 223–240. https://doi.org/10.1016/S1090-9516(00)00036-5.

Cybersecurity Laws and Regulations India 2024. 2023. November 14. https://iclg.com/practice-areas/cybersecurity-laws-and-regulations/india.

DPDP (The Digital Personal Data Protection Act 2023). 2023. August 11. https://www.meity.gov.in/writereaddata/files/Digital%20Personal%20Data%20Protection%20Act%202023.pdf.

EPO (European Production Order). 2018. https://eur-lex.europa.eu/legal-content/EN/TXT/HTML/?uri=CELEX:52018PC0225#:~:text=The%20European%20Production%20Order%20and,proceedings%20for%20concrete%20criminal%20offences.

ESB (European Systemic Risk Board). 2020. Systemic Cyber Risk. chrome-extension://efaidnbmnnnibpcajpcglclefindmkaj/https://www.esrb.europa.eu/pub/pdf/reports/esrb.report200219_systemiccyberrisk~101a09685e.en.pdf.

European Union Directive. 2018. https://eur-lex.europa.eu/legal-content/EN/TXT/?qid=1524129181403&uri=COM:2018:226:FIN.

European Union e-Evidence Regulation (e-Reg). 2018. https://eur-lex.europa.eu/legal-content/EN/TXT/?qid=1524129181403&uri=COM:2018:225:FIN.

Falchetta, T., D. Brown, and K. Rodriguez. 2022. "Opening Stages in UN Cybercrime Treaty Talks Reflect Human Rights Risks." *Just Security*, April 28. https://www.hrw.org/news/2022/04/28/opening-stages-un-cybercrime-treaty-talks-reflect-human-rights-risks.

FSB (Financial Stability Board). 2020. "Effective Practices for Cyber Incident Response and Recovery: Final Report." October 19. https://www.fsb.org/2020/10/effective-practices-for-cyber-incident-response-and-recovery-final-report/.

GDPR. 2016. "European Union General Data Protection Regulation." chrome-extension://efaidnbmnnnibpcajpcglclefindmkaj/https://eur-lex.europa.eu/legal-content/EN/TXT/PDF/?uri=CELEX:32016R0679.

Gopalan, S. 2003. "Transitional Commercial Law: The Way Forward." *Am U. Int'l L. Rev* 18: 803–849.

Ignatov, A. 2022. "The BRICS Agenda on the Internet Governance." *International Organisations Research Journal* 17 (2): 86–109. (in English). https://iorj.hse.ru/en/2022-17-2/663282915.html.

International Law Commission. 2006. Fragmentation of International Law: Difficulties Arising from the Diversification and Expansion of International Law. chrome-extension://efaidnbmnnnibpcajpcglclefindmkaj/https://legal.un.org/ilc/documentation/english/a_cn4_l702pdf.

Johnston, A., and M. Trebilcock. 2013, Jun 12. "Fragmentation in International Trade law: Insights from the Global Investment Regime." *World Trade Review* 12 (4): 621–652.

Kabelka, L. 2022. "Controversy Surrounds New Cybercrime Protocol as Plenary Vote Still Hangs in the Balance." *Euractiv.*, May 16. https://www.euractiv.com/section/data-protection/news/controversy-surrounds-new-cybercrime-protocol-as-plenary-vote-still-hangs-in-the-balance/.

Kobrin, S. 2001. "Territoriality and the Governance of Cyberspace." *Journal of International Business Studies* 32: 687–704. https://doi.org/10.1057/palgrave.jibs.8490990.

Koch, R. 2020. What is the LGPD? Brazil's Version of the GDPR. *GDPR.EU*. https://gdpr.eu/gdpr-vs-lgpd/.

Letter to the United Nations to Include Human Rights Safeguards in Proposed Cybercrime Treaty. 2021. December 2. https://www.eff.org/deeplinks/2022/02/letter-united-nations-include-human-rights-safeguards-proposed-cybercrime-treaty (Joint Letter, 2021).

Li, Y., and Q. Liu. 2021. "A Comprehensive Review Study of Cyber-Attacks and Cyber Security; Emerging Trends and Recent Developments." *Energy Reports* 7: 8176–8186.

Marco Civil Law of the Internet in Brazil, Law No. 12.965. 2014. In Portuguese and English: https://publicknowledge.org/policy/marco-civil-english-version/. (Marco Civil, 2014), April 23.

Mauer, T., and A. Nelson. 2021b. "The Global Cyberthreat." *IMF Finance and Development*. March. 5chrome-extension://efaidnbmnnnibpcajpcglclefindmkaj/https://www.imf.org/external/pubs/ft/fandd/2021/03/pdf/global-cyber-threat-to-financial-systems-maurer.pdf.

Maurer, T., and A. Nelson. 2020a. International Strategy to Better Protect the Financial System against Cyber Threats. November 18. https://carnegieendowment.org/2020/11/18/international-strategy-to-better-protect-financial-system-against-cyber-threats-pub-83105.

NATO. 2022. Interoperability: Connecting Forces. February 22. https://www.nato.int/cps/en/natohq/topics_84112.htm.

O'Neill, J. 2001. "Building Better Global Economic BRICS." *Global Economics Paper* No. 66. Goldman Sachs, November. chrome-extension://efaidnbmnnnibpcajpcglclefindmkaj/https://www.goldmansachs.com/insights/archive/archive-pdfs/build-better-brics.pdf.

PDPB (Personal Data Protection Bill). 2019. Bill No. 373, Art. 33 Restriction on Transfer of Personal Data Outside India. chrome-extension://efaidnbmnnnibpcajpcglclefindmkaj/http://164.100.47.4/BillsTexts/LSBillTexts/Asintroduced/373_2019_LS_Eng.pdf (PDPB, 2019).

Pedersen, T., and S. Tallman. 2022. "Global Strategy Collections: Emerging Market Multinational Enterprises." *Global Strategy Journal* 12 (2): 199–208. https://onlinelibrary.wiley.com/doi/epdf/10.1002gsj.1439.

Radu, Roxana. 2019. *Negotiating Internet Governance*. London, UK: Oxford University Press.

Rodriguez, K., and M. Baghdasaryan. 2022. "UN Committee to Begin Negotiating New Cybercrime Treaty Amid Disagreement Among States Over Its Scope." *Electric Frontier Foundation*, February 15. https://www.eff.org/deeplinks/2022/02/un-committee-begin-negotiating-new-cybercrime-treaty-amid-disagreement-among.

Russian Proposal. 2021. June 29. chrome-extension://efaidnbmnnnibpcajpcglclefindmkaj/https://www.kommersant.ru/docs/2021/RF_28_July_2021_-_E.pdf.

Sheppard, L., E. Yayboke, and C. Ramos. 2021. The Real National Security Concerns over Data Localization. https://www.csis.org/analysis/real-national-security-concerns-over-data-localization.

Shrivastava, A., and R. Lakra. 2022. "Revisiting due Diligence in Cyberspace: Crafting International Law's Arsenal Against Transboundary Botnets." *International Journal of Law and Information Technology*, eaac021. https://doi.org/10.1093/ijlit/eaac021.

Singh, M. 2022. "India Withdraws Personal Data Bill that Alarmed Tech Giants." *TechCrunch+*. https://techcrunch.com/2022/08/03/india-government-to-withdraw-personal-data-protection-bill/?guccounter=1&guce_referrer=aHR0cHM6Ly93d3cuZ29vZ2xlLmNvbS8&guce_referrer_sig=AQAAAN1MYsz9a_ZslrGKCw3bTEPXILJs8CEW4x7eTRdvATuaz5XHHaCLQCBWFGAaPeHchxkG39mC84jbg9Dqgohi8tiqZmzX3Nyrvg2llZcdvF5j2pCaYQRdzu060hgol8rkMS8nieUt2mo_FThmTRU-b-or-M1TzXJegw0AsvsNqm-N.

Sukianto, A. 2023. India's Six-Hour Reporting Rule, July 30. https://www.upguard.com/blog/indias-6-hour-data-breach-reporting-rule.

Sverdrup, U. 2002. "An Institutional Perspective on Treaty Reform: Contextualizing the Amsterdam and Nice Treaties." *Journal of European Public Policy* 9 (1): 120–140. https://doi.org/10.1080/13501760110104208.

Theohary, C., and J. Rollins. 2015. "Cyberwar and Cyberterrorism: In Brief." *Congressional Research Service*. March 27. chrome-extension://efaidnbmnnnibpcajpcglclefindmkaj/https://sgp.fas.org/crs/natsec/R43955.pdf.

Tripathi, R. 2018. "Home Ministry Pitches for Budapest Convention on Cyber Security." *The Indian Express*. January 18. https://indianexpress.com/article/india/home-ministry-pitches-for-budapest-convention-on-cyber-security-rajnath-singh-5029314/.

Turner, L. 2022. "Researching the Harmonization of International Commercial Law." *GlobaLex*. May/June. https://www.nyulawglobal.org/globalex/Unification_Harmonization1.html#introduction.

Twigg-Flesner, C. 2021. *Foundations of International Commercial Law*. London, U.K.: Routledge Publications.

U.N. General Assembly resolution 74/247. 2019. December 27. https://digitallibrary.un.org/record/3847855?ln=en.

United Nations Manual. 1994. International Review of Criminal Policy-United Nations Manual on the Prevention and Control of Computer Related Crime. 1994 United Nations Crime and Justice Information Network. chrome-extension://efaidnbmnnnibpcajpcglclefindmkaj/https://www.unodc.org/pdf/Manual_ComputerRelatedCrime.PDF (U.N. Manual, 1994).

U.N. Report. 2020. U. N. Secretary General, Roadmap for Digital Cooperation 2020. chrome-extension://efaidnbmnnnibpcajpcglclefindmkaj/https://www.un.org/en/content/digital-cooperation-roadmap/assets/pdf/Roadmap_for_Digital_Cooperation_EN.pdf.

Wahl, T. 2018. "Commission Proposes Legislative Framework for E-Evidence." *Eucrim* 1: 35–36. June 29. https://eucrim.eu/news/commission-proposes-legislative-framework-e-evidence/.

Weismann, M. 2005. "The Convention on Cybercrime: A Harmonized Implementation of International Penal Law: What Prospects for Procedural Due Process?" *J. Marshall J. Computer & Info. L* 23: 329–362. https://repository.law.uic.edu/jitpl/vol23/iss2/4/.

Zander, L., A. Mockaitis, and C. Butler. 2012. "Leading Global Teams." *Journal of World Business* 47 (4): 592–603. https://www.researchgate.net/publication/257492674_Leading_global_teams.

Minimising unnecessary restrictions on cross-border data flows? Indonesia's position and challenges post personal data protection act enactment

Faiz Rahman and Cora Kristin Mulyani

ABSTRACT

In the era of massive digital development, data plays an essential role as a 'fuel' in reshaping and creating new opportunities in the digital landscape, especially in the digital economy. The significance of data for Indonesia can be seen from the amount of data created, collected, and analysed in various sectors. However, Indonesia also faces problems of data breaches that happened in recent years, which harm society and need immediate attention. This article examined Indonesia's data and cross-border data flow regulatory and institutional frameworks and its implementation challenges, especially with the recent enactment of a comprehensive Personal Data Protection Act (PDP Act), mainly inspired by the EU GDPR. This article shows that Indonesia is moving to less restrictive data-flow regulations than the previous regulatory regime but is still between the prescriptive and restrictive spectrum of data-flow regulation. This article argues that the enactment of the PDP Act can be momentum for Indonesia to evaluate the current regulatory framework to ensure that Indonesia's regulation is not providing unnecessary restrictions that lead to complexity of implementation and will hinder from benefiting the utilisation of data.

1. Introduction

In the era of massive digital development, data collection has become more accessible, as can be seen from the amount of data created, collected, and analysed in various sectors globally. By 2025, around 465 exabytes of data are expected to be created each day globally (Desjardins 2019). Moreover, the data explosion in the past decade has created new opportunities for data utilisation, which has led to new insights, data creation, and data analysis (Saha 2020). Additionally, given the interconnected nature of cyberspace, it is inevitable for those vast amounts of data to move across national jurisdictions.

In the current global landscape, the utilisation of cross-border data has become necessary. Cross-border data flows are also significant and are even referred to as the backbone of various digital service models (Voss 2020). However, the concept of cross-border data flow at the international level has not yet found consensus, as it is defined variously (United Nations Conference on Trade and Development 2021). For instance, Aaronson describes cross-border data flow as data that move across borders when individuals, companies, or governments allow data to be transferred from one country to another, where the data are processed or used (S. A. Aaronson 2019; Nguyen and Paczos 2020). In a broader sense, cross-border data flow can be defined as the unimpeded movement of data across international borders (Fefer 2020; Nguyen and Paczos 2020; World Economic Forum 2020b).

Furthermore, various concerns are raised when dealing with data that move beyond the reach of state jurisdiction, regarding, for example, asymmetric power relations among firms and between firms and consumers, and also regarding privacy and data protection (Casalini, López-González, and Nemoto 2021; Khumon 2018; LeSieur 2012). Therefore, how a country regulates data will affect how it utilises the data located in its domestic jurisdictions and abroad and addresses various emerging concerns in the cross-border data flow.

The cross-border data flow issue has been increasingly discussed outside of Indonesia in recent years, especially after the proposal of data free-flow with trust in the 2019 G20 Osaka. The Indonesian government echoed the issue through the Minister of Communication and Informatics, especially in response to the cross-border data-related proposal in previous G20 Digital Economy Working Group meetings, given the fact that in 2022, Indonesia holds the position of G20 Presidency. One of the priority issues discussed in the 2022 G20 Digital Economy Working Group meetings is cross-border data flow and data free flow with trust. Beyond that, the discussion on Indonesia's cross-border data flow regulatory framework remains underexplored, including an examination of the broader data regulatory landscape and an assessment of whether substantial changes have occurred following the enactment of the PDP Act (further discussed in Part 3 and Part 4).

Therefore, the discussion on cross-border data flow has its urgency. Indonesia is among the countries with the most extensive data produced globally, considering that 77% of Indonesia's population (approximately 212,9 million out of 275 million) are internet users, and approximately 167 million are social media users (We Are Social & KEPIOS 2023). The report by We are social and KEPIOS above can illustrate the considerable economic potential of data, considering various advanced mechanisms to analyse data produced. Indonesian President Joko Widodo even recognised the importance of data during his presidential speech on Indonesia's Independence Day in 2019, which stated that '*data is a new type of wealth for our nation, and it is more valuable than oil*' (Antara 2020). Furthermore, Hicks argued that the control over the production and dissemination of personal data represents a pivotal struggle in the global information economy, especially for the Global South countries, including Indonesia (Hicks 2021).

Indonesia recently stipulated Law No. 27 of 2022 on Personal Data Protection (PDP Act). This Act has become a legal basis for processing personal data and its enforcement, including transferring personal data across borders. Thus, the comprehensive PDP Act is expected to become a more robust legal basis than the previous lower-level regulations to safeguard against future data misuse and leaks. The enactment of the PDP Act is an important milestone, as Indonesia has faced a series of data breaches and misuses in recent years (BBC Indonesia 2021; CNN Indonesia 2022; Kompas 2020). These leaks have become a pressing issue and need to be addressed to enable safe and reliable data utilisation. Indonesia's development of cross-border data flow regulation will highly impact the way Indonesia utilises cross-border data and its positioning in the regional and global communities.

Before the stipulation of the PDP Act, some global institutions, such as UNCTAD, UNDP, and World Bank, classified Indonesia as a restrictive country or implemented a limited transfer model regulating cross-border data (United Nations Conference on Trade and Development 2021; United Nations Development Programme 2021; World Bank 2021b). Therefore, a further question arises regarding whether the stipulation of the PDP Act is changing Indonesia's position in the global cross-border data flow regulation landscape.

Given Indonesia's potential for data utilisation, recent legislative updates, and the ongoing discourse surrounding cross-border data flow, this article aims to comprehensively evaluate Indonesia's current regulatory framework regarding cross-border data flow. The article is structured as follows. The second part briefly outlines cross-border data flow issues, emphasizing the conflicting perspectives on data localization versus the free flow of data, providing context for Indonesia's evolving data flow regulation. The third part details Indonesia's regulatory approach to data in general and cross-border data flow, covering terminologies relevant to data movement, requirements, limitations, and concerns associated with facilitating data movement, and relevant government institutions responsible for overseeing cross-border data flow. The fourth chapter examines cross-border data flow dynamics following the enactment of the Personal Data Protection Act, assessing its impact on Indonesia's regulatory position and identifying associated challenges. This article endeavours to examine Indonesia's evolving stance on cross-border data flow regulation, offering valuable insights for policymakers and stakeholders.

2. Background: localisation and free flow of data

The discussion of cross-border data flows is inseparable from the issue of data localisation and the free flow of data. Data has become an essential asset for government and business (Arroyo et al. 2023), and therefore, control over data flow become more important in the global landscape and has significant implications for contemporary politics in many areas (Obendiek 2022). Moreover, different approaches to data flow also become a global political contestation, as rules to data flow often overlap and even conflict (Casalini and Gonzálezi 2019), and the emerging issue remains on whether to restrict the data flow by localising data or to enable free flow of data. Efforts to find a balanced approach between data localisation and data-free flow are quite difficult and remain an ongoing issue to address carefully (Mishra 2016; Topornin, Pyatkina, and Bokov 2023; Zimmerman 1982).

In general, the World Bank classifies three models of data transfer approaches, namely: (a) open transfer model, (b) conditional transfer model, and (c) limited transfer model. Each model has its characteristics and implications for cross-border data flow in a country (World Bank 2021b). The main characteristics of the open transfer model are the absence of provisions regarding government restrictions on cross-border personal data transfers and providing flexibility to the private sector in regulation and practice. The conditional transfer model strives to balance the obligation to protect data and the need for open data transfer. The policy goal in this conditional characteristic is protecting citizens' personal data. The limited transfer model is more restrictive and emphasises cybersecurity and other security concerns (The World Bank 2021a).

Furthermore, a report from the OECD highlights four broad approaches to cross-border data flow regulation: no regulation, ex-post accountability, flow conditional on safeguards and flow conditional on *ad hoc* authorisation (Casalini, López-González, and Nemoto 2021; Goodman and Risberg 2021). These broad approaches are perceived through the level of restrictiveness of data movement. According to the OECD, regulation of cross-border data flows varies greatly, reflecting each country's cultural preferences and policy objectives (Casalini, López-González, and Nemoto 2021). Moreover, the approaches above can be used simultaneously within the same jurisdiction, depending on the data types.

Nowadays, the approach to cross-border data flow is no longer rigid, especially in this big data era where cross-border data flow has dynamic and uncertain characteristics (Yang 2021). One of the current cross-border data flow challenges is policies and regulations (Atkinson and Cory 2021), as there is no global consensus regarding the regulatory framework for cross-border data flow (S. A. Aaronson 2019; Khumon 2018). Each country has its regulatory model according to its background conditions and state interests. For instance, the United States (US), the European Union (EU), and China, as actors that currently dominate the digital and economic field, have differing regulatory models and approaches (Atkinson and Cory 2021; Zheng 2021). The US has a more permissive policy, while the EU applies the precautionary principle through specific prerequisites, and China is restrictive towards cross-border data flows (Chin and Zhao 2022; Yang 2021; Zheng 2021).

Moreover, there is also a complex relationship between the free flow of data and trade agreements, human rights, and national security (S. A. Aaronson 2019; Mitchell and Hepburn 2017). With the ease of data exchange across borders in this digital era, finding international agreements solely for data flows has become challenging. States have varying interests in data utilisation and are responsible for protecting and respecting human rights established under international laws, leading to the incorporation of human rights language in data flow regulations (S. Aaronson 2015). Furthermore, trade agreements offer enforceable obligations in practice, making them an appealing venue for governing cross-border data flows (Burri 2014) and involving international bodies in resolving trade disputes. Considering the complicated relationship above, a well-handled cross-border data flow governance will have positive impacts on protecting data sovereignty, national data rights, and the development of the digital economy (Cuihong and Yuanzhi 2021).

3. Indonesia's regulatory framework on data and data flow

This part begins by mapping the country's data-related laws and regulations to grasp Indonesia's regulatory landscape. This mapping effort aims to understand the scope of data regulation within Indonesia, shedding light on regulatory complexity and coherence across different levels of regulations. Based on the collected data, four issues concerning the data flow regulatory framework are analysed: (a) the types of data subject to regulation; (b) terminology used to denote data movement; (c) regulatory requirements and limitations governing data movement within and beyond Indonesia's jurisdiction; and

(d) relevant government institutions responsible for overseeing data flow. The analysis of the four issues above allows for a nuanced assessment of Indonesia's position in cross-border data regulation. It helps validate or challenge the classification by international institutions like UNCTAD, UNDP, and the World Bank, which label Indonesia as a restrictive country in terms of regulating cross-border data (United Nations Conference on Trade and Development 2021; United Nations Development Programme 2021; World Bank 2021b).

3.1. How does Indonesia regulate data?

Data are difficult to regulate, and it becomes a challenge, especially on a transnational level, where it affects multiple issues and actors (Obendiek 2022), both public and private. Therefore, how a country regulates data is essential, not only regarding how they internally govern the data but also how it might relate to the country's transnational relations. The terms 'data' and 'information' are used interchangeably in various Indonesian regulations (hereafter, the term 'data' will be used). There are more than 50 regulations in Indonesia, from the Act level to the ministerial and institutional regulations levels identified to regulate or at least mention data (in specific sectors). The table below shows the mapping of data regulated in various legislation. It should be noted that one regulation might regulate several types of data, both personal and non-personal data (Table 1).

Based on the table above, 52 regulations concerning data are identified. However, not all regulations explicitly define and regulate the data types and requirements or limitations for data movement. Only several regulations define the data being regulated, such as the Geospatial Information Act, Industry Act, Population Administration Act, and the newly enacted PDP Act. Furthermore, the regulated data vary from non-personal to personal data. It is noteworthy that the unidentified data in the table could also become personal data, considering the general wording used in various regulations. Moreover, considering the number of regulations, it essentially shows the extensive scope of data and the high potential of data movement, both in the private and public sectors.

Specific to personal data, the first comprehensive PDP Act was enacted on 17 October 2022. Thus, regulations concerning the transfer of personal data previously regulated in various laws should refer to the PDP Act. However, even though Indonesia now has a comprehensive PDP Act, there is homework to harmonise and synchronise the implementation of data protection in various sectors previously regulated in a silo, as there is a tendency for sectoral institutions to continue using sectoral regulations in implementing personal data protection in that sector. Therefore, the harmonisation and synchronisation of sectoral laws and regulations are pivotal.

Table 1. Mapping of Indonesian regulations related to data/information.

		Type of data	
Regulation Level	**No. of Regulations**	Personal	Non-Personal/ Unidentified
Act	17	21	20
Government Regulation	9	18	16
Presidential Regulation	1	1	1
Ministerial/Institutional Regulation	25	25	17
	52	65	54

Source: Compiled by Author, 2022.

Even after the enactment of the PDP Act, the inconsistency in regulations is still prevalent. Take an example of the Population Administration Act, which was the first Act to define personal data. The Act has a different 'approach' to regulating personal data, as it differentiates 'personal data' (See Article 84) and 'individual data' (See Article 58). Consequently, there is a different degree of protection toward data that is not categorised as 'personal data' under the Population Administration Act, even though, in principle, 'individual data' such as full name, Sex, religion, marital status, are categorised as personal data (See Article 4 paragraph (3) of the PDP Act).

Furthermore, it is also noteworthy that the issue of inconsistency is more apparent in the regulation of non-personal data, which is essentially still being regulated in silos. Some examples of non-personal data include geospatial data (See Law No. 4 of 2011 on Geospatial Information), trade data (See Law No. 7 of 2014 on Trade), and industry data (See Law No. 3 of 2014 on Industry). As there is no standard on data flow, how these data move inside and outside Indonesia's jurisdiction depends on each sector's regulations.

Although many Acts already define their regulated data, another concern that should be noted is that various data types were introduced at the implementing regulation level. For instance, the definition of trade data and information mentioned in the Trade Act only appears in the Government Regulation on Trade Information Systems. Additionally, other types of data that are entirely new also appear in the implementing regulations, such as data related to trade through an electronic system in Government Regulation on Trade through Electronic System, and Traffic Data and Subscriber Information mentioned in the Minister of Communication and Informatics Regulation on Private Electronic System Operator (ESO) as one of the Government Regulation on Electronic System and Transactions Implementation.

It illustrates that the regulatory framework gives the impression of being more flexible regarding data classification, as the meaning of the data is regulated in implementing regulations, which tend to be easier to revise. Therefore, currently considered general data can be regarded as specific or strategic in the future, leading to stricter protection and security. On the other hand, it also shows that data regulations in lower-level regulations do not provide strong legal protection, especially concerning data subjects' privacy protection. However, since Indonesia now has a comprehensive PDP Act, the processing of personal data introduced in lower-level regulations should comply with the PDP Act, meaning that the issue of harmonisation of regulations is pivotal to ensure compliance.

The 'detailing' of data types in lower-level regulations is inseparable from the increasingly technical regulations, which indirectly encourage more detailed data that is regulated. Therefore, the more specialised a regulation, the greater the potential for detailing the data types. Consequently, the regulations are increasingly sectoral, especially the ministerial or institutional regulations. The sectoral approach is prone to potential inconsistencies in the implementation of data utilisation and protection by different ministries and institutions, including data transfer.

3.2. Terminology related to data movement

As aforementioned, there is no consensus on the terminology of cross-border data flow. This article uses a broader interpretation approach as described at the beginning by emphasising the movement of data from one 'territory' of the country to the 'territory' of another country (Arroyo et al. 2023; World Economic Forum 2020a). In general, various regulations in Indonesia do not recognise the term cross-border data flow. Multiple terms describe data movement, both within the country and across borders. These terms include exchanging, giving, sending, conveying, distributing, and transferring.

Furthermore, the terms sending, giving, exchanging, and conveying are dominantly used in various regulations to refer to the movement of data from one place to another. The term data transfer, which is often used in the literature concerning cross-border data flow, is only found in at least 5 (five) regulations, namely the PDP Act, Health Act, Electronic Information and Transaction Act, Government Regulation on Electronic Systems and Transactions Implementation, and Central Bank Regulation on Payment Systems. However, only three explicitly mention the outward transfer, namely the PDP Act (See Article 56), Health Act (See, for instance, Article 349), and Central Bank Regulation on Payment Systems (See Article 109). Moreover, as many types of data are introduced in various sectoral regulations and considering the very general nature of most of the provisions, the potential for data movement, including outward movements, is even higher.

3.3. Requirements, limitations, and concerns in facilitating data movement

Various sectoral regulations also specify requirements for cross-border data transfer in specific sectors, such as trade, finance, banking, and government. For instance, Government Regulation No. 80 of 2019 on Trade through Electronic Systems is one of the implementing regulations of the Trade Act for the trade sector, Minister of Finance Regulations, and regulations by the Financial Services Authority and Central Bank of Indonesia, which mainly focus on financial technology and banking sectors. Among various laws related to data transfer, at least 12 (twelve) regulations explicitly mention or regulate the outward data movement or vice versa (Table 2).

Specific to cross-border data flow for personal data, it is regulated in Chapter VII (Personal Data Transfer) of the PDP Act. It requires the transfer of personal data to a controller or processor outside the Indonesian jurisdiction to comply with the PDP Act. The data controller or processor must ensure that the country of domicile of the party receiving the transfer of personal data has the same level or higher protection of personal data compared to the PDP Act. Otherwise, the data controller must ensure an adequate and binding data protection mechanism and obtain the data subject's consent.

In the new Health Act, data and information managed by Health Information System providers can be transferred outside Indonesia's jurisdiction for specific and limited purposes, based on permission from the central government (See Article 349 paragraph (7)). The outward transfer can be done, for instance, to mitigate pandemics or epidemics, or for international cooperation in the health sector. As the Health Act was enacted after the PDP Act, it is logical that the transfer of health data should be based on data protection principles, especially purpose limitations. Even the PDP Act requires that the transfer of specific personal data, including health data, should employ data protection impact assessments (See Article 34), and the data controller should appoint data protection officers (See Article 53). However, which 'central government' institution can provide

Table 2. Several national regulations related to cross-border data flow.

Legal basis	Type of data regulated
Law No. 27 of 2022 on Personal Data Protection	Personal Data
Law No. 17 of 2023 on Health	Health Data
Government Regulation No. 71 of 2019 on Implementation of Electronic Systems and Transactions	Personal Data, Electronic Data
Minister of Communications and Informatics Regulation No. 20 of 2016 on Personal Data Protection in Electronic Systems	Personal Data
Government Regulation No. 80 of 2019 on Trade through Electronic System	Personal Data
Government Regulation No. 5 of 2020 on Trade Information Systems	Trade Data and Trade Information
Government Regulation No. 46 of 2014 on Health Information Systems	Health Data and Information
Minister of Finance Regulation No. 39/ PMK.03/2017 on Information Exchange Procedures Based on International Agreements	Financial Information
Minister of Finance Regulation No. 70/PMK.03/2017 *jo.* No. 19/2018 on Technical Guidance on Access to Financial Information for Tax Purposes	Financial Information
Bank Indonesia Regulation No. 22/23/PBI/2020 on Payment System	Individual Customer Data
Financial Services Authority Regulation No. 25 /POJK.03/2019 on Reporting of Foreign Customer Information Related to Taxation to Partner Countries or Partner Jurisdictions	Financial Information
Financial Services Authority Regulation No. 5/POJK.03/2022 on Credit Information Management Agency	Financial Information

Source: Processed by Author, 2022.

permission is unclear. Although the provision indicates that it will be the Minister of Health, according to the PDP Act, the PDP Authority also has a role in assessing the fulfilment of personal data transfer requirements (See Article 60 letter f). Hence, it could be logical for the PDP Authority to authorise permission for data transfer, including health data.

Moreover, cross-border data flow is also substantially regulated in Government Regulation No. 71 of 2019 on Implementation of Electronic Systems and Transactions (Government Regulation on EST) and the Minister of Communication and Informatics Regulation No. 20 of 2016 on Personal Data Protection in Electronic Systems (MCI Regulation on PDP). In the Government Regulation on EST, at least two provisions indicate data movement from within the country to abroad and vice versa.

The first can be found in Article 20, which regulates the operation of an Electronic System in the public sector that can process Electronic Systems and Electronic Data outside the territory of Indonesia if the storage technology is not available domestically (See Article 20 paragraph (3)). However, specific requirements must be met to be able to do this (See Article 20 paragraph (4)), considering that, in principle, Electronic System Operators (ESOs) in the public sector must process data in the territory of Indonesia (See Article 20 paragraph (2)).

The second one is Article 21, which regulates the implementation of private sector Electronic Systems that can process Electronic Systems and Electronic Data outside the territory of Indonesia (See Article 21 paragraph (1)). In contrast to the public sector, private sector ESOs are allowed to carry out processing within and/or outside the territory of Indonesia. However, if data processing is carried out outside the territory of Indonesia, the private sector ESOs are obliged to ensure the effectiveness of supervision by the Ministry or Institution and law enforcement (See Article 21 paragraph (2)). Moreover, private sector ESOs should provide access to Electronic Systems and Electronic Data for supervision and law enforcement based on Indonesian laws and regulations (See Article 21 paragraph (3)).

The Government Regulation on EST also opens the possibility of further technical and sectoral regulations. For instance, private sector ESO in the financial sector should comply with regulations concerning Electronic Systems and Electronic Data issued by supervisory authorities of the financial sector. It can be seen from various regulations from the Central Bank of Indonesia, the Financial Services Authority, and the Minister of Finance above. Moreover, the MCI Regulation on PDP explicitly regulates the transfer of personal data by public and private ESOs, regional governments, and citizens. If they want to transfer personal data outside Indonesian jurisdiction, they should coordinate with the Ministry of Communications and Informatics or authorised institution and comply with the regulations concerning the exchange of personal data across the border. However, this regulation must be adjusted as the new PDP Act also has cross-border data transfer provisions.

In the trade sector, for example, Government Regulation No. 80 of 2019 on Trade through Electronic Systems (Government Regulation on TES) requires business actors to store personal data in accordance with personal data protection standards or the prevalence of developing business practices. Government Regulation on TES also prohibits the transfer of personal data outside the Indonesian jurisdiction unless the Minister of Trade declares that the countries have the same standards or level of protection as Indonesia.

In the health sector, according to the new Health Act, the processing of health data may be carried out abroad with the Central Government's permission. The policy to process health data is slightly changed from the 2014 Government Regulation on Health Information Systems. Although the current Health Act also mandated that the health information system be implemented in Indonesia's jurisdiction, it is still possible to process that in accordance with laws and regulations. The provision is still the same as the 2014 Government Regulation. The difference is that in the 2014 Government Regulation on Health Information Systems, the implementation could be done under the Minister's permission. Nevertheless, the current Health Act did not explicitly mention the specific institution, even though it will most likely be the Minister of Health.

The analysis above signifies that Indonesia still emphasises a sectoral approach. The sectoral approach is more prevalent in the context of supervision over Electronic Systems. Government Regulation on EST regulates that ministers or institutions in relevant sectors are required to formulate provisions regarding supervision in their sector, although they still have to coordinate with the Minister of Communication and Informatics. Furthermore, in the context of sending/transferring data outside Indonesia's territory, there are also sectoral provisions. For example, the Government Regulation on TES stipulates that the Minister of Trade decides whether personal data can be sent outward, while in the MCI Regulation on PDP, the assessment is conducted by the Minister of Communication and Informatics. This sectoral characteristic can also be seen in other regulations governing the authority of ministries/institutions related to cross-border data, as described above.

Another thing that should be a concern is the scope of data that can 'cross the border'. Reflecting on the vast scope of data and the various terminologies referring to data movement, the potential for data to 'cross the border' is very high, regardless of the absence of explicit provisions concerning cross-border data movement. The absence of cross-border data movement provisions will undoubtedly become a challenge for the government in the future to be able to classify data that can 'cross the border'. It is inseparable from the character of the data itself, which is multidimensional (Chapelle and Porciuncula 2021). Moreover, issues related to the protection of personal data, cybersecurity, and intellectual property are also issues that are often mentioned when discussing cross-border data flow and need to be considered in formulating regulations related to cross-border data flow (Casalini, López-González, and Nemoto 2021; United Nations Conference on Trade and Development 2021; United Nations Development Programme 2021).

3.4. Relevant government institutions in governing cross-border data flow

Based on the analysis of various data and data flow regulations, at least 6 (six) government institutions are explicitly mentioned as stakeholders related to cross-border data. However, due to the broad scope of data/information used and various regulations that have provisions concerning data movement, other stakeholders (ministries and non-ministerial government institutions) are most likely responsible for cross-border data, either personal or non-personal data.

Based on the current framework, the Ministry of Communication and Informatics is the main stakeholder regarding cross-border data flow (See also United Nations Conference on Trade and Development 2023). The Ministry has been the main stakeholder in the implementation of the Electronic Information and Transaction Act and its implementing regulations, which are reflected in its duties and responsibilities specified in the Presidential Regulation on the Ministry of Communication and Informatics. The Ministry also became the leading government institution in the 2022 G20 Digital Economy Working Group meeting, and one of the main issues proposed was cross-border data flow.

Additionally, the Ministry of Communication and Informatics was actively involved in formulating and implementing various regulations concerning cross-border data, including the Government Regulation on EST and the PDP Act. Furthermore, until recently, the Ministry also actively raised and supported the discussion of cross-border data flow issues during the ASEAN Summit in 2023 (Bestari 2023; Kuncorojati 2023; Ministry of Communication and Informatics of the Republic of Indonesia 2023). Considering the roles that the Ministry has played, it might remain one of the main stakeholders in regulating cross-border data flow in the future.

After the enactment of the PDP Act, the PDP Authority, which at the time of the writing of this article is not yet established, will become a supervisory authority for cross-border personal data transfer, supposedly for all sectors. The President will establish this institution, and further provisions shall be governed by a Presidential Regulation (see Article 58 paragraphs (2) and (3) of the PDP Act). In the data transfer context, Personal Data Protection Authority (PDP Authority) has the authority to assess the fulfilment of the requirements for personal data transfer outside the jurisdiction of the Republic of Indonesia (see Article 60 Letter f of the PDP Act).

However, it is not explained what the PDP Authority must do when conditions are not met and whether it can refuse data transfer or only provide a recommendation (which is substantially not binding). Therefore, the Government Regulation concerning data transfer as mandated by the PDP Act must provide precise technicalities for the PDP Authority in carrying out its various authorities, including the decisions issued by the PDP Authority related to the transfer of personal data issues. Otherwise, further technicalities concerning the implementation of the PDP Authority's power should be elaborated in the Government Regulation on PDP Authority as mandated by Article 61 of the PDP Act.

Unfortunately, under the draft of the Government Regulation on the Implementation of the PDP Act (Government Regulation on PDP) published by the Ministry of Communication and Informatics in August 2023, the authority to supervise data transfer is not further elaborated and remains the same as in the PDP Act. The draft of the Government Regulation on PDP did not even mandate the PDP Authority to regulate the assessment methods, even though it is still possible by law for the PDP Authority to enact regulation concerning the assessment for outward data transfer.

Furthermore, Table 3 above also shows that various sectoral institutions become the main stakeholders responsible for supervising cross-border data implementation in each sector. For instance, in the banking sector, cross-border data flow is supervised explicitly by the Central Bank of Indonesia, the financial services sector is supervised by the Financial Services Authority, and trade in an electronic system is supervised by the Minister of Trade. Consequently, the regulation and implementation will technically be

Table 3. Government institutions responsible for cross-border data.

Government Stakeholder	Legal Basis	Types of Data
Ministry of Communication and Informatics	• Government Regulation No. 71 of 2019 on Implementation of Electronic Systems and Transactions • Minister of Communications and Informatics Regulation No. 20 of 2016 on Personal Data Protection in Electronic Systems 20	Personal Data (all), Electronic Data
Ministry of Trade	• Government Regulation No. 80 of 2019 on Trade through Electronic System • Government Regulation No. 5 of 2020 on Trade Information Systems	Personal Data (related to trade activities), Trade Data, and Trade Information
Ministry of Health	Government Regulation No. 46 of 2014 on Health Information Systems	Personal Data (related to health), Health Data (a specific terminology that is used by Government Regulation on Health Information Systems, but it is not always personal data)
Bank Indonesia (Central Bank of Indonesia)	Bank Indonesia Regulation No. 22/23/PBI/2020 on Payment System	Individual Customer Data
Financial Services Authority	• Financial Services Authority Regulation No. 25 /POJK.03/2019 on Reporting of Foreign Customer Information Related to Taxation to Partner Countries or Partner Jurisdictions • Financial Services Authority Regulation No. 5/POJK.03/2022 on Credit Information Management Agency	Financial Information
Ministry of Finance	• Minister of Finance Regulation No. 39/ PMK.03/2017 on Information Exchange Procedures Based on International Agreements • Minister of Finance Regulation No. 70/ PMK.03/2017 *jo.* No. 19/2018 on Technical Guidance on Access to Financial Information for Tax Purposes	Financial Information
Personal Data Protection Authority	Law No. 27 of 2022 Personal Data Protection	Personal Data (all)

Source: Processed by Author, 2022.

handled by the relevant authorities in each sector, whether in coordination with the Ministry of Communication and Informatics. This condition strengthens the argument that Indonesia's cross-border data flow implementation is still regulated in silos.

As aforementioned, silo regulations are also endorsed by the Government Regulation on EST, which requires the relevant sector to formulate regulations to supervise their sector. Similar provisions also endorse sectoralism in the Government Regulation on EST. For instance, Article 18 paragraph (4) of the Government Regulation requires the deletion of electronic information that is no longer relevant in specific sectors to be regulated by relevant ministries/agencies after coordinating with the Minister of Communication and Information. Furthermore, Article 21 paragraph (4) states that the provisions regarding the management, processing, and storage of Electronic Systems and Electronic Data for private sector ESOs in the financial sector are further regulated by the regulatory and supervisory authorities of the financial sector. Unlike some Articles above, in the context of the financial sector, there is no provision about the necessity to coordinate with the Ministry of Communication and Informatics.

Regarding personal data protection, apart from the PDP Act, the provisions in Law No. 14 of 2008 (Public Information Disclosure Act) and Presidential Regulation No. 95 of 2018 on Electronic-Based Government System (Presidential Regulation on EBGS) require all state institutions, ministries, institutions, and local governments are parties that are also responsible for data protection. The Public Information Disclosure Act obligates all Public Bodies to restrict access to excluded public information, including public information that can reveal private secrets (See Article 17 letter h). Furthermore, the Presidential Regulation on EBGS regulated data and information, which includes all types of data and information owned by the government and state institutions, as well as regional governments, and/or obtained from the public, business actors, and/or other parties (See Article 26 paragraph (1)). Moreover, the Presidential Regulation on EBGS mandated the use of data and information in a data-sharing manner, meaning that any data and information (including personal data held by agencies) can be shared among government institutions.

The examination of regulations and stakeholders above illustrates that the extensive scope of data/information and the increasing technical regulations governing the various data lead to the expanding number of government institutions involved and responsible for implementing cross-border data. Hence, despite the establishment of the new PDP Authority in the PDP Act, the existing silo approach often results in discrepancies in how different ministries and agencies implement and supervise cross-border data flow. Additionally, sector-specific institutions may lean towards applying their sectoral regulations. Therefore, integrating regulation and implementation through a whole-of-government approach is one of the solutions for the governance of cross-border data flows. Ideally, regulating cross-border data flows in a holistic approach should balance the uniqueness of a country's digital development needs, regulatory and technological capacity, and other external considerations (United Nations Conference on Trade and Development 2021).

4. Post-PDP act: Indonesia's position, challenges, and way forward

As aforementioned, Indonesia now has a comprehensive Act as a legal basis for protecting citizens' personal data. Therefore, data controllers and processors must comply with the

PDP Act provisions when processing personal data, including cross-border transfer of personal data. However, does this significantly change the position of Indonesia's cross-border data flow regulatory framework, or does it leave things relatively unchanged?

In 2019, the government revoked Government Regulation No. 82 of 2012 and introduced Government Regulation No. 71 of 2019 regarding the Implementation of Electronic Systems and Transactions (Government Regulation on EST). This 2019 Government Regulation on EST, which serves as the primary implementing regulation for the Electronic Information and Transactions Act, appears to adopt a less restrictive approach toward data flow than the 2012 Government Regulation. The provisions in the 2012 Government Regulation on EST demonstrate a more restrictive approach, characterized by strict limitations on cross-border data transfers, as evidenced by the inclusion of data localisation provisions (Ferracane 2017). For instance, under Article 43 of the 2012 Government Regulation on EST, entities conducting Electronic Transactions were obliged to store their transaction data within Indonesia's territorial jurisdiction and employ national Electronic System networks. However, these obligations were removed in the 2019 Government Regulation on EST.

The alterations within the prevailing regulatory framework, particularly from the transition from the 2012 Government Regulation on EST to the 2019 Government Regulation on the EST regime, are closely linked to the government's endeavours to foster Indonesia's digital economy. These efforts encompass a range of digital-related policies, Indonesia's participation in bilateral negotiations such as the Comprehensive Economic Partnership Agreement (CEPA) with several nations and regions, and involvement in multilateral forums like the G20. These engagements have indirectly pushed Indonesia to adopt a more 'flexible' approach (Burhan 2022).

As an example, within the Indonesia-Australia Comprehensive Economic Partnership Agreement (CEPA) – which was ratified under Law No. 1 of 2020, it was stated in Article 13.11.2 of the agreement stipulates that both parties are obligated to permit the transfer of information, including personal data, across national boundaries through electronic means. That consensus applies to protected businesses. The EU also advocated for a comparable strategy during negotiations for the Indonesia-EU trade agreement. The EU's proposal regarding provisions related to cross-border data flows and protection of personal data and privacy highlighted that cross-border data flows should not be restricted between the Parties, for instance, by requiring the localisation of data in the party's territory for storage or processing (European Union 2018).

Furthermore, in the G20 Leaders' Declaration spanning from 2019 to 2021, there was an assertion that cross-border data flow encourages increased productivity and innovation, so it needs to be facilitated by taking into account the protection of privacy and prioritising consumer and business trust. Even in the 2022 G20 Digital Economy Working Group meetings, discussions were directed to provide a more flexible approach toward data flow. Moreover, Indonesia failed to propose the principle of reciprocity – requiring mutual imposition of advantages and disadvantages in cross-border data flow, including reciprocal safeguards and treatments – as one of the proposed principles of cross-border data flow and data free flow with trust, alongside fairness, lawfulness, and transparency (Chaudhury 2022; G20 Indonesia 2022; Ministry of Communication and Informatics of the Republic of Indonesia 2022). The principle of reciprocity was excluded in the 2022 G20 Digital Economy Minister Meeting's Chair's Summary (G20 Digital Economy Ministers' Meeting 2022).

Moreover, although the 2019 Government Regulation on EST is deemed less restrictive, according to the MCI Regulation on PDP, ESOs still need to coordinate with the Ministry when conducting the international transfer of personal data. Consequently, even though the regulations may give the impression of being less restrictive, Indonesia continues to adopt a conditional restriction approach toward cross-border data flow. This approach requires foreign states and organizations to comply with various requirements stipulated across multiple Indonesian laws and regulations. Therefore, when placed on the cross-border data flows regulatory spectrum established by UNCTAD, Indonesia's regulatory framework remains situated somewhere in the middle, between prescriptive and restrictive/guarded approaches (United Nations Conference on Trade and Development 2021). Furthermore, Indonesia maintains a relatively more restrictive position than its neighbouring countries within ASEAN, including Malaysia, Singapore, and the Philippines (Khumon 2018; The World Bank 2021a).

The situation appears to have changed following the enactment of the PDP Act, with no explicit provisions mandating the storage of personal data within Indonesia's borders. In various public discussions, the Ministry of Communication and Informatics stated that Indonesia drew substantial inspiration from the EU General Data Protection Regulation (GDPR) (See Agustini 2020; Faisal 2020). This GDPR-inspired approach, in terms of cross-border data regulation, is regarded as prescriptive, involving rigorous compliance requirements for cross-border data flows (United Nations Conference on Trade and Development 2021). However, some issues related to cross-border data regulations within the PDP Act must be addressed to ensure the smooth implementation of cross-border data flow.

First, regarding the entities capable of data transfer, the PDP Act explicitly specifies that only data controllers have the authority to transfer data abroad, while data processors remain unregulated. In practice, it is highly likely that data processors not only engage in data transfers but also delegate processing tasks to sub-processors. This practice is also reflected, for instance, in the EU Standard Contractual Clauses (SCC) and ASEAN Model Contractual Clauses (MCC), both of which show that transfers from processor to processor (and sub-processor) or from processor to controller are allowed (See The Association of Southeast Asian Nations (ASEAN) & European Commission 2023). This situation creates a legal void concerning data transfers from one processor to another or sub-processors. Unfortunately, the draft of the Government Regulation on PDP does not provide further clarification on this matter. Consequently, the legality of international transfers by data processors remains unaddressed.

Notably, the provisions within the PDP Act differ slightly from those found in other personal data protection regulations, particularly among ASEAN countries such as Malaysia, Singapore, and Thailand. These legislations permit data transfers to be executed by either data controllers or data processors, subject to specific prerequisites (See Section 129 Malaysia PDP Act, Section 26 Singapore PDP Act, and Section 28-Section 29 Thailand PDP Act). Only the Philippines adopts a similar approach to Indonesia, as the one responsible for the transfer of personal information abroad is the personal information controller (Section 21 of the Philippines PDP Act).

Second, there is a concern regarding the existence of a 'levelling' of cross-border data transfer requirements, similar to what is employed in the GDPR. Article 56 of the PDP Act is structured to move from the most stringent to the least restrictive requirements. In ASEAN, only Malaysia has a similar approach (See Section 129 paragraphs (2) and (3) of

Malaysia PDP Act). On the other hand, Singapore and the Philippines adopted an adequacy approach with accompanying exemptions (See Section 26 paragraph (1) Singapore PDP Act and Sections 28–29 of Thailand PDP Act). Furthermore, the Philippines does not explicitly define its approach and simply states that outward transfers should be accountable (Section 21 of the Philippines Privacy Act).

Moreover, the language employed in the Indonesian PDP Act bears similarities to, yet also notable differences from, the EU GDPR. Under the GDPR, the transfer of personal data is conducted based on an adequacy decision. If such a decision is absent, a controller or processor may engage in cross-border personal data transfers based on appropriate safeguards (See Article 46 of the EU GDPR). Furthermore, if neither an adequacy decision nor appropriate safeguards are in place, specific circumstances allow the data controller or processor to proceed with cross-border data transfers, such as obtaining explicit consent from the data subject. Compared to Indonesia's approach, the formulation of the PDP Act is not as comprehensive as that found in the EU GDPR. This distinction potentially creates vulnerabilities in safeguarding individuals' data during cross-border transfers, particularly in the absence of detailed implementing regulations.

Specifically on the issue of data transfer based on the data subject's consent, the Indonesian PDP Act lacks clarification on the specific obligations required of data controllers when seeking consent from data subjects. This provision presents the potential for exploitation by data controllers, as practical approval can be obtained in a somewhat 'unilateral' manner, such as during user registration on an application. However, the draft of the Government Regulation on PDP appears to address this issue. According to Article 190 of the draft of the Government Regulation on PDP, data transfers based on the approval of data subjects can only be carried out under certain conditions, including non-repetitive transfers, transfers involving only a limited number of data subjects, and transfers necessary for the purposes of compelling legitimate interests without overriding the interests or rights and freedoms of the data subjects. The controllers must assess all the circumstances surrounding the data transfer and apply appropriate safeguards. Furthermore, the controllers are required to inform the PDP Authority and the data subject about the transfer and the compelling legitimate interests involved. The wording in this Article is identical to that found in Article 49 paragraph (1) of the EU GDPR, which regulates derogations for data transfers for specific situations.

While the draft of Article 190 within the Government Regulation on PDP appears to provide necessary details to mitigate the potential abuse in determining the level of data transfer, there remains a need for more explicit clarification concerning specific criteria for data transfer based on the consent of data subjects. For instance, further clarification is needed regarding the definition of a 'non-repetitive' transfer and the specific parameters for classifying a transfer as involving only a 'limited number of data subjects'. These terms could potentially be subject to broad interpretations by data controllers and processors. Further elaboration upon these definitions is crucial to ensure that the preventive measures outlined in the draft of the Government Regulation on PDP do not inadvertently create opportunities for data controllers to exploit loopholes, thereby violating the rights of data subjects.

Moreover, it is also worth noting that although Indonesia has introduced a comprehensive PDP Act, its scope is limited to the regulations governing cross-border personal data.

As previously mentioned, various other regulations govern non-personal data, encompassing categories like geospatial data, industrial data, statistics, etc. Furthermore, given the abundance of laws and regulations in Indonesia, as explained above, it is plausible that the volume of non-personal data exceeds that of personal data. Therefore, the government should also contemplate establishing standards for the transfer of non-personal data to promote consistent practices in data transfer.

Furthermore, Indonesia's active engagement in those mentioned above bilateral and multilateral forums presents an advantageous opportunity for the country to leverage cross-border data utilisation. Nonetheless, several challenges associated with cross-border data flow, such as privacy and personal data protection (Khumon 2018; LeSieur 2012), must be addressed. In light of these challenges, cross-border data regulations within the PDP Act serve as vital safeguards to protect data subjects from potential infringements in data processing by data controllers and processors.

Additionally, from a more technical approach, the growing accessibility of advanced data analysis algorithms and hardware makes it easier to connect datasets and deduce personal data from ostensibly non-personal data (Finck and Pallas 2020). Therefore, reconciling the interests of privacy and data protection with those of the digital economy and trade poses a significant challenge in implementing cross-border data flow, given the frequent conflicts between these spheres (S. A. Aaronson 2019). The complexities related to data governance, digital economy, and trade become more pronounced due to their close ties with non-personal data.

Furthermore, there is a pressing need to prioritise institutional and technical capabilities to complement the regulatory framework. This urgency stems from the numerous cyberattack incidents leading to data breaches that have occurred in Indonesia in recent years. These incidents serve as a stark reminder of the country's imperative to strengthen cybersecurity and personal data protection. Therefore, enhancing institutional and technical capabilities is crucial. In addition to the PDP Act, the enactment of a comprehensive Cybersecurity Act is equally essential to offer robust assurances of certainty and legal protection in the implementation of cross-border data flow.

Finally, the implementation of cross-border data flow needs to be supported by regulations that do not contain unnecessary restrictions to support the implementation of cross-border data flow. It implies that a thoughtful evaluation of the essential aspects requiring restrictions must be undertaken if restrictions are to be imposed. Moreover, some argue that data localisation regulations are perceived as hindrances to economic development (Svantesson 2020). Thus, even in cases where an organization opts for data localisation policies, these should be aimed at strategic data that significantly affects the continuity of state administration and can only be accessed through intra-networks. Conversely, alternative policies akin to those in New Zealand can be adopted, where Electronic System Operators can store data anywhere but must be willing to provide their data when the government requests (Harrison and Fordham 2020). Given the myriad regulations governing data flow and data management, Indonesia needs to implement a whole-of-government approach, not a siloed or sectoral one. This approach should extend to the relevant government institutions tasked with overseeing cross-border data flow, ensuring uniformity in the regulation and implementation of cross-border data flow and personal data protection across all government bodies and state and local government agencies.

5. Conclusion and recommendations

While the economic potential of data is undeniably appealing, the government must be mindful of the importance of protecting citizens' rights to data, especially in light of recent data breaches that have posed significant challenges. The findings and discussions illustrate the complexity of Indonesia's legal framework related to data and cross-border data flow. This complexity arises from the multitude of regulations governing data and the diverse array of government institutions responsible for data governance within their respective sectors.

Indonesia has experienced notable dynamics and changes in recent years, suggesting a shift toward a less restrictive regulatory framework. However, a closer examination of Indonesia's regulations reveals that the overall approach to cross-border data flow remains situated between prescriptive and restrictive paradigms. This is evident in the various requirements governing cross-border data transfers, as discussed earlier. Therefore, the government must avoid imposing unnecessary restrictions that could exacerbate implementation complexities. Hence, adopting a more integrated approach to cross-border data flow regulation is essential, as the implementation of regulations and policies for cross-border data flow might impact multiple sectors. This integrated approach would streamline implementation complexity, provided there is a robust legal foundation at the Act level, particularly concerning data protection and cybersecurity. While the PDP Act appears to adopt a less restrictive stance on cross-border personal data flow, its implementation represents both an opportunity and a challenge for Indonesia to establish a cohesive legal, institutional, and technical framework for cross-border data flow. Moreover, it is worth noting that not all data falls under the category of personal data, and thus, distinct regulatory frameworks beyond the scope of the PDP Act may apply.

Therefore, maintaining consistent regulatory standards for both personal and non-personal data is essential to ensure uniform implementation of cross-border data flow regulations across various data types. This approach acknowledges the multifaceted nature of data in the digital age, recognising its multi-sectoral and multidimensional relevance, spanning from individual citizens to the international level (United Nations Conference on Trade and Development 2021). Nevertheless, it is noteworthy that there are considerable complications in drawing the boundaries between personal and non-personal data (Finck and Pallas 2020), particularly in Indonesia, where numerous laws and regulations are in place. While this article has offered a brief overview of the overall regulatory framework pertaining to data, further research dedicated to exploring the complexities of personal and non-personal data within the Indonesian context is imperative.

Acknowledgments

The author thanks the Faculty of Law, Gadjah Mada University, for providing grants and funding for this research.

Disclosure statement

No potential conflict of interest was reported by the author(s).

Funding

This work was supported by Universitas Gadjah Mada.

ORCID

Faiz Rahman http://orcid.org/0000-0002-2629-0486

References

Aaronson, S. 2015. "Why Trade Agreements are not Setting Information Free: The Lost History and Reinvigorated Debate Over Cross-Border Data Flows, Human Rights, and National Security." *World Trade Review* 14 (04): 671–700. https://doi.org/10.1017/S1474745615000014.

Aaronson, S. A. 2019. "Data is Different, and That's why the World Needs a new Approach to Governing Cross-Border Data Flows." *Digital Policy, Regulation and Governance* 21 (5): 441–460. https://doi.org/10.1108/DPRG-03-2019-0021.

Agustini, P. 2020. "UU PDP akan Permudah Pertukaran Data dengan Negara Lain." Ministry of Communication and Informatics of the Republic of Indonesia. https://aptika.kominfo.go.id/2020/11/uu-pdp-akan-permudah-pertukaran-data-dengan-negara-lain/.

Antara. 2020. "Jokowi: Data adalah New Oil, Bahkan Lebih Berharga dari Minyak." Tempo. https://bisnis.tempo.co/read/1299253/jokowi-data-adalah-new-oil-bahkan-lebih-berharga-dari-minyak/full&view=ok.

Arroyo, V., K. Hess, N. Grünbaum, and G. Ribeiro. 2023. *What specific measures could the US, the EU and China take in order to foster and facilitate cross-border data flows?* Paris: Science Po Digital, Governance and Sovereignty Chair.

The Association of Southeast Asian Nations (ASEAN), & European Commission. 2023. *Joint Guide to ASEAN Model Contractual Clauses and EU Standard Contractual Clauses*. Jakarta and Brussels: ASEAN and European Commission.

Atkinson, R. D., and N. Cory. 2021. "Cross-Border Data Policy: Opportunities and Challenges." In *Consensus or Conflict? China and Globalization in the 21st Century*, edited by H. Wang and A. Michie, 217–232. Singapore: Springer Nature . https://doi.org/10.1007/978-981-16-5391-9

BBC Indonesia. 2021. "Data eHAC milik 1,3 juta penggunanya dilaporkan bocor, 'keamanan data tidak prioritas." *BBC Indonesia*. https://www.bbc.com/indonesia/indonesia-58393345.

Bestari, N. P. 2023. "Jelang KTT ASEAN, Menkominfo Budi Arie Bawa Isu Data Pribadi." CNBC Indonesia. https://www.cnbcindonesia.com/tech/20230830153736-37-467566/jelang-ktt-asean-menkominfo-budi-arie-bawa-isu-data-pribadi.

Burhan, F. A. 2022. "Indonesia Dorong Tata Kelola Data Lintas-Negara di Presidensi G20." Katadata. https://katadata.co.id/digital/teknologi/622184964cf57/indonesia-dorong-tata-kelola-data-lintas-negara-di-presidensi-g20

Burri, M. 2014. *Should There Be New Multilateral Rules for Digital Trade?*. E15Initiative. Geneva: International Centre for Trade and Sustainable Development and World Economic Forum.

Casalini, Francesca, and J. L. Gonzálezi. 2019. *Trade and Cross-Border Data Flows*. OECD Trade Policy Papers, No. 220. Paris: OECD Publishing.

Casalini, F., J. López-González, and T. Nemoto. 2021. *Mapping Commonalities in Regulatory Approaches to Cross-Border Data Transfers*. OECD Trade Policy Papers, No. 248. Paris: OECD Publishing.

Chapelle, B. de La, and L. Porciuncula. 2021. "We Need to Talk about Data: Framing the Debate around Free Flow of Data and Data Sovereignty." In *Internet & Jurisdiction Policy Network*.

Chaudhury, D. R. 2022. "Indonesia Emphasises on Data Governance by G20 States for Cross Border Data Flow." The Economic Times. https://economictimes.indiatimes.com/news/international/world-news/indonesia-emphasises-on-data-governance-by-g20-states-for-cross-border-data-flow/articleshow/93246115.cms?from=mdr.

Chin, Y.-C., and J. Zhao. 2022. "Governing Cross-Border Data Flows: International Trade Agreements and Their Limits." *Laws* 11 (4): 63. https://doi.org/10.3390/laws11040063.

CNN Indonesia. 2022. "10 Kasus Kebocoran Data 2022: Bjorka Dominan." CNN Indonesia. https://www.cnnindonesia.com/teknologi/20221230125430-192-894094/10-kasus-kebocoran-data-2022-bjorka-dominan-ramai-ramai-bantah/1.

Cuihong, C., and W. Yuanzhi. 2021. "Global Data Governance: Challenges and Responses." *China International Studies* 88:20–40.

Desjardins, J. 2019. "How much Data is Generated Each day?" World Economic Forum. https://www.weforum.org/agenda/2019/04/how-much-data-is-generated-each-day-cf4bddf29f/.

European Union. 2018. "EU Proposal for Provisions on Cross-Border Data Flows and Protection of Personal Data and Privacy." https://circabc.europa.eu/ui/group/09242a36-a438-40fd-a7af-fe32e36cbd0e/library/363b4081-c535-4d7c-9365-84a64f9dc582/details.

Faisal, A. 2020. "Kominfo: RUU PDP Indonesia banyak terpengaruh GDPR Eropa." Antara. https://www.antaranews.com/berita/1716870/kominfo-ruu-pdp-indonesia-banyak-terpengaruh-gdpr-eropa.

Fefer, R. F. 2020. "Data Flows, Online Privacy, and Trade Policy." In *Congressional Research Service Report*. https://crsreports.congress.gov/product/pdf/R/R45584.

Ferracane, M. 2017. "Restrictions on Cross-Border Data Flows: A Taxonomy." ECIPE Working Paper (Issue 01). https://doi.org/10.2139/ssrn.3089956.

Finck, M., and F. Pallas. 2020. "They who Must not be Identified-Distinguishing Personal from Non-Personal Data Under the GDPR." *International Data Privacy Law* 10 (1): 11–36. https://doi.org/10.1093/idpl/ipz026.

G20 Digital Economy Ministers' Meeting. 2022. "G20 Digital Economy Ministers' Meeting 2022 Chair's Summary." In *G20 2022 Indonesia*.

G20 Indonesia. 2022. "Minister of Communications and Informatics Emphasizes Digital Sovereignty in Cross-Border Data Flow." G20 Indonesia. https://www.g20.org/minister-of-communications-and-informatics-emphasizes-digital-sovereignty-in-cross-border-data-flow/.

Goodman, M. P., and P. Risberg. 2021. *Governing Data in the Asia-Pacific* (Issue April).

Harrison, M., and A. Fordham. 2020. "Privacy 2.0: Cross-border disclosures – introducing new privacy principle 12." New Zealand Office of the Privacy Commissioner. https://www.privacy.org.nz/blog/privacy-2-0/

Hicks, J. 2021. "A 'Data Realm' for the Global South? Evidence from Indonesia." *Third World Quarterly* 42 (7): 1417–1435. https://doi.org/10.1080/01436597.2021.1901570.

Khumon, P. 2018. Regulation for Cross-Border Privacy in Southeast Asia: An Institutional Perspective. 29th European Regional Conference of the International Telecommunications Society (ITS): "Towards a Digital Future: Turning Technology into Markets?".

Kompas. 2020, 4 May. "Data Tokopedia, Gojek, dan Bukalapak Bocor di Tengah Absennya RUU PDP." Kompas. https://tekno.kompas.com/read/2020/05/04/20170027/data-tokopedia-gojek-dan-bukalapak-bocor-di-tengah-absennya-ruu-pdp?page=all#page2.

Kuncorojati, C. 2023. "Menkominfo Bawa Pembahasan Perlindungan Data Pribadi ke Tingkat ASEAN." Medcom.Id. https://www.medcom.id/teknologi/news-teknologi/zNAAZz3N-menkominfo-bawa-pembahasan-perlindungan-data-pribadi-ke-tingkat-asean.

LeSieur, F. 2012. "Regulating Cross-Border Data Flows and Privacy in the Networked Digital Environment and Global Knowledge Economy." *International Data Privacy Law* 2 (2): 93–104. https://doi.org/10.1093/idpl/ips004.

Ministry of Communication and Informatics of the Republic of Indonesia. 2022. "Kominfo Dorong Tata Kelola Arus Data Lintas Negara yang Lebih Inklusif melalui DEWG G20." Ministry of Communication and Informatics of the Republic of Indonesia. https://www.kominfo.go.id/content/detail/40244/siaran-pers-no-65hmkominfo022022-tentang-kominfo-dorong-tata-kelola-arus-data-lintas-negara-yang-lebih-inklusif-melalui-dewg-g20/0/siaran_pers.

Ministry of Communication and Informatics of the Republic of Indonesia. 2023. "Optimalkan PDP, Kominfo Dukung Pembahasan ASEAN MCCs." Ministry of Communication and Informatics of the Republic of Indonesia. https://www.kominfo.go.id/content/detail/51135/siaran-pers-no-

255hmkominfo082023-tentang-optimalkan-pdp-kominfo-dukung-pembahasan-asean-mccs/0/siaran_pers.

Mishra, N. 2016. "Data Localization Laws in a Digital World: Data Protection or Data Protectionism?" NUS Centre for International Law Research Paper.

Mitchell, A. D., and J. Hepburn. 2017. "Don't Fence Me In: Reforming Trade and Investment Law to Better Facilitate Cross-Border Data Transfer." *Yale Journal of Law and Technology* 19: 182–237.

Nguyen, D., and M. Paczos. 2020. *Measuring the economic value of data and cross-border data flows: A business perspective*. OECD Digital Economy Papers, No. 297. Paris: OECD Publishing.

Obendiek, A. S. 2022. "What Are We Actually Talking About? Conceptualizing Data as a Governable Object in Overlapping Jurisdictions." *International Studies Quarterly* 66 (1). https://doi.org/10.1093/isq/sqab080.

Saha, D. 2020. "How The World Became Data-Driven, And What's Next." Forbes. https://www.forbes.com/sites/googlecloud/2020/05/20/how-the-world-became-data-driven-and-whats-next/?sh=544e96c257fc.

Svantesson, D. 2020. *Data localisation trends and challenges: Considerations for the review of the Privacy Guidelines*. OECD Digital Economy Papers, No. 301. Paris: OECD Publishing.

Topornin, N., D. Pyatkina, and Y. Bokov. 2023. "Government Regulation of the Internet as Instrument of Digital Protectionism in Case of Developing Countries." *Journal of Information Science* 49 (3): 595–608.

United Nations Conference on Trade and Development. 2021. *Digital Economy Report 2021 - Cross-Border Data Flows and Development: For whom the Data Flow*. New York: United Nations Conference on Trade and Development.

United Nations Conference on Trade and Development. 2023. *G20 Members' Regulations of Cross-Border Data Flows*. New York: United Nations Conference on Trade and Development.

United Nations Development Programme. 2021. *Enabling Cross-Border Data Flow: ASEAN and Beyond*. New York: United Nations Development Programme.

Voss, W. G. 2020. "Cross-Border Data Flows, the GDPR, and Data Governance." *Washington International Law Journal Association* 29 (3): 485–532.

We Are Social, & KEPIOS. 2023. "Digital 2023: Indonesia." https://datareportal.com/reports/digital-2023-indonesia.

The World Bank. 2021a. Crossing Borders. https://wdr2021.worldbank.org/stories/crossing-borders/

The World Bank. 2021b. *World Development Report 2021: Data for Better Lives*. Washington DC: The World Bank.

World Economic Forum. 2020a. *A Roadmap for Cross-Border Data Flows: Future-Proofing Readiness and Cooperation in the New Data Economy*. White Paper (June 2020). Cologny, Geneva: World Economic Forum.

World Economic Forum. 2020b. *Data Free Flow with Trust (DFFT): Paths towards Free and Trusted Data Flows*. White Paper (May 2020). Cologny, Geneva: World Economic Forum.

Yang, X. 2021. "Regulatory Approaches of Cross-Border Data Flow in the Big Data Era: China's Choice." *Journal of Physics: Conference Series* 1848 (1): 012026. https://doi.org/10.1088/1742-6596/1848/1/012026.

Zheng, G. 2021. "Trilemma and Tripartition: The Regulatory Paradigms of Cross-Border Personal Data Transfer in the EU, the US and China." *Computer Law & Security Review* 43:105610. https://doi.org/10.1016/j.clsr.2021.105610.

Zimmerman, J. A. 1982. "Transborder Data Flow: Problems with the Council of Europe Convention, or Protecting States from Protectionism." *Northwestern Journal of International Law & Business* 4 (2): 601–625.

Index

Note: Tables are indicated by **bold**.

Aadhaar's constitutionality 69–70
abstract idea 56–7
The Academy of European Private Lawyers 137
The Ad Hoc Committee 136, 138–9
affective design 9
Age Appropriate Design Code 120
AI-for-good approach: applications 35; beneficence not obvious 36–9; Nazi Germany 35
AI migration: behavioural design, affect and consumer protection 7; cybersecurity governance, data flows and sovereignty 7–8; data protection, consent and engineered choice 6–7; duty to serve public good 5–6; patent strategy and immersive environments 6; public decision-making 4–5
AI4SG, definition 37
AI systems 13
Albarrán-Torres, César 109
Appel, Markus 105
Artificial General Intelligence (AGI) 25
artificial intelligence (AI) 51; Act 13
Artificial Neural Networks (ANNs) 26
Asia-Pacific Economic Cooperation (APEC) Privacy Framework 72
Association of Computing Machinery (ACM) 40
The Association of Southeast Asian Nations (ASEAN) 166
attention technique 27
auditory cues 106–7
augmented reality (AR) 48, 49
autonomous vehicles (AVs) 35
avatar 49
Aww factor 105

The 'Baby Schema' 106, 108, 109
Balkin, Jack M. 73
Beauchamp, Tom L. 39
The Belmont Report 40
beneficence 36, 38; biomedical and AI ethics 39–41; human rights and AI ethics 41–2
biometric surveillance 2
Bjork, Staffan 105
blockchain technology 50
Bonnici, Jeanne Pia Mifsud 4
The BRICs approach: Brazil's legislation 141–2; countries 139; India's legislation 140–1
Brignull, Harry 104
Butler, C. 130

The Carnegie Endowment for International Peace (CEIP) 144
Carnegie Endowment for National Peace 146–7
"catch up" model 2–3
categorical imperative 37
Cauldwell, Catherine 106, 108
ChatGPT 'benefit' people 38–9
Chauhan, Krishna Deo Singh 5
Childress, James F. 39
Collaco, Aafreen Mitchelle 6
collective action problem 130
The Commission on European Contract Law (CECL) 137
Competition and Markets Authority (CMA) 104, 105
Comprehensive Economic Partnership Agreement (CEPA) 165
computational governance 3–4
Computer Emergency Response Team-India (CERT-In) 141
computer programs 57
The Congressional Research Service (CRS) 128
consent. *see also* data protection in India: *Aadhaar* Judgement and struck down 66–7; data protection and informational privacy 66, 67
consent managers 74–6, 140
cookie banners 87–8; consent options 92–4; display timing 89–90; position of 90–1; presentation of 92; solution to problems 89; text and language 91–2; way of consenting 94
cookies: automated consent decisions 95; banners 87–8; The EU ePrivacy Directive and GDPR 86; The EU member states 86; GDPR 95–6; regulatory failure 86; session/persistent 85; usability and likeability 94; user input 85–6
copyleft licenses 31

The Council of Europe Cybercrime Convention (the CoE Convention) 127, 130, 131; disagreement over 134–8; treaty harmonization 137–8
Counter Terrorism Committee Executive Directorate (CTED) 144
Cowls, Josh 37
The CRiTERIA tool 17, 19, 20
cross-border data flows: definition 153–4; and localisation 155–6; *see also* Indonesia's regulatory framework; post-PDP act
cute design 103; affiliative behaviours 107; auditory cues 106–7; Aww factor 105; The 'Baby Schema'/'Kindchenschema' 106; code for communication 108; Darwinian associations 106; and data protection 110–18; definition 105; end-user context 108; expressions of emotion 106; human psyche and socialisation behaviour 107; language 106; marketing technique 105; power differentials 107; software and hardware 108–9; technological determinism 109
cuteness and data protection 110–18
cyberactivists 128
cybercrime: The BRICs approach 139–42; European Production Order 133; fragmentation 142; localization 143–4; operability 143; The Russian Proposal 138–9; 2022 CoE second additional protocol 132–3; 2004 treaty 130–2
cyberspies 128
cyberterrorism 128
cyberterrorists 128
cyberthieves 128
cyberwar 128
cyberwarriors 128–9

Dale, Joshua Paul 105, 108
dark patterns 104–5, 120, 121; cookie consent banners 88
Data Fiduciaries 73, 77
Data Governance Act 13
Data Processors 140
Data Protection Authorities (DPAs) 72, 75, 86, 140
Data Protection (DP) Bill 72
Data Protection Board of India (DPBI) 72–3
data protection in India: committee of experts 70–2; privacy and consent 68–70
data residency 143–4
decentralisation 50
Decentralised Autonomous Organisation (DAO) 50
deemed consent *vs.* certain legitimate use 76–7
Defend Digital Me 104
digital cooperation 147–8; UN Secretary-General (2020) 145–6
Digital Personal Data Protection (DPDP) Act 67–8, 72–3; children's and persons with disability's consent 77; consent managers 75–6; Data Fiduciaries 75; deemed consent *vs.* certain legitimate uses 76–7; The EU GDPR 77–9; The EU law 77; India's Data Protection regime 75; jurisprudence pre 73–5
Digital Single Market Strategy 13
digital technologies 1
digital twins 51, 54
direct infringement 59
Doctrine of Equivalents 59
DY Chandrachud (justice) 69

Electronic Information and Transaction Act 159
Electronic System Operator (ESO) 158
empty cyberspace 127–9
end-user autonomy 103
ethical design 41
The Ethics Guidelines for Trustworthy Artificial Intelligence 15
The EU AI act: applications 29; copyleft licenses 31; foundation models 29–31; High-Risk systems 30; high-risk systems 30; LGAIMs 30; recommendations 30–1; social and environmental well-being 31–2; tiers 29
The Eurobarometer on ePrivacy 91
European Border and Coast Guard Agency 19
European Border Surveillance System (EUROSUR) 12, 13
European Data Protection Board 120
European Data Protection Supervisor decision (EDPS) 14, 90
European Innovation Council 47
European Patent Convention 57, 58
The European Patent Office 59–60
European Production Order 133
European Union Agency for Asylum 14–15
EU's General Data Protection Regulation (EU GDPR) 72
extended reality 48–9

facial recognition systems 26
FarmVille, agriculture simulation game 10
Federal Trade Commission (FTC) 104
Financial Stability Board (FSB) 130
first-party cookies 85
5Rights Foundation 104
Floridi, Luciano 36, 37
foundation models 29–31
Future of Life Institute, nonprofit organization 28

game analysis: cuteness and data protection 110–18; mobile gaming and *FarmVille* 109–10
General Data Protection Regulation (GDPR) 140
Generative Adversarial Networks (GANs) 27
generative AI platforms: AGI 25; beneficence 25; copyright issues 28; cybersecurity problems 28; data privacy 28; definition 26–7; description 24–5; The EU AI act 29–32;

foundation models 25; Future of Life Institute, nonprofit organization 28; hallucinations 28; history 27–8; misinformation 28; principle of 25
Generative Pre-trained Transformer (GPT) models 27
global fiancial system 130
Global Internet Forum to Counter Terrorism (GIFCT) 148
Glocker, Melanie L. 106, 108
Government Regulation on Electronic Systems 159
Graphic Processing Units (GPUs) 26
guardianship liberalism 33

Hacker, Philipp 30
The Hague Conference on Private International Law (HCCH) 137
Haidt, Jonathan 107
Harris, Daniel 107
H2020 CRiTERIA project 13
High-Risk systems 30
Hildebrandt, K. A. 106

immersion 48–9
Indian Patent Act 54–5, 57
indirect infringement 59
Indonesia's regulatory framework: data movement 158–9; data regulation 157–8, **157**; government institutions 162–4, **163**; issues of 156–7; national regulations 159–62, **160**
informational privacy 69
informational self-determination 69
Information Commissioner's Office (ICO) 104
infringement of patents 58–60
Institute of Electrical and Electronics Engineers (IEEE) 40
The International Chamber of Commerce (ICC) 137
The International Institute for the Unification of Private Law (UNIDROIT) 137
The International Monetary Fund (IMF) 130
internet cookies 85
Internet Freedom Foundation 140
Internet Service Providers (ISPs) 141
Internet Service Providers Austria (ISPA) 136
interoperability 143
inventiveness 54–6

Jarovsky, Luiza 119
Jibb, Lindsay 109, 118, 120
Johnston, A. 142
Joint Committee of Parliament (JCP) 72, 140
The Joint Letter 136
Joint Research Centre 91
jurisdictional interoperability 60

Kale, Prajakta 6
Kriebitz, Alexander 41
Kshirsagar, Mihir 105
Kumagai, Gakuji 108

Lacey, Cherie 106, 108
large generative AI models (LGAIMs) 30
large-scale data analytics 2
law on inventorship 53
legal concerns 15
Lewis, Chris 105
Lobel, Orly 32–5
Lorenz, Konrad 106, 107, 109
Lütge, Christoph 41
Lv, Xingyang 106, 107

Mara, Martina 105
The Marco Civil 141
Mathur, Arunesh 105
Mattila, Anna S. 106, 107
Mayer, Jonathan 105
metaverse: AI 51; avatar 49; decentralisation 50; digital twins 51; immersion 48–9; intellectual property 47; interoperability 49–50; NFT 50–1; VR headset, AR glasses/wearable lenses 48, 49; *see also* patents in metaverse
Milaj, Jonida 4
Mittelstadt, Brent 40, 41
mixed reality 49
mobile gaming and *FarmVille* 109–10
Mockaitis, A. 130
Model Contractual Clauses (MCC) 166
most favored nation status clauses (MFNs) 142
Mulyani, Cora Kristin 7
mutual legal assistance (MLATs) 132
mutual legal assistance treaties (MLATs) 136

Naithani, Paarth 6
negative framing 88
negativity bias, AI: guardianship liberalism 33; Human/Machine Double Standard 33; ignoring scarcity 34; non-maleficence *vs.* beneficence 32–3; static & fixed 33
non-fungible token (NFT) 50–1
Nottingham, Emma 7
The Nuremberg Code 40

O'Connell, Anthony 7
The Official Explanatory Report 131
Organisation for Economic Co-operation and Development (OECD) 104
The Organization for the Harmonization of Business Laws in Africa (OHADA) 137
The Organization of American States (OAS) 137
ownership: DABUS 52–3; law on inventorship 53; self-learning 53

patent law 6, 52
patents in metaverse: infringement of 58–60; Intellectual Property rights 51; inventiveness 54–6; novelty 54; ownership 52–3; product and process patents 52; subject matter eligibility 56–8
personal assistant 1
Personal Data Protection (PDP): Act 154, 159; Bill 72
PHOSITA 55–6
Polonetsky, Jules 80
Population Administration Act 158
positive framing 88
post-PDP act 164–8
privacy and consent 68–70
process patents 52
product and process patents 52
Puttaswamy (former justice) 68–9

Rahman, Faiz 7
Ramos, C. 143–4
recommendation systems 26
Report of the Committee of Experts 67
reproductive intervention 2
The Research Group on the Existing EC Private Law (Acquis Group) 137
Rieger, Sebastian 120
right to beneficial automation 35
right to liberty 68
risk assessment model 3
The Russian Proposal 138–9

Sachs, Goldman 24–5
Sheppard, L. 143–4
Sherman, Gary D. 107
Shin, Joongwon 106, 107
Significant Data Fiduciary (SDF) 77
Sinders, Caroline 120
Social Media platforms 12, 13; ethical challenges 15–16; legal challenges 14–15; risk assessment systems 16–17
software patent applications 54
Software Patent Registration 57
software patents 52
Standard Contractual Clauses (SCC) 166
standardised banners 89
Stockman, Caroline 7, 109
structural tensions: autonomy *vs.* engineered environments 8; public authority *vs.* private architecture 8; sovereignty *vs.* interdependence 8–9; transparency *vs.* opacity 8
subject matter eligibility: abstract idea and computer programs 56–7; inventions against public order/morality 57–8
subscriber information 132
Sverdrup, U. 143
systemic cyber risk **129**

technical interoperability 49
technical systems 3
technological determinism 109
technological disruption 1
Tene, Omer 80
third-party cookies 85
transformer models 27
transparency and AI: border control 19–20; considerations 18; European Commission 17–18; high-risk AI 18–19; pre-condition for accountability 19
treaty harmonization 137–8
Trebilcock, M. 142
TRIPS agreement 52
Turkle, Sherry 106

The Unique Identification Authority of India ('UIDAI') 68
The United Nations Commission on International Trade Law (UNCITRAL) 137
United Nations CTED 147–8
Universal Declaration of Human Rights (UDHR) 147
usage interoperability 49–50
US National Research Act 40

virtual reality (VR) 48–9

Web 3.0 50
Weismann, Miriam F. 7
World Intellectual Property Organization 47

Yayboke, E. 143–4

Zagal, José P. 105
Zander, L. 130